PENGUIN BOOKS

CAN YOU MAKE THIS THING GO FASTER?

Jeremy Clarkson began his writing career on the *Rotherham Advertiser*. Since then he has written for the *Sun*, the *Sunday Times*, the *Rochdale Observer*, the *Wolverhampton Express & Star*, all of the Associated Kent Newspapers and *Lincolnshire Life*.

By the same author

Motorworld
Jeremy Clarkson's Hot 100
Jeremy Clarkson's Planet Dagenham
Born to Be Riled
Clarkson on Cars
The World According to Clarkson
I Know You Got Soul
And Another Thing
Don't Stop Me Now
For Crying Out Loud!
Driven to Distraction
How Hard Can It Be?
Round the Bend
Is It Really Too Much To Ask?
What Could Possibly Go Wrong?
As I Was Saying . . .
If You'd Just Let Me Finish!
Really?

Can You Make This Thing Go Faster?

The World According to Clarkson
Volume Eight

JEREMY CLARKSON

PENGUIN BOOKS

PENGUIN BOOKS

UK | USA | Canada | Ireland | Australia
India | New Zealand | South Africa

Penguin Books is part of the Penguin Random House group of companies
whose addresses can be found at global.penguinrandomhouse.com

Penguin
Random House
UK

First published by Michael Joseph 2020
Published in Penguin Books 2021

005

Copyright © Jeremy Clarkson 2020

The moral right of the author has been asserted

Typeset by Jouve (UK), Milton Keynes
Printed and bound in Great Britain by Clays Ltd, Elcograf S.p.A.

The authorized representative in the EEA is Penguin Random House Ireland,
Morrison Chambers, 32 Nassau Street, Dublin D02 YH68

A CIP catalogue record for this book is available from the British Library

ISBN: 978–1–405–94651–3

www.greenpenguin.co.uk

MIX
Paper from
responsible sources
FSC® C018179

Penguin Random House is committed to a
sustainable future for our business, our readers
and our planet. This book is made from Forest
Stewardship Council® certified paper.

Contents

Next up on It's an Arty Knockout – Chippenham's forest of manhole covers

Someone has installed a gigantic and rather elegant ladder on Dartmoor. It's not propped up against anything; it just rises up from the middle of nowhere and heads off into the clouds. Many have called it 'the Stairway to Heaven' and soon local officials will remove it on the grounds of health and safety.

They haven't actually said that this will happen but it will, because what if someone were to climb the ladder and then, when they got to the top – where there's nothing but sky – fell off? Someone would have to be sued. Best, then, to take it down and put it in a skip.

Previously, an enormous oak chair lived for a while where the ladder stands now. It was built by a local artist called Henry Bruce but 'Dartmoor chiefs' (that's what the regional newspaper calls them) said it was too popular with tourists and, because of the resultant traffic problems, it must be taken away. So it was, in a big removal lorry.

I wonder. Why has no one taken down the 66ft winged figure that towers over Gateshead? Or the naked men of iron who stand knee-deep in sand on the beach at Crosby on Merseyside? Or the stencil sketches that adorn the sides of various shops in Bristol?

Ah, well, that's simple. All of these things were created by renowned artists. So they are fine. But the ladder and the chair? They were both made by ordinary people, presumably. This makes them litter, so they must be taken away.

I think this is silly. I like the ladder. Without it, Dartmoor is nothing more than a wild expanse of mud and wind. It's fine if you are a horse, or an idiot in a cagoule, or a convicted burglar, but for ordinary, evolved human beings it needs a focal point. Or else it's just something that must be driven past on your way to Cornwall. A big blob of nothing that's holding back Tavistock.

So I say this to the Dartmoor chiefs: put up a small notice on a nearby wall saying they are not responsible if someone is injured while climbing the ladder – and then leave it be.

And then I have an even better idea for the nation's broadcasters. Let's bring back *It's a Knockout*, but with a couple of important changes.* Instead of getting a paedophile commentator to laugh hysterically while people dressed as Smurfs fall into a paddling pool, make it a gigantic nationwide art competition.

I think people are bored with watching gym enthusiasts in the jungle, or Boris Johnson's relations being normal. And we are definitely bored with ducks that can skateboard, shop assistants who think they can sing and poorly children who can do magic tricks. Soon we will even tire of people with two left legs and a sequin jumpsuit, jiggling about to an Abba track.

My new programme idea is still a competition but it's better than the established powerhouses because each week, two whole towns go head-to-head in a battle to create the best municipal art installation. And they will be encouraged by the judges – Antony Gormley, Jonathan Yeo, Keith Tyson and Mr Banksy – to think big.

---

* To be very clear to all television executives reading this: it's my idea.

Think about it. Every town has a bit of waste ground developers don't want. As often as not these days, that area is known as 'the centre'. It's just a row of charity shops and takeaways and it only comes alive at night when it's a blizzard of chlamydia and vomit. So why not turn it into a mile-long Henry Moore?

Sometimes it won't be the centre. It'll be an abandoned factory, or a tower block that's deemed, post-Grenfell, to be uninhabitable, or a park that's used mostly as a dog lavatory. Everywhere has something or somewhere that could do with a makeover.

So a spot is identified by council chiefs and local artists are consulted. Everywhere has some of these too; people who put up their watercolours and their weird taxidermy in the town tea shoppe in the hope that a customer from the Royal National Institute of Blind People will want to buy it.

These consultations will be filmed because we'd all like to see the back story; the prize-marrow-pony-club-small-town bitterness that's bound to surface when one artist is told that his plans for painting all the telegraph poles red is stupid and they're going for a full-scale model of Bilbao's Guggenheim.

This will require a lot of work but that's OK because in every town there's always a lot of busybodies who want to be involved with 'the community'. And an even greater number who want to be on television. The one I'd like involves recreating that old Sony Bravia ad in which gallons of paint are fired from a council estate to create a blaze of colour. Remember that? Well, imagine firing foot-wide paint balls from a cannon at the side of an eyesore. In minutes, it wouldn't be an eyesore any more.

Bristol could produce an installation based around Concorde, Doncaster could make a 600ft-tall bronze miner and Chippenham could create a forest of manhole covers in honour of its most famous son, Jeremy Corbyn, whose ideas for regenerating forgotten towns are nowhere near as good as mine.

Surely there must be a town in Britain somewhere with a company that could recreate that wonderful fountain from the lobby of the Burj Al Arab in Dubai but on a massive scale. I'd far rather watch someone attempting to do this than a girl on a journey, from her checkout till, past Simon Cowell and back to the checkout till again.

And whereas she'd be forgotten in a matter of moments, the fountain could stand for a thousand years. A marvel that puts the town that created it way further up the art map than the next pointless City of Culture. Coventry.

7 January 2018

Keep playing with your files, constable. Let us vigilantes handle this burglar

I know only one thing about the law in Britain: that there is no more expensive place in the entire world to stand than the moral high ground. God himself could appear from the clouds to tell the jury that what you did was correct, but that doesn't mean you're going to win the case. Usually, it means you won't.

And that brings me neatly on to the case of a man called Mark Cardwell, who appeared at Teesside crown court last week. He'd been online, chatting to what he thought were some young girls, but it turned out he'd been asking for intimate photographs from various paedophile-hunting vigilante groups. Who promptly shopped him to the gammon.

That's tremendous, of course, but hang on a minute. What crime had he actually committed? He hadn't been intimate or inappropriate with a young girl. He had merely asked a paunchy man in a Steppenwolf T-shirt to pleasure himself and send photographs. That's weird, I'll grant you, but it's not illegal.

And yet, amazingly, it is, because last Monday, Cardwell was found guilty of attempted grooming and attempting to engage a child in sexual activity, and was jailed for 18 months.

Perhaps there were aspects of this case that were not fully reported but, whatever, the police commissioner expressed his gratitude to the vigilante groups for their assistance in securing the conviction, even though there's no need to help the police because 'we have the whole thing under complete control at all times'.

Except they don't. We know this because they announced last autumn that in a drive to save £400 million they will no longer investigate minor crimes of violence or tiny bits of theft unless the victim can name the person who did it.

Sure, if a baddie uses violence or trickery to enter someone's house, then the desk sergeant will fill in a form, in his best joined-up writing, and carefully file it away in that massive warehouse where the Lost Ark ended up. But if the baddie jimmies a window open and steals a few bits and bobs, the homeowner will be told politely to get lost.

It's the same story with mild violence. If, like most of the country, you are at war with your neighbour over his unruly hedge, you can't hit him in the face with a hammer. Plod's going to come round if you do that. But if you push him over or poke him in the eye, then that's OK.

The idea is very simple: by ignoring minor crimes, the constabulary will be able to concentrate its efforts on the only stuff that matters these days. Terrorism. Being a disc jockey in the 1970s. Splashing a mum with muddy water by driving through a puddle too quickly. Or dropping plastic into the sea.

The trouble is that when you find you've been burgled, it doesn't feel very minor at all. At best, it's inconvenient because you will have to keep your temper while an insurance assessor accuses you of doing the break-in yourself. And then you will have to buy a new toothbrush just in case the thief put yours up his bottom.

At worst, a burglary can be very upsetting. Losing your mother's engagement ring, or your dog, or your photograph albums may look trivial on paper, but in your heart it's huge and heavy and sad. And it's even sadder when you are told to get out of the police station because 'all our officers are currently on a ladder-climbing course'. So how's this for a plan . . .

Warehouses employ night watchmen to keep an eye on things when the workforce is at home. Light industrial estates have men walking round every so often with fierce dogs. And stores have security guards too. I saw one last week, standing in the doorway of a shop. He had big shoulders and an earpiece, and because he was there, the chances of a smash-and-grab raid were, I should imagine, massively diminished.

Pubs and clubs also have their own security teams on hand to sort out the kind of behaviour that no longer interests Dixon of Dock Green. So why, pray, do streets not do the same thing?

The street on which I live in London does. A local was fed up after losing two Range Rovers in a year, so he got his neighbours to club together to employ a man who drives around at night, shining his torch into the face of anyone in a hoodie. And the next year he had three Range Rovers stolen. But I think this is because the lone vigilante he employed is a bit rubbish.

Yours needn't be. And nor would it be massively expensive, because, think about it: if there are a hundred houses on your road and everyone chipped in, you could have a man and a car and an angry dog for, what, £300 each a year?

For a little more, it might be possible to launch your

own legal system. Various Muslim areas of Britain have sharia, or Islamic law, which is obviously tailored to their beliefs, so follow that lead and decide in your street what is appropriate for you and your neighbours.

If you are in a Jeremy Corbyn-type area, you could invite the burglar into your kitchen for some winter-warming soup. If you are Tunbridge Wells, you could tie him to a maypole and sentence him to death. By stoning, if that's what your children would like.

This would take the burden off the normal courts, leaving them more time to focus on the big stuff, such as parking on a yellow line and driving too quickly.

The only thing I wouldn't recommend you get involved with is paedophilia. Because I have some experience of this. No, wait. Let me rephrase that. I once had to call on CEOP – the child exploitation and online protection arm of the police – for help.

And it was outstanding. Dazzlingly brilliant. It's the one area of police work where individuals cannot do better than the police are doing already.

14 January 2018

Four words that could have saved the UKIP leader's marriage: I hate classical music

If your husband wakes one morning, has a big stretch and says, as he opens the curtains: 'I hate all classical music,' you should breathe a sigh of relief and go through the rest of your life with a smile on your face and a spring in your step. To understand why, you need to examine the case of UKIP leader Henry Bolton who at the age of 54 decided to leave his Russian-born wife so that he could be with a young woman called Jo Marney.

She has been described by friends as a 'model, actress and journalist', and by the non-judgmental lefties on Twitter as 'a topless model 30 years his junior', but the affair seemed to fizzle out once the newspapers started referring to her as a 'racist model, actress and journalist'.

So now, presumably, Mr Bolton is on his own in a bedsit while Mrs Bolton is busy at the family home, putting all their wedding photographs in the waste disposal unit.

It's a sad story and it's not unusual. Lots of 54-year-old men wake up in the morning and think: 'Oh no. Soon I shall be a hollowed-out shell with droopy moobs and see-through hair, so I should make the most of my final few days as a man by buying a Porsche, sculpting my pubic hair into the shape of an eagle and taking a 25-year-old out for dinner.'

In order to impress the woman, the poor man will pretend to be interested in Snapchat and why Rita Ora is better than Bouff Daddy. And later he may agree to go clubbing, where he will not realize that no man past the age of 40 should dance with his arms above his head.

Many people will laugh at him. Especially after he's tried K cider to look cool and finished the evening under a park bench, drooling and thinking he's stuck in Roger Dean's head.

It's probable that one day he will get into the 25-year-old's underwear but since this will take place in the Porsche, he will put his back out and wake the next day with half the handbrake up his backside and chlamydia.

But he'll stick with her, they'll get married and for his 60th birthday, when he should be settling down with a book on fly-fishing, he'll get as a present a new baby.

Amazingly, some men are able to resist this option. Some look at the teenage receptionist and think: 'I must not think that way.' But to take us back to the beginning, a wife can never truly relax until the day comes when her husband admits he doesn't like classical music.

I admitted it to myself over Christmas and then out loud at a party last weekend. People were quite shocked. But I ploughed on regardless. Some of it may be catchy because it was used to advertise tyres or ice cream but if you actually listen to all of Nissan Dormobile it's terrible. Longer than a prog-rock drum solo and about as dreary.

Classical music is like Shakespeare. Everyone says his sonnets are brilliant and the bedrock of our language. Really? So how come, then, that nobody in their right mind reads him from the moment they leave school until the moment they die?

Shakespeare is like Radio 3. We are aware of it and the BBC says 2 million people listen to it every week, but we're not fooled. It's just one imbecile in a loft, turning his radio on and off 2 million times.

You'll probably have seen the epically brilliant film *In the Loop*. It was a feature-length version of the television series *The Thick of It* and in one scene an angry Scottish man tells a pompous civil servant to turn off his classical music. 'It's just vowels,' he shouts. And he's absolutely dead right. It's consonant-free communication.

I firmly believe that the Bay City Rollers produced more of note than Mozart, Brahms and Bartok combined. And anyone who says they like opera, doesn't really. They're just showing off.

And that's the point. When we are in the hunt for a mate, we dream up all sorts of stuff to make ourselves look interesting. We are careful not to use the word 'toilet' and we make a point of not having a television in the bedroom. Nor would we lie on a beach openly reading a Lee Child book. Much better to have the biography of some Renaissance painter.

Nicky Haslam, the interior designer and commentator on social matters, recently posted an image of a tea towel given to him by a friend, listing all the things Haslam reckons are common and to be avoided. Ibiza, Richard Branson, personal trainers, being ill, pronouncing the 'e' in furore, vodka tonic, Oxfordshire, dress codes, cufflinks . . .

The list is very long and if you are in the market for a relationship, it's a handy reference guide that you can hang on your Aga. Hang on. Just checking. Nope. Agas are fine, it seems.

But think of the effort needed to do this, to always be doing the right thing in the right place at the right time with the right people. Once, I arrived with a girlfriend at the house of a posh woman who said to her as we walked through the door: 'Would you like to look in a mirror.' She meant 'Do you want a pee?' but couldn't actually say that because it somehow wasn't correct. She's the sort who'd listen to Bach. And sit on a train with a copy of the *Economist* even though in her heart she'd far rather be reading *Hello!*.

The only reason we live such a wicked life of fakery is because it makes us look cleverer and more interesting and better-read than we actually are. And the only reason we do this is because we want to be attractive.

But the day will come when no amount of squinting into the mirror helps. You just know that you're not attractive any more. And that is the most blessed relief because it means you can say and do and wear whatever you want.

21 January 2018

Before you lynch any Oxfam workers, remember the lives they've saved

I have probably got this all wrong but so far as I can tell, a hard-working charity worker may have slept with a prostitute after a gruelling day spent handing out fruit and silver foil blankets to earthquake victims in Haiti and now there are calls for anyone who's walked past an Oxfam shop to be shot in the head and buried in an unmarked grave on the edge of town.

Let's be in no doubt here, I've always had my doubts about Oxfam. I've never liked the way it used global warming and austerity and Margaret Thatcher as a three-pronged assault weapon on our guilt juices, and I've long suspected that any organization run by a bunch of BBC and Labour Party stalwarts would spend far more on South African nuclear-free peace crisps than it did on bandages for the needy and the dispossessed.

Oh, and not even when I had a brief flirtation with punk on or about 1 August 1976, have I found anything in an Oxfam shop that's caused me to think: 'Hmmm. That's ironic.' It's all just tat.

It's not just Oxfam either. I've been to Muslim trouble spots around the world and – during Ramadan – seen UN workers sitting on street corners in hot pants, smoking and drinking beer. And I've heard people out there in do-gooder land wondering how every single UN Toyota Land Cruiser hasn't been daubed with a blue 'C' and 'T' as well.

Then you've got UNICEF, which we were told last week is riddled with paedophiles, and all of the other non-governmental organizations that you just know are run on the ground by the sort of happy-clappy vicar-people you'd never have round for dinner.

I get the appeal of signing up for this kind of work. You get sent to somewhere hot for a few months and you are doing the sort of important work that will make you look interesting and tanned.

Plus, if something does go wrong and you are trapped or eaten or blown up, you know your old headmaster will say glowing things at your standing-room-only funeral and the local paper will call for a roundabout to be named in your honour. Yeah, John Lennon got an airport for his egg man, but you? You got a roundabout. With geraniums on it.

And when the work is done for the day, you can hang around the pool at the house where you're staying, drinking beer in the warmth of the evening and maybe do sex. And that seems to be the nub of Oxfam's problems.

One of its chaps, a Belgian, working in Haiti, may have actually paid for some women to do whatever it is they are said to have done and that's gone down very badly with everyone who has no idea what they're talking about.

Haiti is very poor. There is very little work. And then along comes a Belgian with a wad of dollars. What happens next, says everyone, puts the Belgian up there with the dentist who shot that lion and Jimmy Savile and Hitler. I'm sorry, but I don't understand the hysteria.

There are prostitutes in the world. They sleep with men for money. It has been happening since I was born. Some say it's been happening since even James May was born. Sex workers are a fact of life. Yes? Right? So what happens to these women if there are no customers? They take a job in a nail salon? In Haiti? Get real.

It's much the same argument we saw recently with grid girls in Formula One. It was decided they didn't fit the sport's image so now they've been dropped. Which means that several hundred young women from all over the world now have less income.

What this Belgian does with a prostitute is a matter for his wife. Not a bunch of barking mad lunatics back in Britain. I'm distraught to see that since this story broke, Oxfam has been bleeding direct-debitors – 1,270 went in just 3 days. And now we have flocks of former international development secretaries denying they've heard of Oxfam and the hairy-armpit brigade burning people in the street for looking in a charity shop window.

We can be absolutely certain that this story will run and run. In the same way that Harvey Weinstein led to Kevin Spacey, who led to everyone else who's got a scrotum, and the Presidents Club fiasco consumed the nation to the point where Great Ormond Street Hospital handed back money given to help sick children because it had been raised by young women in matching underwear, so other charities will be dragged into the mire.

And by this time next week you'll be afraid to roll a 10p piece into the Royal National Lifeboat Institution's tin in case it spends it on bats for clubbing seals.

Yes, some charities are quite inefficient and only spend 60 per cent of what they're given on good causes. But most do better than that and spend only 1 per cent of their income on running themselves.

I used to know a chap who worked for a well-known

charity and when he was back in Europe after six months on a battlefield or in some hellhole, he would regale us with horrific tales of sewing people's legs back on back to front and nailing coffin lids down on people who said 'Ow!' when the first hammer blow landed. Those who didn't know him well were appalled by this and in today's climate he'd be hanging from a lamppost while the idiotic threw vegetables at him.

But the fact is this: for every one mistake he made while utterly exhausted, and in a bloodbath, he saved hundreds, maybe thousands of lives.

I fear that's what the world is doing to the Belgian man. I could be wrong, of course. He could be a terrible wrong 'un. But let's be sure before we lynch him for sleeping with prostitutes – he's not the first to do that – after a day spent saving the actual lives of hundreds of others.

In the meantime, here's a tip. Give Oxfam a bit of money next time you're passing one of its shops.

18 February 2018

Keys, gum, corkscrew . . . ah yes, here it is. I knew I'd put my masculinity in my man-bag

Keen to learn more about the alarming claims that Jeremy Corbyn was once mincing around London with a poisoned umbrella and a briefcase full of atomic launch codes, I turned to the BBC's sprawling news website and found . . . nothing about the story at all. There was, however, an interesting piece about the history of the man-bag.

Obviously, no mention was made of this on the BBC but they've always been seen as a bit, you know, gay. There was an episode of *Friends* in which Matt LeBlanc – whatever happened to him, I wonder? – bought a bag that provided his co-stars with many opportunities to make out that he may, in fact, be a lady.

Then there was an episode of *Seinfeld* in which Jerry told friends, indignantly, that his man-bag was not a purse. 'It's European,' he said. As we know, when an American describes something as European, such as not carrying a gun or smoking a Disque Bleu, he means 'homosexual'.

My dad used to have a handbag and God I teased him about it. He argued that no one in the hard, men-are-men mining town of Doncaster would ever steal such a thing and he was dead right. It was, in fact, stolen while he was in the European city of Amsterdam. 'Presumably,' I said, 'by someone who wanted something to hit his boyfriend with.'

According to *GQ*, the man-bag first became popular in the 14th century when chaps would attach a small pouch to their belt or leg that was filled with spices and herbs to make them smell nice. It was a sort of Renaissance deodorant. Right Guard. Only with a hint of parsley.

Things, of course, have changed since then. Homosexuality is now pretty much compulsory and exhibiting its traits is de rigueur if you want to get on. Which is why David Beckham, Lewis Hamilton and various other chaps who live their lives in the *Mail Online*'s sidebar of shame are regularly seen 'jetting into LAX' with a three-grand leather pouch tossed casually over their shoulder.

Sales are up. Fifteen per cent of the male population of Britain bought a bag last year and that jumped to a quarter among the under-34s. And here it comes. I have one. It wasn't made by Stella McCartney. It doesn't have any leather trimmings. It's more in the style of Indiana Jones's satchel but it's mine and I'm a man and it's a bag and I simply couldn't manage without it.

Think about it. When you went out in the past, everything you ever needed – chequebook, condom and Blockbuster membership card, for when the condom wasn't necessary – fitted in a wallet. And that fitted in the pocket of your Oxford bags.

Today things are different because when you go out you need a phone, a laptop, an iPad and chargers for all of them. Then there's your Kindle and your credit cards and a bit of cash, and there's no way you're going to fit that lot in your pockets.

You may say that a briefcase could accommodate all of these things and that's probably true. But a briefcase makes you look like you go to meetings and say that you'll 'reach out' to various people, which is not acceptable unless you are in the Four Tops. It also suggests that you play golf at weekends and that's not a message you want to be sending out. Much better to have people think you bat for the other side.

What's more, no briefcase could accommodate all the other stuff that the modern man needs if he's truly ready to move at the drop of a hat.

My bag, for instance, contains the laptop and the chargers and so on. But in addition, there are headache potions, all the malaria pills I've never finished taking, the key cards for every hotel I've ever stayed in, two packets of nicotine gum, a bottle opener, a torch, a corkscrew, a passport, pictures of my children, plug adaptors for every country in the world, spare house keys, two pairs of sunglasses, a spare pair of reading spectacles, noise-cancelling headphones that I use to drown out the sound of James May on aeroplanes, a bag of tissues, a card saying I won't catch yellow fever, $40, €40, coins for airport trolleys, spare batteries for the James May-cancelling headphones, a laser pointer for annoying dogs and, critically, no liquids or penknives or anything that could cause a delay at an airport.

I could get an emergency call this afternoon to be in the Arctic or an equatorial swamp and I wouldn't have to think for a moment because I know that everything I'll need is in that bag.

There is a drawback, of course, because we've all been there, with a woman, standing outside her front door as she rests her handbag on an elevated knee while she rummages around for the house keys. Well, it's the same story with my bag. I know everything is in there but I can never locate anything. I've cancelled cards that have turned up a week later and once even changed the locks on my flat having decided I'd definitely lost the keys. Only to find them six weeks later, tangled up in some iPhone cabling. Which I'd just replaced at one of those Apple shops where nothing makes any sense.

God knows how David managed. The Bible tells us that when faced with Goliath, he reached into his man-bag and took out a stone that he threw at the Philistine. The truth is that if it had been a real man-bag, he'd have been standing there for half an hour in a puddle of chewing gum wrappers and old boarding passes saying: 'Hang on, hang on. I know it's in here somewhere.'

The thing is, though, I'd rather know that I have something I need somewhere about my person than know for sure that it's on my hall table. And for that, you need a bag.

25 February 2018

A proper lunch – that's all millennials need to stop getting fat and miserable

Last week an old man in a chalk-stripe suit woke up and said the panna cotta of celeriac that he'd been given for his subsidized lunch in the House of Lords canteen was nothing more than a petrified carrot swimming in a pool of egg. Also, his beef had been 'uneatable'.

Naturally, this went down badly with those of a hairy-armpitted disposition who all said something or other about hard-working families and austerity and Trump and how the poor can't even get any food at KFC these days.

It also went down badly with me because I love lunch, and since AA Gill died I can't find anyone else who does. Apart from a lot of dead people in clubs in St James's who are propped up in front of a spotted dick that was cooked in black and white during an air raid.

If I do talk someone into joining me for a spot of gossip and a wine, they tut when I order a starter, spend the main course looking at their watch and become wide-eyed with incredulity when I suggest a second glass.

Normally, I could rely on women to come and play, but not any more because – and I am not making this up – they have started having FaceTime lunches. This involves doing something pointless to an avocado, pouring a splash of gently carbonated water into an overpriced glass and then sitting at their kitchen table and nattering away on an iPad to a friend who's done exactly the same thing at her kitchen table.

It's no good in the office either, because when I ask if anyone would like to go to the pub at lunchtime, everyone looks at me as though I've just said, 'Would anyone like to come outside and kick a homeless person to death?'

Only the other day I was in our conference room and noticed someone from the previous meeting had eaten half a custard cream. Who does that? Who takes a bite from a small biscuit and then thinks, 'Mmm. I'm stuffed'?

The problem, probably, is that most of the people in our office are about nine, and as we know, nine-year-olds claim to eat only leaves that have been shade grown by well-paid organic farmers in Borneo. A plate of not-sustainable fish and full-fat chips at the pub? Cooked by an immigrant on the minimum wage? Or an entire biscuit made by an American corporate giant? They'd rather eat their shoes.

Or would they? Because figures just released by the nanny state show that today's millennials are on course to be the fattest generation in history. More than 70 per cent will need a weighbridge to determine their weight by the time they are 40, say researchers. Others won't make it that far because they will explode at the age of 29.

So, the message is clear. If by some miracle they make it to old age and need an MRI scan, they will have to be sent to the vet and put in a tube normally used for horses.

I have no idea how millennials are getting so fat. Perhaps it's because, as we've learnt, they prefer lunching via telephone to getting off their arses and going to an actual restaurant.

But I think the real problem is that they are a very miserable generation who believe that Theresa May set the Grenfell Tower alight by herself and that the country would be better if it had a man called Stormzy in the hot seat. They are steered through life by campaigning websites, leftie tweets and inspirational hashtags, and as a result see inequality and injustice all around them. Especially on Instagram, where everyone else is always on holiday. And has a better-looking dog.

This causes them to seethe with bitterness. In their minds, Margaret Thatcher is from the same page in history as Adolf Hitler, all men are rapists and all white people suffer from institutionalized racism. Lily Allen is cleverer than Stephen Hawking, Cara Delevingne has a point, Jeremy Corbyn is a god and all Tories are bastards.

Last week they had a new champion. A woman with big teeth announced that she isn't paid very much by the BBC, not because she's penis-free, but because she has some kind of regional accent. And before I could say Cilla Black or Huw Edwards, the *Guardian* was jumping up and down and squeaking a lot about how she has a point, right? #TimesUpAttenborough.

Let's have a bit of 'Ee bah gum' on t'news. And some 'Calm down, calm down!' on the weather forecast. Actually, that's not such a bad idea. 'Bit chilly' would have been more helpful last week than 'Beast from the East'.

The trouble is that if you wear a shell suit at the next awards ceremony to show your solidarity with the riff-raff, you'll be castigated for not wearing black and thus supporting all the women who've slept with attractive rich men over the years. Or a white glove. Or whatever fashion statement Lily Allen has decided is important that week. #ColdandHomeless.

Keeping up with this pressure, with nothing but an avocado for company, is hard work and stressful and lonely and it will make you sad. Which will cause you to eat crisps when your FaceTime lunch is over. And that's probably what's causing the weight problem.

And that takes us back to the beginning. Because if you want to lead a full and happy life, don't bother with breakfast or dinner but do have a nice long lunch, with a bottle of wine, a lot of laughter, and maybe a small zizz afterwards. Doctors say a run would be better. They say exercise stimulates the mind, but they are wrong. There are no very bright athletes.

And there are no very happy people who spend their lunch hour eating weeds while scrolling through a ream of electronic misery on their laptop.

4 March 2018

Use your loafers, with the right shoes you'll beat the jungle, illness and Corbyn's reign

I have never really seen the point of opening a bank statement. Because it either says you have money in your account, in which case, so what? Or it says you are overdrawn, in which case, you're going to what? Magic the balance from behind the sofa? Sell the dog for medical experiments? Kill yourself?

Last week, however, while I was on holiday, I did open a statement and, worse, I read it. And I've never had such a panic in my whole life, because suddenly I could see how much everything was costing. The little wi-fi dongle, for instance, that I plug into the cigarette lighter in my car. That costs more to run than putting three children through Eton. And Ocado? I spend less on lawyers.

Over the years, I've wandered round the world with my data-roaming on, watching amusing clips of cats in washing machines, imagining that because it's the internet it's all free. But it isn't free. It's pricier than my car.

Of course, in a time of plenty, which is what the world's been enjoying these past 10 years, this recklessness isn't too bad, but in the past 2 weeks I've met my accountant and a woman from my bank, and both say with solemn faces that the end is nigh; Corbyn is coming, and everyone with a mortgage and a car and enough for a family holiday in the summer should make preparations.

'Yes,' I said sagely. But, actually, what preparations can you make for the arrival of a card-carrying lunatic? We have no idea what madness he will ejaculate into the economy or from where his attacks on the fabric of common sense will come.

We know only that if your parents were born in Britain and you have more than 25p to your name, you will be visited in the night by his brown-suited henchmen, who will take away your money and give it to Hezbollah or that annoying man on the pavement in town who has a dog on a piece of string.

So how do you get ready? Do you put all your money in a biscuit tin under the bed? Or cover yourself in woad and move to the woods? Should you be getting lessons in how a crossbow works and how to gut a rabbit? Or stocking up on soup and other tinned foods? Or getting in a sledge and going to the countryside with Julie Christie?

Well, you can start – bear with me on this one – by looking at what you spend on shoes. According to figures that are now 5 years old, the average British woman buys 13 pairs a year. That, in a lifetime, is £34,000. You could almost run my wi-fi dongle for that.

You'd imagine men spend less, and you'd be right. But it's not much less. In the US women spend $30 billion on shoes each year, and men a not-far-behind $26.2 billion. Whereas in the past 2 years, the amount I've spent on footwear is £360, this being the price of one pair of Tod's loafers.

Now I will admit that on a wet shopping-centre floor the Tod's loafer is useless. I visit the giant Westfield arcade in west London extremely infrequently, partly because it is full of horrible people buying horrible things from horrible shops but mostly because I almost always fall over.

However, in every other environment the loafers work

brilliantly. You can wear them for lunch in the Wolseley restaurant on Piccadilly, and you can wear them while climbing to the highest point of a jungly island in the Seychelles. I know this because I did it last week.

I have worn the same shoes pretty much every day since I bought them. I wear them to host my television show, and I wear them in the field, so to speak. I wore them while crossing Colombia in January, and I wore them in the snow we had recently. They are the SUV of shoes.

You may argue that for various sporting activities they would be hopeless, but no. I have played football in them, and tennis. I have also slept in them. Well, one of them.

This morning, while on the beach, I was alerted by some rumblings in my tummy that I had only a few seconds to reach a lavatory. And the nearest was up 142 steps, behind the hotel's reception desk.

Now bear in mind that this was midday in the tropics. The equator was only 4 degrees away, and I can spit that far. The steps would therefore be very hot, so I'd need shoes. Flip-flops would be quick to put on, for sure, but they'd slow me down on the steps. Training shoes would be ideal for the run, but doing up the laces would mean getting as far as the reception and then making a mess of its marble floor.

Happily, I had the trusty loafers to hand, which meant – and it was close – that I made it to the loo in time.

They are also good in airports. You see people struggling to get out of their Doc Martens or their over-the-knee boots in the security area, whereas you can kick off your loafers in a second and overtake.

Then, when the plane journey is over and your feet have swollen to the size of barrage balloons, you can hear the grunts of fellow passengers as they try in vain to put their normal shoes back on, whereas when you have a loafer, you can just put the front of your foot in the shoe and the job's a good 'un.

You may find the idea of wearing the same shoes every day ridiculous, but trust me: when Corbyn has put a red flag over Downing Street, you'll be very glad of this advice. You will also be glad if you look at your bank statement and note that you haven't spent half your wage that month on what, when all is said and done, is nothing more than an insurance policy in case you tread on a piece of Lego.

Last week I accidentally alluded to the fact that Cara Delevingne is pointless. She isn't. I meant Meryl Streep.

11 March 2018

If you're so happy you could die, I have a suggestion: move to Finland

Following on from the success of its International Women's Day, soon after which we learnt that several extremely well-paid newsreaders are not paid quite as much as their extremely well-paid colleagues, the United Nations is preparing to stage its International Happiness Day this week.

Ahead of this global event, its annual World Happiness Report has just announced that the happiest place on earth is now – drum roll – Finland.

And how have experts arrived at this conclusion? Well, it was simple. They went to all of the countries in the world and, in essence, asked the people they met if they were content. And more people said yes in Finland than anywhere else.

'Joo. I am very happy,' said Erik from Helsinki as he washed down his 50th sleeping pill and climbed into the bath with a Stanley knife and a gallon of cheap whisky.

I wonder if the UN thought about this. Seriously. Did it sit down at any point and think: 'Hang on. If these Finns are as happy as they claim to be, how come so many of them while away the day by committing suicide?'

According to the World Health Organization, the only people in the civilized bits of Europe who kill themselves significantly more often are the Belgians, usually because officers from their equivalent of Operation Yewtree are at the door.

Mozambique is one of the world's poorest countries. Life there is hard and hot but they do better than the miserable Finns. And it's the same story in Rwanda and even the Democratic Republic of Congo. Although to be fair, in the DRC, few people have the ability to kill themselves because some drug-crazed warlord has thrown them into an acacia tree.

Other spots in Europe where suicide is relatively popular include Iceland and Norway. And both of these are in the top five on the UN's happiness report.

So what's the disconnect then? How can people claim to be happy when they are sitting in a car, with a hosepipe coming through the window? Well, I think the answer is simple: the UN's report is complete claptrap.

Let's take Britain as an example of the problem. We finished in 19th place, which is not bad, but I suspect we'd have been a damn sight lower down the running order if the UN had done its research in Wakefield on a wet Tuesday evening in November.

When the first 'Beast from the East' was on its way, the BBC found a woman from somewhere grey and miserable in West Yorkshire who, because she couldn't afford to heat her house, spent all day riding around town on a bus. 'It's t'only way to stay warm,' she said.

I'm guessing now, but if you asked her to rate her level of contentment, to keep some halfwit at the UN's office in New York busy, she'd say minus a million and then tell you to eff off.

Whereas if you asked a family from Fulham who were playing in the waves outside Padstow on a beautiful June day if they were happy, they'd offer you some prosecco and say: 'Yes, very.'

Happiness is hard to pin down because there's the undercurrent and there's the moment. The undercurrent says that Jeremy Corbyn is coming and that makes me sad. But, as I write, the moment says that I'm going to the Cheltenham Gold Cup and that makes me happy.

There's more. If you are expecting the surgeon to cut off all your limbs and he announces at the last minute that he can save your left arm, you will be the happiest person in the world. Even though you won't be opening any cans any time soon.

Then you can have someone who's just got out of Cameron Diaz's bed. Happy? Not if he's just trodden on a piece of Lego.

According to the UN's report, money definitely makes you happier. But among its footnotes – and this will warm the cockles of Corbyn's heart – there are references to a previous study that suggests this is only true if you earn $75,000 (£54,000) a year. Any more or less and the happiness tails off.

The authors of this earlier research, both of whom have won Nobel prizes – for services to communism, probably – note that an increase in income beyond this point no longer improves a person's ability to do what matters most, such as 'spending time with people they like, avoiding pain and enjoying leisure'.

I see their point on that, if your idea of leisure is bowling or knitting or having a pint after work. But mine is going on a superyacht in the Caribbean, so not earning enough to do that would make me sad.

All of which brings me back to Finland, which is one of the most aggressive places I've been to. Other Scandinavian countries are full of socialism-lite people paying voluntary taxes and riding their pastel-coloured micro scooters to the recycling plant.

But Finland's not like that in my experience. It's often dark. There are many mosquitoes. Passers-by in the street will often – and for no reason – invite you to eff off. One man took out his penis and waved it at me. And in every bar I visited, there was always someone looking at me as though they were wondering how I'd look without skin.

It was more like Scotland, really, which is why it's no surprise to me that Finland's biggest export in recent years was the mobile phone app called Honey, Puppy Dogs and Kisses.

Oh no, wait. Sorry. It was Angry Birds.

PS: Don't worry. The UN's much anticipated World Toilet Day is coming, though not until November 19.

18 March 2018

Ignore the Scandi-killer on the TV, there's a real murderer just outside your window

When you come to the end of a box set that you've really loved, it's like coming to the end of a long-term relationship. You need to spend some time whittling wood and listening to Phil Collins before you can move on.

I felt like that when I finished *Black Mirror*. 'Nothing will ever be as good ever again,' I wailed into my snotty hanky. But last week, having swiped left on the remote for about a month, I came across a show called *Modus*. It's set in the snowy wastelands of Sweden and, as is usual with Scandi-dramas, it features various weirdly attractive people staring into the monochromatic scenery while solving a set of improbable murders.

Modus is not as good as *Black Mirror*. It's not even close. But it certainly satisfies the masochistic trend that compels us all towards a drama that makes us feel afraid, cold and miserable. We seem to like the violence and the slowness and the reminder that, deep down, happiness is something to do with the devil.

However, if all you want is a bit of misery, might I suggest that until the writer of *Black Mirror* stops collecting awards for the four series and gets on with the fifth, you turn off your television and go for a walk . . .

Last week, I didn't do that, obviously. But I was outside, seeing how much of my oil had been stolen that day, when a barn owl swept no more than 8in over my head. I didn't see it coming and, more astonishingly, I didn't hear it either. This was a medium-sized bird with a face that has the aerodynamic properties of a satellite dish, travelling at maybe 40mph, and it wasn't making a sound.

It swooped over a hedge and then, out of nowhere, it was attacked by a brace of crows. The owl twisted and turned but the bastards kept at it. Pecking. Grabbing. Ramming. Not since the late summer of 1940 had the skies over Britain seen such a dogfight.

I can only assume the owl was out early that night, before the sun had set, because it was hungry. And because it was hungry, it wasn't as strong as it should have been. Plus, it was like a Stuka, designed for fast dive-bombing, unlike the crows, which were the F-15s. The result of the drama was inevitable and soon, owly was dead.

We're always told that in nature everything is bright and beautiful and animals kill only for food. It's only humans in general, and Scandinavians in particular, who strangle and stab for fun. So I figured that the owl-versus-crow contest was a one-off and that I'd witnessed something unusual.

It seems not. Three days later, the papers ran a large photograph of a sparrowhawk standing on an upturned starling. You could see the panic in the starling's face and the cold detached killer look of a Nazi zombie in the eyes of the hawk. It was a brilliant picture with more drama than you'd get in a week of television.

And it gets better. After I'd finished the newspapers, I picked up a copy of *Country Life*, where there was an even more amazing photograph. It showed a great grey shrike standing by the carcass of a mouse that it had impaled on a large thorn. Not even the girl with the dragon tattoo thought to do that to her victims. Small wonder its nick-name is the butcher bird.

This is a creature that can peel the skin off a toad before eating the innards. It can lure other birds into an ambush by mimicking their cries. Oh, and it kills by beating vic-tims to death with its beak.

It is a rare sight in Britain these days, but if you can't find one, don't despair because the much more common thrush can entertain you by smashing a snail to pieces on a rock.

Abroad, things get even more gruesome. On one Afri-can holiday, I was watching a little monkey preening itself in a tree when, out of nowhere, an eagle arrived. There was a bit of a kerfuffle during which the bird quite simply emptied the monkey. When the dust settled it was sitting on a branch with a bloodstained beak and what appeared to be a monkey glove puppet on its foot.

Then, on holiday last month, I sat at the breakfast table each morning, watching all the birds fight over which one would get to the breadbasket first. There was a sparrow with a wonky leg we called Peg, and all the other birds, sensing his disability, picked on him. For them, a bit of warm croissant was less important than annoying Peg.

During the day, I liked to sit in a treehouse watching the fairy tern chicks – almost certainly the cutest crea-tures on God's green earth – defending their patch from adult ingress. They'd stick their arms out and fluff up their down and charge at birds four times bigger.

As Sir Attenborough was not on hand, I had no idea why they were doing this. But being confused didn't detract from the show. I mean, I hadn't a clue what was going on in *Inception* either but I still watched to the end.

There was a story last week about a singer who decided to take the money she'd earned and start a bee farm in the sticks. It all sounded a bit yoga and yoghurt to me at the time but now I'm not so sure.

Because all the things you see and love on the television – apart from *The One Show*, obviously – can be found, for nothing, in your garden: murder, violence, intrigue, bullying, beauty and heroism.

Plus you can get involved, rewarding the heroes and punishing the villains. Which is why, after the crows had killed the owl, I got my shotgun and, with a plaintive cry of 'Don't pick on the little guy,' blew both their heads off.

25 March 2018

45 litres of red from pump No 4, please – that's how I want to buy my wine

Do you know what our biggest problem is today? We are burdened with far too much choice. A surprising claim, I know, but think about it. If you arrive in a car park and there's one space, life is easy. But if you arrive in a car park that's empty, it's almost impossible to decide which space would be best. So you end up driving round and round for hours.

Margaret Thatcher taught us that choice was a good thing, that state ownership of gas, telecommunications and the railways didn't work because there was no alternative to bad service, grimy sandwiches and high prices. We all bought into that. We were all urged to 'tell Sid' as we invested in gas shares, and we flicked the 'V' at Arthur Scargill as he was dispatched back to his bungalow with his tail between his legs.

But hang on a minute. In Chadlington, in Oxfordshire, there is a village shop. It is the best village shop in the world. Everything is fresh. The cheese doesn't cost more than a car. And the young women who work there are chummy and trusting and wonderful. That shop? It would have Thatcher drooling.

But if you take her vision of Britain to its natural conclusion, there should be two village shops in Chadlington, and the owners should compete with each other for business. That's capitalism, and capitalism is how the world goes round. So one of the owners would eventually buy one of the two shops in another village to use economies of scale to keep his prices down. And this would drive both his rivals out of business.

Pretty soon he'd buy another shop, and then another, and then you'd end up with only five village shops in the whole country. These would be called supermarkets. Then one day someone called Jeff would come along and think: 'I can undercut these supermarkets if I do away with the actual buildings. I shall therefore sell everything online.' So then there are no village shops and we are back where we started, with no choice about where we buy our stuff.

And is that a bad thing? I'm not just saying this because I make a television show for Amazon but, seriously, have you ever been on its shopping site and thought: 'I wish there was an alternative to this cheap and convenient way of buying my washing-up liquid'?

Yes? Really? OK, then think about this. One day you're at work and you get the call you dread most of all. One of your children has been hurt, and before you can get all the details, your phone's battery goes flat. Happily, because you have an iPhone, other people at work can lend you a charger. But what if you've been a clever clogs and bought a Samsung instead? You'll feel a proper idiot as you stand in the local phone box wondering what half-wit decided to turn it into a defibrillator.

When I have a hangover, I don't want a menu; I want a McDonald's. And when I order a Coke and the barman says, 'Would you be OK with Pepsi?', I always reply: 'Sure. If you'd be OK with Monopoly money.'

This is at its worst in an off-licence. You want a bottle of red and the Frenchman behind the counter shows you a wall of choice. He talks about how one offers you hot handbags in a Bovril factory and another some notes of Angela Merkel hovering over a cauldron of sawdust. And as he drones on, you're just thinking: 'I want to get pissed.' Wine should be sold like petrol. While I'm at it, cheese should be sold like logs.

I've a similar problem in art galleries. I don't need to know how the artist began at a street cafe in Hoxton or how Damon Albarn bought his last work. I just want something 2ft by 3ft for about 50 quid. I do like a choice in a shop that sells paint. But nothing like the choice we have now. Someone needs to tell Farrow & Ball there's only one beige, not 500.

We waste an enormous amount of time making decisions based entirely on this fanciful notion that we like alternatives. On the morning I wrote this column I asked a waitress for poached eggs on toast and was given a list of toast options that went on for about a week. Toast is toast. It's made from sliced white bread. The end.

The day before that, I needed to get from somewhere called Are, in Sweden, back to Britain. The airlines would like to think I spent hours with their brochures and based my decision on the quality of their food and the smiliness of their stewardesses. But I didn't. I ended up in the communistical squashed world of a one-class-for-all SAS Boeing because that set off at the most convenient time.

That brings me neatly on to the vexed question of where Britain's next runway should be built. If you live in Crawley, the answer is Gatwick. If you live anywhere else in the entire world, the answer is Heathrow.

And while we are on the subject of transport, you can set yourself up as an owner-operator taxi driver, billing yourself in your adverts as a clean, safe chap who knows where he's going and isn't even slightly predatory. But you won't get anywhere, because people don't want a choice. They want Uber.

The government tells us that football fans should be given the choice of going to the World Cup in Russia this summer. Why? Because if you go, you will be stabbed, and if you don't, you won't. And what kind of choice is that?

It's like the choice we will face come the next election. Do we want a madwoman with silly shoes or a man who appears not to like Jewish people? They had the same problem in America, where they were asked to choose between a lunatic and a woman with a stuck face.

Whereas when we were given someone whether we liked it or not, we got the Queen. And that hasn't worked out too badly, has it?

1 April 2018

Hard cheese, Corbyn, you will never fly the red beetroot over No 10

So let's see if I've got this straight. Jeremy Corbyn is besieged on all sides by people accusing him of being an anti-semite. So he decides, in the midst of the storm, to go to a party held by a group of Jewish radicals. He doesn't take a bottle of wine or some soap – that would be too bourgeois. Instead he rocks up in an anorak, obviously, with a bundle of fresh beetroot, which is the most right-on thing I've heard of.

He was greeted with chants of 'F*** the police' and 'F*** the Tories', and there were exhortations to have a revolution. And that's all fine and what you'd expect, but weirdly the event was full of people who reckon Israel is a 'steaming pile of sewage'.

So he's being depicted on social media as Hitler and he's chosen to quieten the noise by passing the evening with people who allegedly booed when the name of the president of the Board of Deputies of British Jews was mentioned and do everything in their power to annoy the nation's rabbis. As PR strategies go, it's up there with Harvey Weinstein choosing to address his issues by going to the Presidents Club dinner.

Now I know that in 2015 I said in one of these columns that I would leave Corbyn alone. I saw no need to ridicule his beard or his tracksuits or his collection of photographs of manhole covers, because then he seemed to have no chance of becoming prime minister. Now, though . . .

He spent his earliest years in the agreeable-sounding Wiltshire village of Kington St Michael, where nothing has happened since the 17th century. And nothing happened then either. He went to a fee-paying prep school and in his teens became a left-wing lunatic.

This is quite normal. Many young people dally with communism because they are too busy worrying about spots to get much of a handle on how the world works. They just want to stay in bed and have the government send them tickets for Glastonbury once in a while. Capitalism, to them, means getting up.

Of course, most people give up on socialism when they get their first pay packet and see how much has been deducted in tax. A friend of mine's son became a dyed-in-the-wool Tory overnight when he was told the money had been taken by the government to pay for schools and hospitals. He accepted that, but rang his mum in a panic when he got his second pay slip. 'They've done it again,' he wailed.

Corbyn was different. He clung on to his socialism and got a job teaching geography in Jamaica. But that was far too colourful and enjoyable, and there is no space in the world of Marx for jollity and sunshine. So he went to north London instead and enrolled at a polytechnic to study trade unions. Sadly, he left after a year, having spent most of his time arguing with the tutors.

This means he's the only person in the world with fewer qualifications than me. He admits he hasn't read any books on the economy but says he's looked at a few. I'm not sure this equips him to run the country. I mean,

I've looked at a few elephants over the years, but that doesn't mean I'd be a good zookeeper.

As a backbencher he made it his mission to object to just about everything anyone said. When Labour was in power he defied the whip a staggering 428 times. And he built a reputation for supporting absolutely anything that was anti-British. So just weeks after the IRA's Brighton hotel bombing in 1984 that killed five people, he invited the then Sinn Fein leader Gerry Adams to visit the Commons.

He was later arrested while protesting against the show trial of the man convicted of setting the bomb. And naturally he supported the men who were convicted of bombing the Israeli embassy in London. He nearly went to jail over the poll tax, and once defied Labour policy on law and order by saying only the National Front would want greater police powers in Britain.

Naturally, he was passionate about the plight of dispossessed people from the Chagos islands, even though literally no one has ever heard of them. I'm fairly sure they haven't even been an answer on *Pointless*.

He also supported the miners, cross-dressers, Middle Eastern terrorist groups, Campaign for Nuclear Disarmament and so on and so on, and opposed privatization in all its forms. He was a walking cliché. A poster boy for the permanently disillusioned.

He's been married three times but still found time to take Diane Abbott on a motorcycling tour of East Germany. And who would do that? I've been to East Germany, and apart from some beautiful cobbled towns, it is in no way a match as a holiday destination for France, Greece, Spain, California, Italy, Portugal,

Switzerland, Vietnam, the Seychelles, Austria or indeed West Germany.

In fact, if I had to choose the worst place to go on holiday, it would be Algeria. But East Germany runs it a close second. And I certainly wouldn't go on a motorcycle and it definitely wouldn't be with Diane Abbott.

But I'm not Corbyn. He looks at a situation and thinks: 'Once I've worked out what everyone else is doing, I'll do the exact opposite.' His unpredictability is completely predictable. I knew he was going to side with Russia on this Salisbury thing long before he did.

This is almost certainly why he went to that weird leftie gig last week. It was all a gigantic middle finger to everything Tunbridge Wells holds dear. Apart from the beetroot, obviously.

And I like that in a man. I like someone who stands at the back and throws bricks. And I especially like it from the leader of the Labour Party. Because it means that, despite what my gut thinks, he cannot and will not ever be prime minister.

8 April 2018

Choose life, Scotland. Choose a job. Choose exquisite views. But forget independence

One of the things I've never really understood about the people who voted for Brexit is why they thought they would be better off if British people were making British laws. Do they think British people are all the same? Because I'm not sure we are.

I, for example, have very little in common with an equally British Welsh hill farmer. And Princess Anne has only a basic facial arrangement in common with people who go to Millwall's away matches. Some people in Britain like painting watercolours. Some like doing wheelies on motorcycles. Some enjoy campanology. Others – me, for example – think all church bells should be made from kapok. Or the severed limbs of those who think bronze is better.

Even if you went further than Brexit and allowed the town I live in to govern itself, it would still be impossible to ensure everyone was happy. Because even in a small market town in the Cotswolds you have those who want to burn the supermarket down and those who like its cheap prices. Then there are those who want the roads to be more bicycle-friendly and those – me again, I'm afraid – who think all cyclists should be sent to prison.

The only way I could truly be happy is by making my house a nation state. And even then there'd be some issues about using mobile phones at the kitchen table, general demeanour among the under-25s and: who put an empty jar of horseradish back in the bloody fridge?

This is why I was in favour of a United States of Europe. I know I have nothing above a biological connection with a Romanian teenage gypsy or a Milanese fashion designer or a Swedish detective, but once you have two individuals being governed by the same person, you may as well have 200 million.

And that brings me on to Scotland. It had a vote on independence in 2014, and sanity prevailed. Then those who lost immediately decided they'd like another vote. And so it will go until, eventually, they win, and we will have to post soldiers on the road out of Gretna Green.

I don't understand the need for Scottish independence. The Battle of Falkirk was a very long time ago. And it's not as if England can win the Calcutta Cup any more. What's more, the Scottish have exactly the same problem with going it alone as we'll have post-Brexit.

The bi-curious artisan who's opened a craft shop in the Highlands selling jumpers knitted from her own armpit hair does not want the same things from Nicola Sturgeon as a heroin enthusiast from the tenements in Glasgow. They may think that getting rid of the English will unite them all and bring Sean Connery back. But it won't.

I spent several days recently up beyond Inverness, and I'm not trying to suck up to the Scots, but it really is absolutely eyes-on-stalks beautiful. We often talk about breathtaking views, but in the Highlands they literally do that.

I drove on Wednesday along the coast road north of Ullapool, and never have I gone so slowly. Sometimes the views were so spectacular, I coasted to a halt and never even noticed. The sky was the colour of a Norwegian model's eyes. Tendrils of cloud spilt over snow-capped mountains before being whipped into nothing by the wind.

And it went on and on and on. Past turquoise water like you find in the Maldives and islands as weird and as enticing as those in Ha Long Bay. This was – and I will take no argument on the matter – by far the most beautiful place on Earth. As far removed from anything we have in England as Timbuktu.

And yet on the radio there was the travel announcer talking about jams on the M25 and news reporters talking about Theresa May's policy on Syria and DJs discussing that night's opening of Soho House in White City, west London. They might as well have been talking about life on the moon.

Is that a bad thing? Really? Would the people who own the wonderful Kylesku hotel, which is just outside nothing at all, on a road that goes nowhere, be less interested in Syria or celebrity gossip than someone from Hemel Hempstead? Maybe they would find the M25 jams a bit boring, but the Scotland-first political correctness at the BBC means the report always begins with roadworks on the A9.

Do they want different laws? Really? What laws? Legalization of burglary? The age of consent raised to 48? Compulsory yodelling for anyone on a bicycle? No. They want the same things as you and I. Something to do in the day and some disposable income at the weekend.

At this point I should like to talk about the film *Local Hero*. It's about an American oil company that wants to turn a Scottish village into a refinery. But the longer the

Texan negotiator spends there, the more he wants to keep it as it is. It's a fabulous film. One of my favourites.

What I love most is the anarchy. The locals up there are all mucking in – so completely, they aren't really sure who has fathered the community's baby. They catch lobsters and paint their boats and at night they all meet in the pub for a chat and a few beers with the Russian trawlerman who's dropped by, totally unnoticed by anyone in authority.

Oh, sure, Whitehall is droning away 600 miles to the south, and the EU is making laws in Brussels, and there's a police station, probably, in the next town. But none of these things concern the villagers. They just want the oil money. And then to be left alone again.

Isn't that better? Just living your life while serious-faced people in suits make serious decisions about things that in the big scheme of things don't really matter? Politics exists only to keep David Dimbleby in a job.

And Scottish independence and Brexit and Catalonia? Yup. Same thing.

15 April 2018

Why the fuss about chemical weapons? The blowy-up ones kill you just as dead

If you believe the reports, Britain's contribution to the recent attack on Syria was a bit My Little Pony. While the French and the Americans were launching sophisticated missiles from a range of sleek warships and supersonic aircraft, we were lumbering about in our Sopwith Camels, shouting tally-ho and generally being a nuisance.

One report said that our only warship, HMS Austerity, had to be moved out of the way of the USS Gut Buster because, to save money, it hadn't been fitted with any actual weapons. Another suggested our planes had been built in 1979. In other words, Biggles was flying around in an airborne Morris Marina and winding the windows down to drop gravity bombs on the target.

My favourite story, though, was that the Rivet Joint, our top-secret spy plane, was monitored constantly by President Bashar al-Assad on his mobile phone's flight-tracking app.

Indeed, it's said that all Britain did to support the raid was provide the maps. Yup, forgetting perhaps that most people now have pretty good maps on their phones, the Royal Geographical Society sent over its cartography, drawn up by TE Lawrence himself, so that the gung-ho Americans and lackadaisical French would not hit Persia or Mesopotamia by mistake.

The message here is clear. We turned up with two 40-year-old biplanes, a ship with the armaments of a rowing boat, a spy plane that can be tracked by anyone with an iPhone and Sir Ernest Shackleton's map of South Georgia because Enid in the government's post room had got a bit muddled again.

However, to try to convince everyone that Britain had been a valuable part of a massive international effort to punish an evil dictator, Mrs May made a serious-faced speech in the House of Commons. And there was much wailing and gnashing of teeth on all sides.

Some said she should not have sent our maps without first consulting parliament. Others said she'd only sent them because Donald Trump had insisted. And Mr Corbyn said that he'd need irrefutable proof before making his mind up that Syria is a country, that President Assad is its leader and that there is such a thing as 'nerve gas'.

Meanwhile, in America, Mr Trump was busy on Twitter telling Wilbur and Myrtle that the USA would prevail just like it had done at the Bay of Pigs and in Vietnam. And everyone was clutching their baseball caps to their chests and weeping while Billy Ray Cyrus belted out 'The Star-Spangled Banner'.

I, however, was wondering what on earth just happened. Assad had launched a gas attack on his own people. I'm not Corbyn. I believe that. And to punish him, America and France had been given Dr Livingstone's maps to rain fire on a factory that they'd suddenly identified as a chemical weapons plant.

But hang on a minute. When Russia launched a similar attack on Salisbury, the world didn't respond by firing sophisticated weapons at the facility where they'd been made. It simply sent a few Russian diplomats home. We seem to be saying that the punishment for using chemical weapons will be used only if you are weak.

That's by the by, though. The main thrust of my concern is: why are chemical weapons treated differently from any other sort of weapon?

Around the turn of the last century, two separate treaties were drawn up in the Hague, banning the use of 'chemical agents'. But within a matter of years Germany was lobbing chlorine at Tommy in the trenches. This caused the allies to respond in kind, and pretty soon everyone was wandering round Belgium coughing up their lungs.

After the First World War was over, everyone had a meeting in Versailles and decided that, in future, Germany and, er, Bulgaria would never again be allowed to use chemical weapons.

In June 1925 they decided that everyone should be covered by the ban, so they sat down in Switzerland and agreed that while it was perfectly acceptable to mow down thousands with sustained machinegun fire, it was not acceptable to use gas of any kind.

Everyone went home and began to make as much as possible, because everyone else was probably making it too. So in 1972 there was another meeting, where everyone agreed to stop producing, transporting or even storing it. Nuclear weapons? Yes, they're fine. As is napalm. And anyone can have a Daisy Cutter and an Apache gunship. But nerve agents? Still the big no-no.

Why? We are told that, in the recent Syrian attack, many died, including children, but if you look at footage taken in the aftermath, it looks as if everyone is suffering from hay fever. Maybe that's what Assad did. Bomb them with pollen.

And then there's Salisbury. Russia made a nerve agent and transported it secretly all the way from Moscow to Wiltshire, and yet despite this Herculean effort it made only three people a bit poorly for a while. If it'd simply used a pistol, Sergei Skripal would now be dead, there'd still be a full complement of spies in the embassy and Plod would still be sitting around wondering why someone had shot such a nice old man.

Remember the Ebola outbreak? We were told everyone in the world would be dead in a fortnight. But after it swept across six countries, the eventual death toll was just over 11,000. That's how many die on the roads every four days.

This, then, is my suggestion. The world needs to sit down again and get rid of chemical weapons once and for all, because they don't work properly.

And, in future, the good guys will break out John Blashford-Snell's maps and retaliate against anyone who's been an arse, no matter what sort of weapon they've chosen to use.

22 April 2018

If this farm-supplies store folds, my pigs – and the Hamster – will starve

My colleague from the television, Richard Hammond, is a rural halfwit. In my mind, he lives in a medieval village where there are maypoles and stocks and the street lights are lit each evening by a man in a three-pointed hat. When you die there, you go to the plague pit on a cart.

Certainly, Richard doesn't like London. He finds it confusing and bossy and is never quite sure where he's going. The other day, he caused much merriment by announcing proudly that he'd finally swallowed his fear of going underground without being dead first, and come to work on 'the tubes'.

Then he caused more merriment by saying that he likes to take his family out for their Sunday lunch to Countrywide. Countrywide, for those of you who have two eyes, is a chain of agricultural supply hypermarkets dotted around the southwest. It sells horse blankets and fence posts and work boots. And Richard Hammond has his Sunday lunch there at the in-store cafe. He says it's very cheap.

I can't even begin to imagine what this lunch looks like. And how badly things must have gone for the chef so that he has ended up boiling vegetables for two hours, because that's the way his customers like them. I'm picturing the meat now. It's not something I'd want to put in my mouth. Unless the alternative was the chef's tongue.

'Don't tell me,' I said to a bewildered-looking Hammond. 'You also buy your wine there?' 'Yes,' he stammered, wondering where else you might buy it.

He wasn't joking. Between the crossbow cabinet and the boxes of weed killer, the store had a fridge full of wine that had been created, by the Wurzels and Pfizer, solely to take away the taste of the pork you'd just ingested.

Whatever, Richard came to work the other day with a long face because incredibly, to his mind, Countrywide had gone into administration. He was fearful that he and his family may have to start eating in confusing local pubs where the chefs cook the chips three times and write bits of their menu in French.

I too was slightly incredulous, but for different reasons. Because I also use Countrywide. Not as an off-licence or an alternative to the cafe at Daylesford but as the only place within a day's drive where I can get six padlocks, some baler twine and a pair of secateurs.

Doubtless, the people who have piloted this fine institution into a hillside will argue that their customers were getting all their rural needs online, but they are missing the point . . .

You may remember the British summer. It arrived suddenly 10 days ago, and despite no gardening knowledge whatsoever, I was consumed with an immediate need to go outside and plant the beautiful wisteria that my daughter had bought as presents for my birthday.

This meant I needed six railway sleepers and a pile driver for creating a bed where they could grow. Not quite understanding what 'administration' meant – I know less about accountancy than I do gardening – I went to Countrywide, where I've had an account for years. And while it was open for business, all it had for sale was washing powder. I doubt this is a strategy that will save the business, unless everyone suddenly falls over in the mud.

Of course, I could have gone home and ordered what I needed from Amazon, who'd deliver it all within a day or two. But this was a British summer and by then it would be over. As indeed it was.

If you live in the countryside and you have more than a garden, you need Countrywide. It'd sell you the LPG for your machinery, and half-ton sacks of horse muesli. It would then take what you'd bought to your pick-up truck in a forklift and there'd be someone on hand to mend anything that went wrong.

I'm not Hammond. I can eat elsewhere and I can sure as hell buy my wine elsewhere, but on my farm I have more than 120 gates, all of which need to be maintained and painted, and how can I do that without Countrywide? My pigs also face an uncertain future now, that's for sure.

I am aware, of course, that there are many shops in London that sell wellies but these are for Glastonbury or shooting weekends. If you need a pair of wellingtons for going into the woods and pulling a horse chestnut tree out of the pond, you need Countrywide. If you want to shoot squirrels or mend a wall that's been destroyed by one of Brian May's badgers, you need Countrywide.

Losing it is like losing the police. Yes, it would be possible to hire private security and sit up all night, cradling a shotgun in your lap, and yes, it's possible to make a citizen's arrest. But that would require complicated planning, and all things considered, it's better to have Plod on the other end of a phone.

There were plans to rescue at least some of the stricken chain's 48 stores, but they were stymied by the announcement of an investigation by the Competition and Markets Authority (CMA), which used to be called the Office of Fair Trading. The suggestion was that if the takeover went ahead, there would be a monopoly on farming supplies, to which I scream: 'So bloody what?' The fire brigade has a monopoly but no one is suggesting we should have a choice of whom to call when our deep-fat fryer bursts into flames.

In my local town, Chipping Norton, many small shops have been squeezed into oblivion by the arrival of a hideous new Aldi supermarket. And no one from the CMA is moaning about that.

Which is why, this morning, I'm urging them to back off. Because otherwise all my fences will rot and Richard Hammond will starve to death.

29 April 2018

Here's the million-pound question – why have me instead of Stephen Fry?

It's 20 years since *Who Wants to Be a Millionaire?* first aired on British television, and to celebrate the anniversary, it's back for just one week with, er, me as question master. The first show was transmitted last night, and I appreciate some of you will want to watch it on catch-up so I won't say what happens. Apart from the fact it didn't exactly go as I'd hoped.

Everyone has their own ideas about why this brilliant show was canned back in 2014 but here's mine: people began to realize that if they could get into that chair, it was extremely easy to win a not inconsiderable £8,000.

They had to answer five quick-fire questions that even a toddler could get right and then they had a guaranteed £1,000. That's £1,000 for knowing that Abba were Swedish and the first man on the moon was not Joe Pasquale.

They could then use their three lifelines to get £8,000, and that meant they had enough to take the family on a nice cruise for two weeks. So then they'd jack it in, and the audience, I reckon, started to find this annoying. Certainly, I used to sit screaming at them for their lack of drive and empty nutsacks. And then later, after a wine or two, I'd tell anyone who'd listen that the problem was bound to be down to 'diversity'.

They fiddled with the format to address the issue but I'd still wail: 'It's the producers. They'd rather have a transgender person with a cute northern accent win small than a well-spoken woman from Fulham win a million.

'It should be a show,' I'd go on, 'that celebrates the brainpower of the well-read and the bright. And maybe even the lucky. Stupid people who just want enough for a bit of decking in the garden should be told to get lost. You don't see hunchbacked greasy young women on *Britain's Next Top Model*, so why should numbskulls be allowed on *Millionaire*?'

Chris Tarrant was brilliant at looking happy for someone who was going home with enough to buy a new fridge-freezer, whereas I used to figure that if they wanted to watch people winning money for no effort, they should film customers buying scratch cards in corner shops.

I always said if I'd been in Tarrant's shoes, I'd snarl and snap at hopeless contestants for wasting everyone else's evening. And now I am. When the call first came, asking if I'd like to do it, I said yes immediately. I am a ginormous quiz-show fan and watch *Pointless* every day. So the idea of hosting the biggest game show of them all . . .

Later, after I'd signed the contract, they gave me the bad news. The show would be recorded over four days in Manchester. It takes a lot to get me to the northwest. But hosting *Millionaire*, I was there two hours early.

Rehearsals were tricky because the Autocue – something we don't use on my car shows – was located about 500 yards from where I was standing. 'Good morning,' I said cheerily, 'and we're comb to How Wants to He a Billionaire.'

It wasn't just the eyesight that was letting me down either. The contestants, softly spoken and mumbly through nerves, were seated 8ft from my ears, which meant I couldn't hear a word they were saying. Especially with that constant music track playing.

So I couldn't hear the answers and I couldn't read the Autocue, and there was worse. To make the anniversary shows different, the producers came up with a fourth lifeline. Ask the host.

I'm not quite sure why they thought this was a good idea. Maybe they reckoned at the time they could get Stephen Hawking to be the question master. Or Stephen Fry. But they didn't. They got me, and all I know about is the 1979 Volkswagen Golf GTI. Art, literature, chemistry, sport – I'm clueless about the lot.

And that's a worry, because let's say someone has come to me for help with the £250,000 question. If I give them the wrong answer and they go for it, they'll lose a fortune. What if that happened? What face would I pull? It's something I've been practising in the mirror a lot.

And then it was time for the dress rehearsal. A proper show with proper contestants on the actual set. And immediately I ran into a problem I simply hadn't thought about.

On a quiz show, you can't just talk normally. You have to use trigger words, which instigate the lighting moves, the sound effects and the dramatic music. And when these are happening, you have to just sit there, not saying anything at all. This is not something I find easy.

Eventually, though, with night falling and the cameramen starting to mutter stuff about how Phillip Schofield would have been a better choice – or his dog – I started to get the hang of it.

The trouble is, I was concentrating on the sound effects so much, and straining my ears to the point they were giving themselves tinnitus, that I wasn't really looking at my screen. There's a lot of information on it – no, not the answers – but there is a little box telling me when to go to a commercial break.

In 28 years on the electric fish tank, I've never had to worry about this before. It just didn't occur to me, and it kept on not occurring to me right up to the point when the message changed from a solid 'break' in 4-point italics to a flashing 72-point missive saying: 'Oi f***face. Go to the break NOW.'

I have flown an Apache helicopter and I have now hosted *Who Wants to Be a Millionaire?*, and let me tell you: the chopper is much less complicated.

And that's before we get to the promise I made to myself that I'd snarl and snap at contestants who shouldn't really be there. I tried it on the first show and afterwards my girlfriend was cross with me because I'd been 'horrid'.

I can't win. Unlike the contestants, who, we should never forget, can.

6 May 2018

Ich bin ein Mancunian – Britain's Berlin throbs with hot bars and fit bodies

Disastrous news, I'm afraid. Never mind the customs union or the Irish border; we have already been told by the EU that we can no longer submit candidates to become the European capital of culture. We will, from now on, have to rely on our own competition, the UK city of culture. The judges scoured the land looking for somewhere with a vast but underfunded cultural movement to assume the title from 2013, and alighted upon Londonderry, which wasn't a PC decision at all.

When the time came to choose a city to take over the role four years later, competition was fierce. Leicester, which is very like Rome and Paris except on a cellular level, was up against Dundee, Swansea and Graham Norton, who reckoned the award should go to Bexhill-on-Sea. You get the impression that if Stuart Hall hadn't been banged up, they'd have got the contestants to wear big yellow shoes and fall over in a paddling pool.

Hilariously, the title eventually went to Hull, where it resides now – a city famous for its weird phone boxes and Philip Larkin, who, shortly after he arrived on Humberside, wrote to a friend saying: 'I'm settling down in Hull all right. Every day, I sink a little further.'

A third winner – Coventry – is already chosen for 2021, but I reckon we have a more pressing issue. Where exactly is Britain's second city? Historically the answer has always been Birmingham, but I wonder if that's the case any more, because while other cities in the UK have re-invented themselves in recent years, Birmingham seems to be stuck.

My colleague Richard Hammond has an anecdote about a professor at Birmingham University – and before Noddy Holder calls to complain about this, I should explain both Hammond and his professor are local men – who said that there's a very good reason for this: 'The problem with people from Birmingham is that they like crap.'

So if it's not Birmingham, where is it? Well, there's a case for making it Glasgow, but if that happens, we're going to have people from Belfast and Cardiff doing a palms-up shrug and feeling left out. This is always the problem with making politically correct decisions. You open a lavatory to transgenderists and immediately the feminists are waving placards outside your offices and there's dog dirt on your doormat.

A number of years ago the BBC decided to survey the population on the matter and found that nearly half thought Britain's second city was Manchester. Ha-ha-ha, I thought.

I guess that at around this time the corporation was in the process of moving many of its shows to the north-west and wanted to make staff feel better about having to up sticks. It didn't work very well, though, because even the man it put in charge of getting people up north remained resolutely in Richmond upon Thames.

I'll be honest. I've never been a fan of Manchester. The much-missed AA Gill and I once wrote at some length about how we disliked the rich towns and villages around what we both agreed was a run-down, jumped-up, drizzle-soaked swamp. Imagine my despair, then, when I received the contract to host *Who Wants to Be a Millionaire?* and noticed that it was to be filmed in Salford.

On the first night I took two of my children to a very grand-looking Italian restaurant called Rosso. Being from London, where people go out for dinner because they can't be arsed to do the washing-up, and from a family who think that dining out on special occasions is odd, we were wearing ordinary clothes. And so, as we walked in, there was a marked drop in noise. People couldn't believe it. There were actual white people in the restaurant. Not orange.

Everything on everyone else in there was extended. Lips, breasts, hair – you name it. And if you're planning on opening a bra shop in Manchester, forget it. Bras, plainly, are for the weak.

Then there were the men, all of whom had Action Man bodies, Ken doll hair and shrink-wrap suits. Their shoes were pointy and their cheek bones chiselled.

And it wasn't just in that restaurant either. It was everywhere. Manchester makes Marbella look like La Paz. It's bonkers and – whisper this – absolutely brilliant. Maybe it's the football or maybe it's the massive 'media city', but something has turned Manchester into a British Berlin. And that, I assure you, is high praise.

I was mostly stuck in a studio, but on the way I did see some magnificently restored Victorian warehouses jammed up against genuinely interesting modern architecture. Amazingly, the sun was shining – this happens about once every 14 years in Manchester – and, boy, were the townsfolk making the most of it. The men peeled off their hermetic suits and replaced them with Orlebar

Brown shorts, the women slipped into some dental floss and everyone headed for the waterside bars to hang out and mate.

Me? Well, I needed to get a haircut, so I found a nice Alsatian with a ponytail, who sat me down and insisted we chat before he broke out the scissors. 'It's important I get to know your personality before I start,' he said. I tried to explain that I have the sort of personality that wants my hair to be made shorter in the least possible time, but he was having none of it, and soon I was sobbing on the floor while talking about my mother.

When I arrived back in London, it felt dowdy and monochromatic, and now I've made a decision. Manchester is not Britain's second city. It's the first. And it should be the next city of culture too, not because it was once home to Geoffrey Chaucer – it wasn't – but because it is the city that best represents the culture we have now. Fake breasts, Ferraris and football.

13 May 2018

I'm sure you'll be dying to hear about my plans for a population implosion

We are forever being told that to save the planet, we must forgo soap while showering, use soggy paper straws while drinking, eat like budgerigars and have our heads crushed under the wheels of an articulated lorry while cycling to work. And now there's a new thing: a racing driver in America called Leilani Münter has said we must not have children.

Don't be cruel. She may be called Münter but she isn't one. In fact, she earns some of her living as a Catherine Zeta-Jones lookalike and is to be found on the internet in a selection of dresses that expose a great deal of flesh. Take it from me, her decision to not have children has nothing to do with the fact she can't get a suitor.

A lot of people will be very cross with her for saying this – Mr Pope, for example. But also a great many couples whose bits don't work properly. I have many friends who have gone – sometimes literally – to the ends of the earth so they can have children. And I absolutely understand why.

Yes, it's true, you can only be as happy as your least happy child and they are a constant font of worry and stress. But I cannot imagine what life would be without them or the fizz I get when I know I'm going to spend time with them. They are, quite literally, the point of my existence.

I'll go further. We are all nothing more than life support

systems for our genitals. We exist for only one reason: to pass the baton on to the next generation. And if we choose not to do that, then we are not being human. We are nothing more than furniture.

However, the problem is that Ms Münter has a point. In the early 19th century, which isn't that long ago, the global population reached a billion. It is now more than 7.5 billion and growing at the rate of at least 1.5 million a week so that in just over 30 years it'll be up to about the 10 billion mark. If we carry on doing what we are designed to do, therefore, we won't keep the species going. We will kill it off.

Already, the world's farmers are struggling to keep up with demand and the simple fact is that this won't be possible when there are 10 billion mouths to feed. Especially if those idiots from Greenpeace keep rolling around on experimental crops. There won't be enough water either. There won't be enough of anything, in fact.

That's why it's not just Ms Münter who reckons that to keep the human race going she must sit there with her legs crossed. Her views are shared by Sir Attenborough and lots of scientists with bad hair and plastic shoes.

But their thinking isn't practical. Asking for volunteers to remain childless is silly. You might get a few weirdos on Planet Corbyn to put their hands up, but not doing what you're designed to do requires a level of willpower that we just don't have. It'd be like asking a washing machine to mow the lawn.

Of course Ms Münter will say, as she stands there pouting, that she is raising awareness, but when people say that, they mean they are doing nothing at all. It's like those 'marine biologists' who announced last week that

they are going to sail around the tropics, fishing plastic
from the sea. This is raising awareness, for sure, but what
they're actually doing is sailing around the tropics. If they
were doing it in the Humber estuary, in November, we'd
all have a bit more sympathy for their cause.

Certainly, I'd have a bit of sympathy for the cause of
Ms Münter and Sir Attenborough if only they'd look at
other ways of controlling the population. Speed limits,
for example. Now that we are all restricted to 20mph in
cities and not much more than 50mph anywhere else, it's
very hard to die in a car crash. Whereas in India, which
has recently raised its speed limits, more than 150,000
died on the roads in 2016 alone.

Then there's the issue of those signs in shopping centres that advise visitors the floor is slippery when it's wet.
Without those, we could probably cull 20 or 30 people
every year, and they'd be the stupid ones too, which is
good for natural selection.

To get population numbers down dramatically, though,
we should think about invading Russia. At present, we
are allowing Vladimir Putin to get away with blue murder. He's taken over parts of Ukraine and is dropping
bombs all over Syria. Well, in one fell swoop we could
put a halt to his antics and reduce the population by millions in months. I wonder if Ms Münter would like that?

I notice that there's been an outbreak of Ebola in the
Democratic Republic of Congo. This is a country with
one of the top 30 birth rates in the world so how's this for
a plan? Instead of sending aid, and doctors and hazmat
suits, let's just sit back and enjoy the sunshine.

Oh, and while we are at it, let's close down the Samari-
tans. If people want to jump off the Clifton suspension

bridge, let them. In fact, let's start a new charity that encourages people to top themselves. Maybe Sir Attenborough would be the patron.

Or should we use tax to solve the problem, forcing couples who have more than two kids to pay for the privilege? They tried that in China, as I'm sure you know, and it meant a lot of dead baby girls were thrown into sewers.

And that's the problem with population control. A voluntary system won't work and every other method requires a level of cruelty that no sane person has.

It's possible you haven't seen the new Avengers film – *Infinity War* – in which the bad guy is obsessed with overpopulation in the universe and wants to kill half of all the living souls.

The idea Sir Attenborough would be cheering him on seems faintly weird.

20 May 2018

Puffins or seals? Easy – let's get clubbing the Labrador-faced swimming machines

On my farm this year, 175 acres is being used to grow oilseed rape. Yes, the dust it gives off in the breeze drops my voice an octave or two and makes visitors look tearful but its beautiful yellow flowers are a welcome break in the endless patchwork of green, and as crops go, it is extremely versatile.

It can be used to make candles, food for cows, sexual lubricants, margarine, soap, plastic and green fuel for power stations. When mine is harvested, it will be taken to a factory in London and crushed to make cooking oil, which will fill 100,000 bottles on the supermarket shelves next year.

There's no money to be made from farming, but I quite like the idea that my land is being used to make the bread and the bacon needed to offset the effects of the beer I also grow. It makes me feel all warm and fuzzy.

However, last week a man called Stephen Moss, who is the president of the Somerset Wildlife Trust, said that rape may be pretty but that if you ingest the oil it produces, your heart will become deformed and diseased. And that's just the start of it. He also says that no other arable crop requires so much help to grow and that the fertilizers used invariably get into the water supply, which produces many swollen babies.

I suppose I could point out that the long, cold winter this year killed off many of the bugs that would normally attack a field of oilseed rape, so much less spraying has been necessary. But this, of course, is a one-off.

Most years, as Mr Moss explained, rape must also be sprayed with chemical insecticides, and that, as we all know, will eventually kill all the world's bees. And without bees 70 per cent of the world's crops could not grow, which would cause massive global food shortages, leading to looting, violence and, ultimately, a thermonuclear world war.

Mr Moss goes on and on about the evils of rape, saying that the herbicides it needs kill off wild flowers and that it's so dense, it forms an impenetrable barrier to ramblers. I was going to ask him what on earth a rambler would be doing walking through the middle of a field of crops, but there was no time – and no point either, because the cagoule enthusiasts are a law unto themselves. Legally speaking, you can't even shoot one. Mr Moss carried on, banging on about dead chaffinches and voles and how rapeseed oil used to fuel power stations isn't green at all.

After I had finished reading his spittle-drenched rant, I looked out of the window at my fields of rape and was filled with guilt and shame. I'm a warmongering baby-killer and I should immediately put on a hazmat suit and roll around on my fields, Greenpeace-style, until everything is dead.

But then what? The world uses soya oil instead? Doubtless, at this point, the nation's ramblers and tofu enthusiasts will be bouncing up and down, shouting: 'Yes, yes, yes'. Soya beans are about as Shoreditch as food gets. It's not just nourishment. It's a statement of political intent.

Unfortunately, soya bean production needs a lot of

land. In 1940, before Jeremy Corbyn had been invented, 1,700 acres of Brazil were needed to grow it. But today there are so many vegetablists in the world that about 74 million acres of Brazil are used to keep them healthy.

What's more, most of the world's soya beans are treated with hexane, which you get from crude oil. Oh, and then there's the problem with soil erosion and the loss of habitat for millions of species around the world. Remember that next time you have a bit of tofu. Yes, you've declared solidarity with Diane Abbott, but you have also killed a panda.

So what about palm oil? Same sort of thing, really, only this time it's the orang-utan that's at risk as farmers chop down more and more trees to keep up with demand from Britain's ramblers. The problem is acute, but, happily, I have a solution.

You may have read last week that the gorgeous little puffin has become an endangered species. This is saddening news for me, as I like puffins very much. So much so that it's one of the few things I haven't ever eaten. Once, a restaurateur in Iceland offered to grate some onto my whale steak, but I had the guillemot instead.

When they are six weeks old, puffins drag themselves into the sea and don't see dry land again for five years. They just bob about, helping themselves to little fishes that swim by and preening their feathers to keep them oily and waterproof.

Naturally, the little bird's decline is blamed, by those who said diesel was good and then said it wasn't, on global warming. But that's nonsense. Then you've got the other fall-back excuses: oil spills and plastic in the sea.

But I fear everyone is skirting around the real culprit.

Johnny Seal. Ever since some supermodel or other decided not to wear fur, people who clubbed seals for a living became more ostracized than paedophiles. The Labrador-faced swimming machines were regarded as deities, and all sorts of laws were drawn up to make sure they thrived.

Which they have done, and then some. Since 1978 the seal population has risen by 500 per cent, and it's said that by 2030 we will be able to walk on a bed of seal from Cork to New York.

And here's the thing. Seals eat puffins. And ruin the habitat where they breed. So how's this for a plan: we stop getting our oil from rape and palms and soya plants and get it instead from omega-3-rich seals. That's good for pandas, puffins, orang-utans, ramblers, trawlermen, babies and world peace.

27 May 2018

Real diamonds are clearly designed to ruin men. Give me a Didcot knock-off any day

As we know, it is completely impossible for a normal human man to buy jewellery for his wife or girlfriend. And soon it's going to be harder still. In the run-up to last Christmas I was given a subtle hint that I should buy some drop earrings. And when someone says, 'I don't have any drop earrings and I would like some,' even I'm able to work out the hidden meaning.

So I went online to see what a drop earring was and then went to London, where I reckoned I'd be able to buy some.

There were many on show, but after 20 minutes of staring at them, with the same level of interest as I use on red traffic lights, I was fighting back the urge to curl up on the pavement and die of boredom. But then one pair caught my eye. They were blue, and as I like the colour blue, I went into the shop and asked the orange lady behind the counter if she would get them out of the locked glass case.

There was a lot of pomp that went into granting this simple request, and as the door swung open, I half expected to be serenaded by Beethoven's 'Ode to Joy'. But eventually the earrings were laid out on a cushion for me to inspect. This was like asking my mother to inspect a ship's boiler. I had no idea what I was supposed to notice, so I said: 'Mmmm. Yes. They're lovely. I'll take them.'

There was then more pomp, and I was offered a glass

of champagne while the earrings were wrapped, and then I was presented with the bill, which was, and there's no other way of saying this, £67,000.

It was hard to work out what I should do at this point. My mind was spinning and my eyes were suddenly full of sweat. 'Hmmm,' I said. And then, 'Hmmm,' I said again, buying some time until a solution presented itself. Eventually, I'm delighted to say, it did. I turned and fled.

Why don't jewellery shops put prices on the jewellery they're selling? Do they like humiliating their customers? Or are they practising for some kind of world smirking championship? And, while we are at it, why don't they also provide a handy guide next to each piece explaining why it is worth £67,000 more than the stuff you get in seaside trinket shops?

Bridegrooms in Britain spend around £500 less on engagement rings than brides would expect. But, apart from in Yorkshire, where the figure is lower, they still blow around £1,500. You could get a pretty good car for that. Certainly it'd buy you a very stylish oven. Whereas all you get from a ring is some metal and a rock.

To me all jewellery looks exactly the same. A gold bracelet that you win if you are good at hooking a fairground duck is identical in every way to a bracelet that you buy from one of those Bond Street shops that are guarded by former soldiers with curly earpieces.

And diamonds? You can tell a good one from a bad one only if you have 30 years of training and a very powerful microscope. Or if you are a shallow woman in Monte Carlo. To me they are all sort of silvery and see-through and small. Carats, in my book, are like DEFCON numbers. Are the higher ones better, or is it the other way round? I'd be as useless at being a billionaire as I would at being a president of America.

And now things are about to get even tougher, because in a U-turn in policy on synthetic diamonds, De Beers has decided that it's silly to wait 4 billion years for a diamond to form and has announced that it's to start a production line in its factory in Oxfordshire that can make them in three weeks. Now I happen to know that in Namibia, once every so often, mining companies use hundreds of bulldozers to push the beach out to sea at low tide. This creates a flimsy sea wall, which holds the incoming tide at bay while thousands of workers scamper onto the seabed with toothbrushes to look for diamonds stuck in the cracks of the rock.

Of course, I can see that something that needs this level of danger and expense to recover is going to be a bit pricy. Whereas something made in Oxfordshire by squeezing and heating a small honeycomb of carbon isn't. Yes, the squeezing is quite intense – the same pressure as the Eiffel Tower sitting on a fizzy drinks can, in fact. And the heating is more than you can get from a Primus stove. But we are not talking about kryptonite here. Carbon is the fourth most abundant element in the universe. So charging big money for it would be as daft as charging big money for hydrogen and oxygen. Actually, strike that – Evian does.

Whatever, when De Beers is up and running with its new diamond factories, I shall be presented by an orange shop lady with two diamonds. One has taken billions of years to form under Africa and has been recovered by the performance of dental work on the seabed, and the other has been made, like a pencil, in Didcot. And to my eye they will appear to be identical. Which is because they are identical. Because they are both diamonds.

De Beers itself has spent millions over the years on machines that can tell laboratory diamonds from the real thing. So why, it must be asked, bother with the real thing at all?

Giving me the choice in a shop of spending £2,000 on the real thing or £600 on something that is also real, but that will get me a slap should the receipt ever surface, is just another unnecessary burden of difficulty for the human male.

Still, at least we don't have to buy wedding dresses. Because – and I will take absolutely no argument on this – they are all identical as well.

3 June 2018

See the ruins of a lost civilization before the tourist hordes arrive – in Detroit

I was recently in a bare-brick-and-zinc-type restaurant in Detroit, enjoying a bowl of duck dumplings in a light broth, when I noticed I was only a couple of hundred yards from the city's derelict railway station. It was in there, just 20 years earlier, that an angry drug addict had held a semi-automatic shotgun to my head.

The next night I was in a Shoreditchy-type bar, sipping an excellent Chilean rosé, when I realized it was located on Michigan Avenue, and that back in the 1990s you would not even think about going there unless you were in a tank.

Most of us know the story of Detroit. It was the Motor City. Motown. It made a lot of cars that are now made in Mexico and music that is now made in Los Angeles. So the city withered, went bankrupt and died. Except my recent visit there demonstrated that it didn't die. And that now it is far and away the best tourist destination in the whole of North America.

Yes, according to the FBI, it is still the most violent city in America. Most people there are killed at least three times a day. But that means very few foreigners pay it a visit, which in turn means there are no queues at passport control. And, what's more, you don't get a surly official who knows for sure you're a terrorist and is determined to prove it. You get a guy who stands up, hugs you and thanks you profusely for coming.

Hotels. This is a new concept in modern Detroit, which means none of the staff have been infected with that overbearing American niceness. Most days at the converted fire station where I stayed, they ran out of orange juice at breakfast and made it very plain that this wouldn't have been an issue if I'd ordered something else.

If this doesn't appeal, you could buy a house. Many are on the market for about $10, but these are a bit run-down and some smelt of crystal meth. However, further up the scale I found an absolute gem for £40,000.

This, said the particulars, came with 'multiple ballrooms'. And that raises a question. How many ballrooms must a house have before the estate agent gets bored counting them? These low prices are attracting lots of young people, who are starting up tech companies and microbreweries and cool restaurants. In my experience only New York can match Detroit for food these days. Only in New York it isn't actually growing in the streets, whereas in Detroit it is.

The urban farming initiative is nowhere near as big as you might have been led to believe. We've been told that huge swathes of the city have been turned into allotments, but the fact is that of the million or so available acres, only three are being used to grow organic peace vegetables.

The other 999,997 acres beggar belief. You drive for mile after mile and every building is either burnt out or boarded up. Many have gone altogether and have been replaced with hay. It's like Chernobyl, only bigger and more empty. You'll do more Instagramming here than anywhere else in the world.

Occasionally you come across a giant factory, which

back in the day made Packards or Cadillacs but is now just a creaking, groaning shell full of nothing but drips and the faint whiff of asbestosis. People travel for thousands of miles to see the ruins of Siem Reap in Cambodia and none is as eerie or as impressive as those in Detroit.

And when you've looked round, and it's evening time, you can visit one of the city centre's many lap-dancing bars, all of which take equal opportunities so seriously that even the cleaning ladies are encouraged to get up on stage and give it a go.

There are also some shops. I counted three. And that's good, because no one wants to waste their time buying stuff they don't need from exactly the same retail cathedrals we have at home. What we do not have at home, however, is the very beautiful Detroit Institute of Arts.

Built and filled when Detroit was pretty much the richest city in the world, it's enough to cross the eyes of even a philistine like me. In one room there's a Picasso just hanging there. No guards. No alarms. No bulletproof screen like the one they use to protect that cracked stamp known as the Mona Lisa in Paris. And this is the best bit: it wasn't even straight. Who has a Picasso and puts it on the wall cock-eyed?

Then there's a Rodin you can stroke and countless other priceless pieces that are displayed like the trinkets in a Stow-on-the-Wold junk shop. You can forget all the world's other museums; if you want to get up close and personal with a Monet, Detroit's where you need to be.

Further up the road, there's the Henry Ford museum, where you can lean on the actual car in which John Kennedy was shot, and there's also the financial district, where the grit-and-grind four-square skyscrapers now sit cheek by jowl with little greenhouses selling more kale and artisan T-shirts.

Many bore the encouraging slogan 'Say nice things about Detroit', which is what I'm doing here. Even though I do slightly miss the attitude on the shirt I bought last time I was there. It said simply: 'Detroit. Where the weak are killed and eaten.'

I spoke to one waiter who said that without noticing it he'd walked home the other night. 'For the first time in my life, it didn't occur to me not to,' he said. So, yes. Detroit is still a cracked and unused car park, but now there's a rose growing out of it. A sense that life will prevail.

Which raises an interesting point. If Detroit can go to the brink, peer over the precipice of doom and then stage a comeback, maybe we shouldn't worry quite so much about those industrial towns in the north of England that seem these days to have no real point either.

17 June 2018

A little gift I'd love to give the man who stole my TV – extreme police brutality

A report in *The Sunday Times* last week revealed that in England and Wales only 4 per cent of robberies and a mere 3 per cent of burglaries are solved by the nation's policemen and policemen women. Things aren't much better when it comes to knife attacks, sexual assault and moped-related thefts. And Plod still hasn't found the man who nicked my television, even though I published a pin-sharp photograph of him leaving my flat in the *Sun*.

Naturally, every commentator in the land spent all of last week trying to work out why the figures are so lamentable, with many blaming the parents. I'm not sure this is relevant, though, as the man who nicked my television was in his thirties, and with someone that age, his mum and dad aren't really responsible for his whereabouts. It's the same story with the kid riding round on a small motorcycle with a large knife in his coat pocket. Chances are his parents are not around.

If you've just arrived in Britain, it doesn't take long to work out that you can make a safe and pretty decent living here by breaking into people's houses and stealing their things.

You know that the police are busy closing motorways and checking on foxes and ensuring school-run mums are not smoking in their cars, and that after the homeowners report the burglary they will be given the offer of some counselling, and that will be the end of that.

You know, therefore, that there's a 97 per cent chance you'll get away scot-free and that even if you're caught red-handed by the homeowner and hit over the head with a pickaxe handle, he'll be arrested and Jeremy Corbyn will bring you flowers in the free hospital.

And if you are one of the unlucky 3 per cent who are caught after the event, the arresting officers will make sure you don't bang your head when you get into the police car and will give you some nice soup at the station while they wait for a translator to turn up. Maybe a chicken sandwich as well.

If you are subsequently convicted, you will be given a short spell in a prison that is better than most of the hotels in the country from which you came. And while you're in there, a hand-wringing member of the shadow cabinet will make lots of speeches about you and how you were driven to crime by bankers and members of the Conservative Party.

All of this makes us – you and me – cross. So when we are apprehended by the police for doing 24mph, we tend to say things such as: 'Have you caught the man who stole my television yet?' This always makes Plod cross, but the truth is, it's a good question.

So the vast majority of law-abiding people have no respect for the police because we only ever encounter them when they are being pedantic and because they don't do anything about our stolen televisions. And they treat us like Fred West when we dip momentarily into a bus lane.

And then you have criminals who actually quite like the police because they're so much kinder than the forces of law and order back home.

And this is where I think the politicians can make a difference. If you are caught breaking the law in the more benighted countries of the world, you will be taken into a cell and kicked repeatedly in the testes.

That's what we need here, really, if we are to deal with the knife crime and burglary issues: extreme police brutality.

Obviously this would cause those of a criminal persuasion to think twice before climbing onto the moped that night. They'd know that there was only a slim chance they'd be caught, but that if they were, they would be attached to the mains through holes in their nipples until a week next Tuesday. Many, if they knew this, would get straight off their mopeds and start up a small business instead.

There's another advantage too. We, the good guys, would know that if the police caught the man who had stolen our television, he would not be given a sandwich and then sent home with an ankle bracelet. He'd be taken to where they keep the police dogs and treated as food.

Many of us would prefer that. I know I would. We've had to fill in insurance forms and deal with assessors, and then we've had to go online and buy another television and then wait for the delivery driver to stick a note through the letterbox saying: 'While you were in, I tip-toed up to your door and posted this because it's easier for me if you come to the depot and pick up the television yourself.'

It'd be satisfying to think that bits of the man or woman who caused all this nuisance were in a dog. Certainly, it would help restore our faith in the police if, when we popped round to the station to see if they'd found the man who stole our phone last night, the desk sergeant asked for a moment of silence so we could better hear the culprit trying to pull the fluorescent light tube out of his bottom without breaking it.

Also, we might be a little more understanding if, when we were pulled over for checking text messages while sitting in a traffic jam, we knew that the man who stabbed our son last month was not playing ping pong while deciding what TV dinner he'd like, but was in an unheated, damp cell, trying to suck moisture and nutrients from the moss on the walls.

None of this would improve the clear-up rate. But it would dramatically cut the number of people who wake up in the morning and think: 'Hmmm. I'm going to be a burglar.'

24 June 2018

I'd rather take another six-day battering in Mongolia than a World Cup penalty

On Wednesday I woke up in a tent, in a field, in Mongolia, and as I sat on the aluminium bucket that had been provided for my morning ablutions I ruminated on how I could possibly survive the coming day. It was just past six in the morning and after I'd eaten a boil-in-the-bag army breakfast, it was time to adopt that camper-man stoop and thrash about in my tent, huffing and puffing as I squeezed all my mysteriously damp things into a suitcase. And then the day began.

First up, we had to film the sort of scene that would cause most American actors to demand three weeks off in the Bahamas, but because we were against the clock we had it done by nine and were ready to film a river crossing. It was a big river and it was fed by melting snow, so it was what people who've just dived into an unheated pool and want you to follow suit call 'very refreshing'.

Sadly, the car got stuck after about six inches so I had to get into the water, which wasn't refreshing at all. It was bloody freezing, and it was travelling so quickly that by the time I surfaced I was about a mile from the action. Happily, though, I was soon caught up in some shallow rapids, which meant that after a lot of light bruising I was back where I'd started. Only with one shoe instead of two.

By eleven I had stumbled and swum and sworn my way over the boulder-strewn river and was faced with a cliff

that I'd have to climb. Until this point, my six-day camping trip across Mongolia had been lovely. There had been
no noticeable temperature, the whole place smelt of a
herb garden and there hadn't been a single insect of any
kind.

This is because they were all on that cliff face. And
they were the sorts of insect that are only really bothered
about getting into your ear. So you're clinging on to a
rock, and you're thinking that you're nearly 60 and you're
frozen from the river and hurting, and all of a sudden you
have a panicky fly in your ear and you can't dig it out
because you'd fall to your death.

But eventually I was at the top, in what looked like Julie
Andrews country, and the herb fragrance was back and
all I had to do was drive 70 miles to the town of Moron.
Unfortunately, there was no road of any kind. So it was
70 miles of absolute violence. At one point, after I'd hit a
particularly enormous marmot hole, I really did think my
spine was sticking out of the top of my head.

We stopped for lunch in a thunderstorm and I had a
boil-in-the-bag army curry before taking on the last leg
of what had been a six-day orgy of exhaustion, animal
lavatory facilities, discomfort, dirty fingernails, damp
camping-trip clothes, army food and James May's
spinnaker-sized sinuses.

At eight in the evening, though, it was all over . . . except
it wasn't. Because after a glass of wine – the first for a
week – it was time to make for Moron's airport and a flight
to Ulan Bator, or, if you prefer, Ulaanbaatar, which would
be a very handy bad-Scrabble-hand clear-out if only
proper nouns were allowed. Here I checked into an airport hotel, where the receptionist showed me to my room

and spent half an hour explaining to me how the door to the minibar worked and what I might find inside.

I just wanted a shower. So, having interrupted her spiel on what Heineken tastes like and ushered her out of the door, I put on my broken spectacles to examine the plumbing setup. It turned out that the shower had two settings: off and scalding.

Even though my head was burnt off and my lips were cracked and bleeding, I selected scalding and stood in the jets for a full 10 minutes, soaping away at all my small, delicate places until I was clean. Except, after drying myself off and examining the now grey towel, I realized I wasn't. So I went back into the lava and tried again. And after that I turned another towel grey, so I tried again. But the water had run out. So now there were still two settings but both of them were off.

No matter. I put on clean clothes, went downstairs and, after explaining to the disappointed receptionist that I hadn't touched the minibar, checked out and went into town to find the Moustache bar, where the film crew was meeting up to listen to a Russian commentator talk us through the England match.

It was two in the morning when that started and getting light when Colombia equalized. Watching the half an hour of extra time would have meant missing the flight to Beijing, so off we went to the airport, where we arrived just in time to see Eric Dier do his thing.

Two hours later I was in China, using the three-hour stopover to write a script for the film we are making in Switzerland on Tuesday. And then it was time for the 10-hour flight to London, where I reflected on what I'd done in the past 24 sleep-free hours.

Climbed. Swum. Wrapped a show. Driven. Flown. Drunk. Watched a football match. Flown again. Written a script and then flown some more. And all of this after a week that would have flattened Sir Fiennes.

It had been the busiest day of my life and I was so tired that some people in the plane stopped to ask if I was all right. I wasn't, if I'm honest. I was broken.

But I'll tell you what. I'd do that every day for the rest of my life rather than stand in front of a billion people thinking: 'Right. Half the people in this stadium hate me, and if I can't make this ball go past that man and into that net, everyone will.'

That is the definition of pressure. And let's not forget, shall we, that those World Cup footballers give their international earnings to charity.

8 July 2018

We don't need no condescension – so, hey tweeters, leave that Trump alone

The Dark Side of the Moon was very much the soundtrack of my youth and the track 'Time' was entirely behind setting me on the road to where I am now. 'No one told you when to run, you missed the starting gun.' And so on.

As a result I was very much looking forward to seeing former Pink Floyd frontman Roger Waters perform in Hyde Park at the start of last weekend. Especially as the sun was shining, and I had backstage passes and I was going with friends who are fans, rather than the sort of non-Seventies people who stand there with long faces wondering why the song 'is still going on'.

It all began well enough but pretty soon old Rog was prancing about the stage with a banner saying 'F*** the pigs'. The pigs? This might have had some relevance in the US race riots in the Sixties and even here in Britain, in Orgreave, in the Eighties. But people don't call policemen pigs any more.

As I was digesting all of this, the giant screen at the back of the stage started to depict Donald Trump, with a micro-penis, vomiting, and then we had something about how black lives matter and Grenfell Tower, and then Roger committed the cardinal sin of playing a song from his latest album – *Is This the Life We Really Want?* – which has a sixth-form common room vibe about the awfulness of everything.

Well, I had a good look at the crowd and the fact is that

they all had Volvos and they were all drinking rosé wine in the sunshine and not a single one of them could find much to moan about. Except perhaps the £150 they'd paid for a ticket to this Barclaycard-sponsored event. And how, owing to safety and health regulations, it was being played at about 40 decibels, which meant that the only vocals you could really hear were those of the stock-broker standing next to you.

Roger hadn't finished. Not by a long way. Because now he was wearing a Palestinian keffiyeh and quoting lines from the Universal Declaration of Human Rights. At this point, I decided I'd heard enough, and having circum-navigated the locked gates to make sure everyone stayed to the bitter end, I went to the Dorchester where I bumped into Julian Fellowes, who was a refreshing tonic.

Naturally, we spoke about London mayor Sadiq Khan's decision to allow various squatters and unemployed people to fly a weird Donald Trump balloon over Parlia-ment Square while the president visits Oxfordshire – and Scotland.

Even my leftie friends reckon this is poor form. Yes, it poses no threat to public safety and, yes, peaceful dem-onstrations are enshrined in the spirit of Britain but, I dunno, it seems to fly in the face of something else that's enshrined in our spirit: good manners.

I mean, I don't like what Jeremy Corbyn says, or does, or thinks, or is. But I wouldn't fly an effigy of him, naked and shrivelled and under-endowed above my apartment, partly because that would be insulting but mostly because someone would come round and set fire to me.

It's the same story with Waters. He can stand on a stage and tell 65,000 solicitors they should adopt a Somalian but if I went to Speakers' Corner and told a collection of bewildered Chinese tourists that Rog had a Lexus and membership of one of the most exclusive golf clubs in the Hamptons, the thought police would arrive and put me in a van.

I'm not sure how this has happened but we've reached a point where Waters can say what he thinks, and that's fine. But Trump cannot. Because unseen forces in the ether have decided that Roger is right and Donald is wrong.

We see this all the time on Twitter. If someone of a Theresa May disposition says something, they are threatened and forced to back down and apologize and then eat rat poison. Whereas if Gary Lineker says something nice about refugees and Diane Abbott he is held aloft as some kind of suntanned god.

Last week the RAF managed to creak a few of its planes into the air and stage a flypast over Buckingham Palace. It gave many people an opportunity to put pictures on social media, with a statue of Sir Winston Churchill in the foreground and a Spitfire overhead. Some chose to caption their work with the line about how so much was owed by so many.

Big mistake. Because straight away the forces of good were on their high horses, saying that the very people flying those planes had spent the past few years murdering women and children with their wayward bombs in Syria.

There's no point arguing or talking about the defence of the realm, because you're wrong. The armed forces are wrong. War is wrong. The people who fight it are wrong.

Throughout the World Cup, we've been told by these same people that the tournament was a joyous celebration of the world working together as one. Well, it wasn't on my social media feeds, which – every morning – were filled with pictures and captions that could have come straight from an episode of *Till Death Us Do Part*.

Even the one-time Labour luvvie Lord Sugar, who almost certainly campaigns in public to kick racism out of football, was caught out, reckoning the Senegal team looked like lads flogging sunglasses on a beach in Marbella. Whoops.

The problem is that social media, which is seen as the pulse of the nation, is actually nothing of the sort. It's the pulse of the young and the idealistic. Waters will have looked at Twitter after his gig and seen that what he had done was good. Even though most of his actual fans will have walked back to their Volvos with a line from the last song echoing in their heads. 'Your lips move but I can't hear what you're saying.'

15 July 2018

Thunderbirds are go, but Elon 'Brains' Musk needs rescuing from himself

When you are a famous person you can never be rude to someone who isn't. Being famous is like being a banker. You are wrong. Always and in all things. It's like driving a Porsche. If you are sitting in a lay-by, eating a sandwich, when a little old lady drives into your rear end, it's your fault. You will be called a 'Porsche driver' in the newspaper and we all know that's code for banker.

You should certainly bear this in mind if you are thinking of becoming famous. Yes, you will never have to wait for a table at your local Harvester and you will be able to sleep with people who are orange, but do please remember before sending off your application to sing in front of Simon Cowell, or have sex in a televised house, that once you have appeared in the sidebar of shame, people will immediately express a fervent hope that cancerous things happen to your family and your lungs.

And you cannot fight back, because if you do, everyone will say that you used your talent-show voters to become Uttoxeter's most famous export, so you can hardly turn round now and call the internet trollist 'spotty' or 'fat' or 'poor'. And you certainly cannot – ever – call him a child molester.

This brings us on to Elon Musk, who got into a Twitter spat over a British caver who helped rescue the boys in Thailand and called him a 'pedo'. When it was pointed out to Musk he hadn't even got the spelling right, he went on to tweet: 'Bet ya a signed dollar it's true.'

Now it is true to say, unfortunately, that southeast Asia is something of a mecca for fifty- and sixty-something single men. You see them milling about, and you know it's possible that they're there, as they claim, for the interesting monasteries, but in your head you're sneering and singing the lyrics: 'D'you wanna be in my gang, my gang?'

Unfortunately for Musk, however, the caver who helped rescue those children is not a paedophile. It's unclear why he moved to Thailand, but he's married to a local lady who is said to be in her forties. So old Elon, despite deleting the tweets and making a mealy-mouthed apology, is now in a spot of bother.

You'd imagine I'd be happy about that, as the South African-born weirdo and I have history. He sued me after I said firm but fair things about one of his Teslas. He lost the case, appealed and lost that too. But if you go online, there he still is, banging on about how I'd cheated and decided not to like his car before I'd even sat in it. The man's a walking litigation magnet and, by rights, I should be hoping that he really does come a cropper.

However, I do have a bit of sympathy for him over this cave-rescue malarkey. As you know, 12 boys and their coach decided after a bit of football practice that they were all male, and males are programmed to look in caves. We can't help it.

Unfortunately, when they were looking about, they were cut off from the outside world by flood water, and that, in my book, is as bad as things can be. Last year, while holidaying in Mallorca, I was told of a secret lagoon that could be reached only by swimming under a boulder for about two seconds.

The water was calm and clear and warm, but I simply couldn't do it. So the idea of swimming through a cave, for miles, in the darkness, wiggling through cracks and getting wedged? I just cannot imagine anything I'd rather do less.

But thank God there are people who do enjoy being cold and frightened and blinded by impenetrable blackness, because they sure as hell were going to be needed to get those boys out. They had many plans and many ideas, and before any of them could be executed, Elon arrived from his own personal Tracy Island, where there are space rockets and electric cars and, he said, an underwater rescue torpedo that could be taken to Thailand by Thunderbird 2.

It's possible, of course, that this was – as our British hero caver said afterwards – a gigantic PR stunt. And that his rescue torpedo was nothing more than a kitchen swing-top bin filled with cancelled orders for the new Tesla hatchback.

But let's just say it wasn't. Let's give Brains the benefit of the doubt. He'd seen the plight of the boys and felt moved to help. He had the resources, he had the facilities and, who knows, he maybe even had some folding palm trees.

So he got the dimensions of the cave and the dimensions of the boys and he got the go-ahead from on-the-scene rescuers and he got to work. I like to think that if I'd been in his shoes, I'd have done the same thing.

And if I had, I'd be jolly cross if someone had said afterwards I should push my torpedo into my bottom. Of course, Musk must have known he could not go after the little guy who said this, because he is the celebrity banker in the Porsche. But he obviously decided that enough was enough.

And I was right with him when he said he would take his rescue torpedo to Thailand anyway to prove it could have got round all the corners. I felt his indignation. I was rooting for the way he was standing up for big guys everywhere.

He was the new James Blunt. The only famous person who can belittle the trolls on Twitter and get away with it.

But then Elon called the hero Brit little guy a paedophile. Which means he blew it. And now, like everyone else, I hope that he's sued so hard, he ends up like that other great puppet hero, the good-looking actor in *Team America: World Police* who becomes a vomiting drunk in a back alley.

22 July 2018

Our holiday on the canals was a blast, but at one hotel my dad caused a stink

I have argued quite a lot over the years, usually with idiotic tax exiles, that home is where your friends are. I really do believe that. You can be surrounded by all your things, and close to your parents, in a house you love, but if your friends are elsewhere, it'll never be home.

At this time of year, however, all my friends are in Mallorca or Corfu. I scroll through Instagram every morning, and there they all are, miles away, in the sunshine, pretending that they're not bothered about the exchange rate, which has caused a plate of calamari at lunchtime to cost more than a BMW M5.

Many will be using social media to contact people they barely know, and don't like, so they can spend the afternoon together, because it's better on Instagram to be gurning and drinking with other people than it is to be with your bored kids, looking round some ruins.

By the time you read this, I will be abroad too, trying desperately to find someone I know, rather than saying to the kids that a look round the colonial hill fort will be very interesting. There is nothing interesting about a rusty cannon. I know that, and they know that too. Or a bird sanctuary.

I could go on about drunken greengrocers from Luton and Entero-Vioform tablets and Watneys Red Barrel, but Monty Python has done this already, so I shall move on to the second-worst word in the English language* – staycation.

According to mutterings in the travel industry, England's better-than-expected performance in the World Cup caused many families to abandon the idea of a foreign holiday and stay at home watching television. Then came the heatwave, which turned the germ of an idea into a family fist bump of agreement.

I don't believe any of this. I think it's just the PR agency for a guesthouse in Blackpool trying to drum up business by taking advantage of the slow-news silly season. The sun can shine, the pound can collapse and Cornwall's beaches can top as many polls as they like for beauty and cleanliness. But people would still rather spend a week up to their knees in sewage in Portugal because it's exotic.

But is it? Because if home is where your friends are, and all your friends are also up to their knees in foreign faeces, then surely the truly exotic thing to do is to be the black sheep and stay at home.

Cornwall is the obvious spot, because the sea is slightly above freezing and the restaurants are rather good these days. But you do run the risk of being debagged by a drunken Etonian whose Brexiteer parents have jumped the gun and come on holiday with the FitzTightlys, whose equally drunken son will then vomit on you. Before giving your daughter the clap.

Devon? Absolutely beautiful, no doubt about that, but there's literally nothing to do. And it's much the same story right along the south coast until you get to the New

---

* Chillax has the top spot.

Forest. This has a motor museum and some horses. Then there's nothing all the way to Dover.

The Cotswolds? Nope. Ghastly. You'd hate it here. Don't come. It's hideous. Take your caravan and your rambler's sense of entitlement somewhere else, please. Somewhere like the lighter shade of grey that you get in Norfolk. There are a couple of drawbacks, of course. It's further away than Helsinki, and the staff at petrol stations will look in a toothless, confused way at your credit card, and then put it in the till.

The Lake District sounds appealing, but even during the deepest heatwave I can pretty much guarantee it won't stop raining. Speaking of which . . .

Scotland. As I said in this column only recently, it's fabulous, particularly way up past Ullapool on the northwest coast, but it makes Devon look like Las Vegas when it comes to entertainment. Which means that sooner or later someone's going to suggest you go for a walk. Possibly to a ruined castle of some kind. This will make your children, who wanted to go on holiday to Ibiza, or with the FitzTightlys to Cornwall, even more sullen than usual.

It all sounds too impossible, but there is one person I follow on Instagram who's taken her kids on a narrowboat holiday. It looks ghastly and sounds worse. There are pictures of the kids sheltering from the rain under a road bridge and shots of bicycles being retrieved from the canal after being swept overboard by low-hanging branches. And that's before we get to the interior, which is like a caravan, but flimsier, and which you know will smell lightly of leaking Calor gas.

The thing is, though, that as a teenager I went on a

couple of narrowboat holidays and they were brilliant. We stood at the front and let off the fire extinguishers at the person who was 50ft away, doing the driving. We crashed into every lock gate at full speed (4mph) to see if it would open. And there was never any worry about finding stuff to do, because the only option on a narrowboat holiday is 'going to the pub'. Which was fine by us.

It's not glamorous. It's not even close. And it's hard in September when people ask where you've been and you have to say 'Uttoxeter'. But you will see Britain in a way you didn't think was possible and you won't get burnt and you won't get a funny tummy.

And if you do, you can do what my dad did and take the overflowing chemi-lav into the reception of the poncy Compleat Angler in Marlow and ask if they had anywhere for him to empty it out. I laughed so hard at their pained faces, I haven't quite stopped even today.

5 August 2018

Argue with today's youth and they'll call you a racist – then start blubbing

Over a lovely lunch on my holiday this year, one of the 'old people' around the table said that Britain's super-slack immigration policy means we are letting an army onto our shores. Well, the mood couldn't have changed more quickly if she'd said: 'I've just murdered 14 tramps.'

One of the young people began to sob. Actually sob. And another fixed the old person with a stare made from rage and bile, and explained that everyone from any-where should be allowed to live wherever they like. And between mouthfuls of padron peppers, I agreed with this, saying that I'd love to live in George Clooney's house on Lake Como.

This went down badly, so, as the lovely lunch was turn-ing into a bit of a disaster, I changed the subject and began to speak about the hot summer in England, which turned into a debate about global warming, or climate change or whatever it's called these days. Only the other day, the former Labour spin doctor Alastair Campbell said that to deny man's involvement in this should be a crime and it seems he has full support from those who are under 25.

They certainly hadn't got the science worked out, with many believing that the purply grey fog that sits over Los Angeles and Geneva has something to do with carbon dioxide in the upper atmosphere and that everything would be better if people didn't drive diesel cars.

Like I said. Twaddle. But my attempts to provide some kind of enlightenment fell on deaf ears. They were right and that's that. Cars are bad. Central heating is bad. Donald Trump is very bad. Kale is good. And I should shut up because it's not my world any more. I'm simply a guest who's outstayed his welcome.

I agree with them on this. When I was sort of their age I'd had enough of old people banging on about the Goons and whippets and industrial action and warm beer and 'bloody foreigners'. I knew they'd lived through rationing and bombing and rickets but I didn't care. Yuppies, in my book, seemed to be having a much better time so I moved to Fulham and got a GTI. And I figured out quite quickly that if I worked hard and eschewed society in favour of individual effort, I could go to St Tropez for my holidays in future, and not St Austell.

My generation came up with a whole new type of comedy and a whole new type of music. We had interesting hair and didn't use braces simply to stop our trousers falling down. We loved Gordon Gekko. Asset-stripping meant thousands would lose their jobs but that didn't matter because, hey, it meant we could party harder that night in Annabel's.

Other people? They didn't matter. You could laugh at the homeless and the weak, and if anyone was offended, you could laugh at them too. I used to make detours to laugh at the lesbians chained to a fence at Greenham Common and earned a living by thinking up similes for Arthur Scargill's hair. It wasn't hard.

Our parents would explain, in much the same way that Martin Sheen explained in *Wall Street*, that we were building a house made from straw, but just like Charlie Sheen in the same movie, we paid no attention. We were convinced of our righteousness. I mean, what could possibly go wrong? It's not like any of us were going to catch Aids.

Of course, not all of us thought the same way. I had friends who reckoned Michael Foot's jacket was an acceptable garment at the Cenotaph. And others who said that disco produced nothing of any value. Ben Elton and me? We were on different roads but we were going to the same place. And that, emphatically, doesn't happen now.

Maybe it's because young people live in a social media world of cyber-bullies who do not allow anyone to stray from the party line, but whatever, people under 25 have become as different as milk bottles. They have a hive mentality about all things. They know that tramps should be called homeless people, that cycling is good and the NHS is better. Oh and, of course, they all know for sure that everything anyone says is racist.

In a debate about transgenderism the other day, I wondered out loud how sport would work if people were allowed to choose their sex before kick-off, and I was called a racist immediately. Then there's Boris Johnson, who learnt to his cost while I was away that it's racist to comment on how another culture dresses. Which means I can't say that a German beer enthusiast in leather shorts looks idiotic. Because that's racist too, and possibly homophobic.

You are not allowed to disagree with any of this, obviously, because then you're being judgmental, which means you are a racist, and that's before we get to the concept of #MeToo, which means I can no longer ask the tea lady at work to get me a cup of tea.

I'm as confused by it all as my dad was when I asked him to listen to *Tubular Bells*.

But what does it matter what I think because I'll be dead soon, and so will you, and our children will have the baton. If they choose to run off the course to lick Jeremy Corbyn, or free a hen or smash up a patio heater, that is their right. It is not our course and it is not our baton. We did not own Britain. We just lived here for a while.

Of course, the problem all the young people have is that next year we will leave the EU. I can't see that working out very well. Maybe that's why they all like an immigration free-for-all, so that they can move to Ibiza when the time comes.

Sadly, of course, that won't be possible. They're stuck here, on their non-judgmental rock in the north Atlantic. And that's their fault because on referendum day none of them could be bothered to go to the polling station.

19 August 2018

The next arrival at Heathrow's eco-haven is a million tons of concrete for the third runway

Heathrow may be only the world's seventh-busiest airport these days, but it's still a gigantic stat fest. Almost 215,000 people pass through it on average every day and in a year they consume nearly 1,000 tons of chips and more than 300,000 bottles of champagne.

Eighty-one airlines use this former Second World War airbase to fly to more than 200 destinations, with a plane taking off or landing every 45 seconds. And if you emptied all the perfume in its duty-free shops into one container, it'd be deep enough to drown everyone in the town of Loughborough.

I may have made that last one up but, whatever, there are more than 76,000 people who work there and it's hard to decide which one has the most important job. Is it the person who's responsible for keeping it all profitable, or the person who must prevent any of 'Jihadi John's' mates from getting through the passport booths? Or is it the sweaty kid in the control tower who must ensure that none of the planes bump into one another?

Sadly, however, I fear that in this day and age the most important person at Heathrow is actually a chap called Adam Cheeseman because – mysteriously – he is the airport's biodiversity manager. Which, on the face of it, is like being in charge of health and safety at a Bangladesh shipbreaking yard. Noble but pointless.

The problem is that boards of directors in Britain are obliged to adhere to a code called corporate governance. It was dreamt up by sensible people with side partings and intended to make sure that directors didn't deliberately crash a company to line their own pockets, or pay themselves more than was realistic.

Today, though, someone who says 'reach out' in his emails has decided that to meet the requirements of the code, a company must also demonstrate that it's at least trying to be carbon-neutral and organic and sustainable and all the other nonsense words that have come to pollute our lives.

So, in order not to be sacked, Heathrow's board of directors has had to set aside some of its land for natural habitat schemes. And then it has had to employ Cheeseman to run them.

He's been given a web page to explain what he's up to. Moths and fungus, mostly. Encouraging birds would clearly be a mistake. 'Cheeseman, you idiot. You've filled your plot with pelicans.'

In the winter, however, everything is quiet, so he is free to review management plans and write updates on his Heathrow Wildlife page on Flickr. As of last Wednesday it had 30 followers.

Now I want to make it plain that I have nothing against Cheeseman. He is necessary to keep Heathrow going, and if he wants to spend his life fitting his beetles with headphones to protect them from the roar of a departing Airbus A380, that's fine. His impact on you and me is no bigger than his impact on anything at all.

But last week I went to Lyons, which has recently been

classified as a carbon-neutral airport. By which they mean there are some flowerbeds on the roof.

Sadly, though, it's fairly obvious that all the people who should be manning the passport booths and luggage trolleys are up there deadheading the roses. Because, my God, you wait a long time for your suitcases. Traveller's tip here: if you need to be in the Lyons area for whatever reason, fly to Prague and get a cab. It'd be quicker.

I can understand why a small artisan bakery in Harrogate would want to boast about its commitment to the planet's wellbeing. Because people who like bread with bits of gravel in it are interested in carbon-neutrality and will be enticed through the door.

It's the same story with footwear. We all know when we buy a new pair of training shoes that there's a very strong chance they were made by a six-year-old in the Far East. Some people will handle the guilt. Some won't. And they will buy a much more expensive pair of shade-grown cardboard peace shoes next time they are in Islington.

This is called choice and it's the cornerstone of all we hold dear. If we think that someone's running a mini-Bhopal on the outskirts of Dundee, we will vote with our wallets and buy from someone who isn't. If we think that a guesthouse is being run by the Ku Klux Klan, we will stay somewhere else. And if we discover the leader of a main political party is a screaming anti-semite, we will vote for . . . actually, I'm not sure what we'd do on that one.

It's the same story with investors. If you are a right-on hand-wringer, it's very unlikely you will invest in a company that owns airports, no matter how many bits of interesting moss Cheeseman has grown. So his work is box-ticking for people who aren't interested.

I have no idea who's decided that corporate good governance should include stuff about the upper atmosphere and weeds, but it just seems to be so unnecessary. And maybe even counterproductive.

Think about it. If the bods running Heathrow were to adhere to the code and say, 'No. We shall not expand. We shall ring-fence our award-winning environmental work and protect it for future generations,' then they would not be able to build a third runway, which means they wouldn't be acting in their shareholders' best interests.

Perhaps that's why the third runway will go straight through many of Cheeseman's weed beds, burying his moths and fungus under 2ft of concrete. And no one apart from his 30 followers will give a damn.

Because what's the option? Fly out of Luton? I'd rather die.

2 September 2018

The Very Old Bill – my pensioner police force will put the fear of God into baddies

A friend announced last week that he is retiring and I was staggered. It feels like only 12 minutes since we were at journalism college together, listening to Harry Chapin on the pub jukebox and deciding that, yes, it would be better to have another pint than to go back to the classroom to do shorthand.

We're only 58 now and that's no age to stop working. I mean, I can still go to a drinks party at seven and not get home till Thursday. And recently, at work, I ran down the roof of a moving Winnebago as it careered across a dried-up lakebed in Nevada. I feel young. I feel fit. And I'm not alone.

Other people who are 58 are Simon Cowell and Jonathan Ross and Hugh Grant and Colin Firth. Any of those ready for the corduroy trousers and gardening gloves yet? No. Then you have Liz Hurley and Elle Macpherson. They're both in their fifties now and there isn't a magazine editor in the world who wouldn't put either on the cover.

The trouble is, of course, that there are some people in the country who do not earn a living from driving round corners while shouting, or hosting chat shows, or wearing a swimming costume on Instagram. Some of them earn a living being in a furnace, or a warehouse, or a genitourinary clinic in Rotherham. And they would like to retire tomorrow morning if possible.

However, as we all know, this is going to become increasingly difficult as time goes by. At present, nearly 20 per cent of the population is older than 65, and with better medicines and new laws making it illegal to have any sort of accident, that number is going to grow. Some reports say that soon 42 per cent will be pensioners, and obviously that's unaffordable.

B&Q – I'm not sure what it sells, but it has big super-stores near ring roads – has had a policy of employing older people for some time. And Barclays Bank and National Express have more recently opened their doors to the elderly.

This makes a deal of sense. I'd far rather drive a coach than sit in the garden all morning, arguing with myself and wondering if it's too early to go to the pub for a drink I can't really afford. I'd rather do anything than that.

Sure, an old person cannot be a professional footballer, but they could work in a restaurant, that's for sure. In fact, if I owned a restaurant, I'd far rather employ a gentle old soul to show people to their tables than some unin-terested thief who spends most of his time at work in the lavatories doing coke.

Old people are less interested in chatting up colleagues and are less likely to arrive late with a hangover. They have lost the awkwardness of youth and will not suffer from the millennials' absurd notion that after a week in the job they should be chief executive. And, having grown up in a more enlightened time, they'll be less likely to sob and sue every time anyone says or does something that Twitter has deemed to be inappropriate these days.

Last week a man with a big title and an important job said that old people should become fitness instructors. I'm not sure about that one. There is nothing so distressing as watching someone with creaking joints trying to hop about. I know this. I've seen a video of myself dancing.

However, there was another idea from last week that makes a huge amount of sense: getting retired Metropolitan policemen and policemen women back into the force. Or the service. Or whatever it's called these days.

Critics immediately branded the idea stupid and blamed the Tories and Margaret Thatcher and Brexit, but I reckon that it's brilliant and should be expanded so that anyone of good character can join up, even if they are 80. No, wait. Especially if they are 80.

You may say that an 80-year-old policeman couldn't possibly chase down a youth who's off his head on disco biscuits, but I put it to you that a 25-year-old officer couldn't either. Because he hasn't had the correct ladder training and because he's back at the station, painting rainbow motifs on his squad car.

There's more. If a young officer does corner a baddie, the chances are he will be stabbed. But no one would stab an officer if he looked like Godfrey from *Dad's Army*. It'd be like stabbing a seal.

And while a young officer is happy to sit at the station, polishing his Taser, an old person would welcome the opportunity to go for a little walk. This would mean more bobbies on the beat.

Solving crime? Well, let's think about that. Young people are far too busy sending pictures of their body parts to one another on Snapchat to concentrate for very long on any given task, whereas old people are perfectly happy to spend all day working on '7 down': 'Weapons minister runs backwards in portfolio we hear perhaps.'

Let me put it this way. Inspector Morse had a limp, but you'd rather he was assigned the task of finding your stolen quad bike than, say, Harry Kane was.

It's the same story with the emergency response. You're holed up in your cellar by an armed gang. A fast police interceptor has been dispatched and is on its way, sirens blaring. So. Who would you like the driver to be? The three-time Formula One world champion Sir Jackie Stewart, or your teenage son?

The more I think about this, the more I think that the minimum age for becoming a policeperson should be 60. In fact, I think it should be compulsory for everyone to join when they retire. Of course, when you are stopped by one of these old bobbies and they say, 'Do you know why you've been pulled over?', it's possible they have actually forgotten.

But they have wisdom gleaned from a lifetime of experiences, they have patience, they are less easily distracted and they don't need to be trained how to use a ladder. Because they already know.

16 September 2018

Lefties will love my West End blockbuster, Neil Armstrong – the Hip-Hop Musical

There has been much discussion recently about who should replace Daniel Craig as James Bond. Some say that in these colour-blind times it should be someone who's black. Then there are those who say it should be a woman. Who knows? Perhaps it could be someone who's both. Thandie Newton, anyone?

We have seen similar modern-day issues with the theatre production of *Sylvia* that closed last night after a disastrous week at London's Old Vic.

Someone decided that in these #MeToo times of feminism and a woman's right to walk down the street without being talked to, looked at or admired in any way, it would be a good idea to stage a play about the Pankhursts and the suffragette movement.

Absolutely. Emmeline Pankhurst was a full-on good person. Ruthless. Determined. And, because she helped earn women the right to vote, rightly hailed as one of the 20th century's most important people. I'd go for Neil Armstrong myself, but I get why Emmeline is on the list.

However, for some reason the producers and the writers decided that the play should actually be about someone called Sylvia Pankhurst. Which is a bit like making a play about the birth of the Nazis and concentrating on Adolf Hitler's little-known brother, Ron.

Sylvia – and I had to look this up – was Emmeline's

communistical daughter, who contributed to the suffragette movement by designing the leaflets. She then
encouraged men not to fight in the First World War,
before eventually moving to Ethiopia, where she did
nothing of any great consequence until her death in 1960.

Why make a play about that? If you're going to do suf-
fragism and female communists from the olden days,
why not look at Emily Davison, who tried to bankrupt
various hard-working butchers by not eating meat, and
then cost thousands of working-class gamblers the
chance to win enough to feed their children by hurling
herself in front of the King's horse at some dreary race in
Epsom?

At least a play about that would have been quite
funny. 'Oops. Here comes clumsy Emily, fighting for the
rights of the downtrodden by accidentally making them
worse off.'

But no. They stuck with Sylvia, and to try to enliven
what had been a dreary and unnoticed life, the play's
writers decided it should be a musical set to hip-hop. I
can't imagine where they got that idea from. And then
they reckoned that Sylvia and her mum should be played
by actresses who are black.

I'm well aware, of course, that there are a number of
people who would want to see this kind of politics used
in this kind of story and set to this kind of music. But,
sadly, the number in question is about four. And that's
not enough to keep the lights on at the Old Vic.

To make matters worse, the centenary of the act of parliament that gave women the vote was back in February,
but the complications of organizing various lefties to
stage a musical and sell tickets and get stuff done meant

they simply couldn't make it on time. That's the trouble with centenaries. You never get enough warning.

Then there were illnesses, which meant that in some performances understudies were on stage reading their lines from a script. And even when things did run smoothly, the show was three hours long. And no one can sit in a theatre seat for that long without becoming suicidal. We're told that some walked out but that those who stuck it through to the end stood up and cheered. I bet they did.

No story takes three hours to tell. Unless you fill it up with anti-Tory jokes and asides, which is exactly what happened in *Sylvia*. That's another problem with lefties. They couldn't even get through a rendition of 'Jack and Jill' without making some spittle-infused reference to Margaret Thatcher.

This is going to have a profound effect on the arts if they aren't careful. I've seen *Hamilton* and I enjoyed it, even though my arse had gangrene by the time it was over. But that was a one-off. You can't go around setting everything to hip-hop, because what's next? A biopic of Sir Frank Whittle set to grime?

And then there's this business of colour-blindness. I'm well aware that Laurence Olivier and Orson Welles played Othello, and I can quite understand why black people might be a bit miffed by that sort of thing. Othello is black and should be played by a black actor. Fact. Definitely. One hundred per cent. So if you're doing a musical about RJ Mitchell, the inventor of the Spitfire, could he be played by Idris Elba? I honestly don't know the answer. I mean, for a kick-off, I have no idea whether Idris can sing.

What I do know is that if you allow yourself to get

worked up about this kind of issue, you lose sight of what you're there for. To provide entertainment for people in exchange for money.

When I was at the BBC and the lefties had really got a grip on senior management, I spent 90 per cent of the week thinking up new ways to annoy them and only 10 per cent thinking about the actual audience. It showed in some episodes.

I'm forever being told about 'an excellent new play' that's just opened, but it's always about immigration or civil rights. Or it's a musical of some kind. And I can't help thinking I'd much rather go and see *Ten Times Table* or *Noises Off*. Which, so far as I could tell, had no political ambition at all. And no singing.

It's idiotic to suggest that there should be no politics in the arts. There's almost nothing I like more than a protest song. And from what I can gather, Jez Butterworth's play *The Ferryman* – which was about the Troubles in Northern Ireland – was bloody brilliant.

Perhaps because it wasn't set to techno. And because the cast was predominantly Irish, not French. Which wouldn't have made any sense.

23 September 2018

In my house we go by my rules, whether we're playing croquet, Scrabble or war

The house in which I spent my summer holidays this year had a croquet lawn in the garden. And croquet is like Buck's Fizz. No one wakes up thinking, 'What I'd like now is a glass of champagne and orange juice,' but when it's presented to you, even if it's a Tuesday and it's raining and you're late for work, it's hard to say no.

And so, after breakfast on the first day, while the women went off to search for holistic wellness by bending over on the terrace, I suggested to the men that we break out the mallets. This went down well because croquet is fundamentally cruel, and that makes it a man's game.

You really can decide, when it's clear you're not going to win, that Dan isn't either. You can pick on the little guy, endlessly sending him into the flowerbeds a quarter of a mile away. And you can drink. In fact, you should drink. Six beers makes the misfortune of others so much more hilarious.

Unfortunately, however, at our idyllic summer retreat in Sri Lanka — go, by the way — there was a problem. The actual rules of croquet were lost long ago, probably by EM Forster, so everyone has developed their own. Some say you can put your foot on your ball while sending an opponent into the hydrangeas; some say you can't. Some say it's a team game; some say it isn't.

Every aspect has its own interpretation, which means several hours can elapse between deciding to have a game and the game actually beginning. Once, many years ago, a friend – you know who you are, Matthew – threw his mallet down and went home rather than play by someone else's rules.

We see a similar problem these days with Scrabble. Last week American enthusiasts of the game listed 300 new words in their bible, including 'zomboid', 'botnet', 'sheeple', 'puggle' and 'nubber'. This has enraged British fans, because here these words are not allowed.

One day that may change, but it won't make any difference in my house, where visitors face a simple choice: my way or the highway. I have my own very simple set of extra rules, which are: the word must be in common usage and you must be able to explain its meaning.

So, while Rachel Johnson – who loves the game, to judge by her Instagram feed – may know that 'qi' is a life force that governs a lot of Chinese medicine, she can't use it because – and I don't care what she says – she hasn't actually spoken it out loud, ever. So it's not in common usage.

And even if she did say it out loud at the greengrocer's that morning, and he's on the phone verifying the fact, she still can't have it, because it's not in common usage in my house. And it's the same story, while I'm at it, with 'jo' and 'za' and 'ob'. Having in your head a list of useful little two-letter words doesn't make you clever. It makes you a parrot. And they crap on their own legs.

The other problem with Scrabble is that it's been completely ruined by technology, because now, when you are staring at a set of letters that won't join up in your head, you can quietly tap them into your phone and a cheat app will come up with the best solution.

Obviously this doesn't work for me, because I almost always pick up an 'I', followed by another, and then five more. Occasionally, if I'm having a good day, I'll get an 'O', and once I had a 'V'. But usually it's seven 'I's. And there's no interpretation of the rules or app that can solve that one.

Then there's rugby. There are now so many new rules that the players need a man on the pitch to remind them – constantly and out loud – what they are.

And that brings me on to the taxman. I'm dimly aware that many years ago a man in a suit put some of my savings into a film production scheme and afterwards he said that two of the movies I'd invested in had done quite well. I was very pleased until years later the taxman said that while this scheme had been legal at the time, he'd had a think and decided that now he'd actually like to put his foot on his ball and send me into the flowerbeds. So I ended up giving him enough to buy one of the navy's new aircraft carriers. That was a bit annoying, if I'm honest.

Mind you, it's nowhere near as annoying as it must be for soldiers who have to abide by the rules of engagement. Rules that, so far as I can tell, aren't written until after the conflict is over.

In Iraq you couldn't shoot someone unless they'd shot at you first. But if they shot at you and then put the gun down, you couldn't shoot them either. You could, however, arrest them and put their head in a bag.

Or could you? Well, yes, you could at the time, but then afterwards the international criminal court said that putting a man in a bag is inhumane and therefore illegal. Which means squaddies who'd done nothing wrong could have found themselves in court.

It's weird. Genghis Khan waged war by invading a city and then building a pyramid at its centre from the heads of the children who had lived there. That's definitely not allowed now. Nor can you use the gas that was commonplace in warfare just a hundred years ago.

In the Second World War many Germans were shot after they'd surrendered, and a blind eye was turned, and then in Vietnam people looked the other way if unpopular officers were hand-grenaded by their men as they slept.

The rules of war, then, have always changed as a reaction to the conflict that's just been fought. But after the last bout of serious fisticuffs and the lawsuits that followed, it's now possible that war cannot be waged at all.

And, after watching the harrowing and brilliant Vietnam War series on Netflix last week, I find that doesn't sadden me at all.

30 September 2018

For a petrolhead, bathing in crude oil was a must. But, ooh, it gave me the willies

Every week the vain and the underemployed are invited to try out a new type of diet involving nothing but cucumber sandwiches, or a new kind of yoga-based exercise routine developed by monks in China. Gimmickry is the key. No one's going to try something they've tried before. Because if it had worked, they wouldn't be back.

In fact, no one's going to try anything anyone's tried before. Everything needs to be the next big thing.

Spas are particularly susceptible to this. You can't just ask customers to eat lettuce and go for a long walk. They need to get their nourishment by nicking the rear end of an organic cow and sucking the blood that spurts out.

And they need to exercise at absolute zero while humming excerpts from *Tubular Bells*. And everything has to have a Tibetan name. 'Tara. It's time for your Vajrayana bath.'

Bathing used to happen in water, but that's no good any more. Unless it's piped directly from Lhasa. You need to bathe in honey, or liquefied yak's cheese. In Georgia there's a spa where you can bathe in wine. And I don't buy into any of it.

However, on a trip last week to Azerbaijan I was told of a clinic where customers could bathe in oil. And I don't mean olive oil or the oil you get from an orang-utan's house.

I mean crude oil. The raw material that's used to make everything that matters: balloons, skis, crash helmets, pens, speedboats, elderly film stars' faces, doors, coffee machines, bottles and, of course, at the top of the list, petrol.

I had to try it. It would be like baptizing myself in the church of speed.

So it was off to the back streets of Baku, where I found the clinic. It was not like the sort of thing you see in the Emmanuelle films. There was no steam or pebbles or whale song played on pan pipes.

It was, as you'd probably expect in this former Soviet colony, a bit Russian. Wipe-down walls, furniture from the People's Chair Factory No 45 and an ECG machine that you felt could monitor electrical activity in the body and, at the flick of a switch, increase it dramatically.

A nurse ordered me into a room with flickery fluorescent lighting and asked: 'How old you are?'

I replied: 'Twenty-four.'

So she wrote '24' on her form.

'I was joking,' I said. 'I'm 117.'

She fixed me with the exact same look as the fake general got from his nurse in *Where Eagles Dare*.

Later a doctor explained that I needed to be checked because bathing in crude oil is not for the weak. More than 10 minutes in there, for example, and you get cancer.

That's a downside, for sure, but the upsides seemed immense. 'It is good,' said the doctor, 'for your kidneys, your liver, your skin, your circulation, your heart and your, how you say, penis.' With that I was taken into what was easily the most disgusting room I'd ever seen in my whole life. And this is a man who went to the lavatory once on a Chinese steam train in the Eighties.

They'd tried to enliven things with a pot of fake

flowers and some battery-powered candles – the real thing might have been a bit risky – but the walls looked as though they'd been decorated by Bobby Sands, and the ancient bath from the People's Bath Factory No 12 was full of what looked like hot sewage.

I climbed in and at first it was nice. I can see why sea-birds are so happy to take the plunge whenever a tanker crashes into Alaska. But then it was time to get out, and that led to the most humiliating and revolting episode of my entire life.

You'll be able to see the bathing scene on *The Grand Tour* next year, but what happened afterwards? No. Not a chance.

The first problem was getting out. Oil is skiddy, which means you simply cannot stand up in the bath, let alone lift a leg over the side, which means you need assistance.

This comes in the shape of a small Azerbaijani man, whose face, when he's finally got you standing, is level with your gentleman sausage.

Hanging on to him for dear life, I'm eventually out of the bath and clinging desperately to a coat hook, while matey-boy reaches for a shoehorn. He uses this to scrape the oil off my back and thighs, but even I can see he's getting nowhere. As guillemots know, oil clings.

It is also entirely unbothered by water, a point that becomes obvious as he slithers me across the tiled floor to the tiny shower. Here, I look down to see what benefits have been bestowed on my penis, but other than the fact it's now black, there appear to be none.

Someone is going to have to make it white again. And I can't see how that might be me. The floor is now coated in a thick veneer of soap and crude oil, and that means I need both hands to hold on to the shower-head mounting, and . . . oh my God, he's washing it. And now he's on his knees and he's washing it quite quickly and I'm worried that, unless he stops, this could result in a very unhappy happy ending. And then we had to get it out of the cavities.

It took half an hour to get enough oil off and out of my body that I could walk past a naked flame without exploding, and an hour in a bubble bath before my toenails became visible. And did I feel any better?

No. All the organic Tibetan downward dogs and all the whale song bathing are just anecdotes to keep the dinner party going until everyone gets talking about what box sets they're watching. If you want to get thin and healthy, eat less and walk more. The end.

14 October 2018

Ties? Rubbers? Five equals 11? Learning to play bridge left me vulnerable to a large glass of red

As a general rule, I'm a big fan of card games. I spent a great deal of my formative years playing blackjack because, even if you're gambling only tiny amounts, casinos give you free drinks. And since then I've whiled away many happy hours playing Between the Sheets, Queen of Spades and, best of all, Oh Hell.

It's hard to understand how playing cards came about. Who thought: 'Right – we have invented a printing press, so let's use it to make 52 bits of paper divided into four suits'?

And then, once someone had worked out how they could be used to play a game, why did someone else develop another? And then another? And then another? No one did that with chess. They came up with the board and the bishops and the prawns and they left it at that. Today no one ever says: 'What sort of chess are we playing?'

With cards, though, people did keep inventing new ways of using them until one day a soldier in the Crimean War decided that, to take his mind off the disease and how Wilfred had just been blown up again, he'd invent the most complicated game of them all: contract bridge.

I've avoided this in the past, mainly because I had better things to do and I'm not 87. But last week it was time to step into God's waiting room and take it up.

When you play blackjack you are usually surrounded by

serious-looking Arabs and chain-smoking Chinese men in a room with no windows, and when you play everything else you are at someone's kitchen table surrounded by several empty wine bottles, some overflowing ashtrays and a bit of sick.

Bridge is different. It's serious. So we'd be playing it in one of those clubs in St James's where everyone is dead and you have to wear a tie. I used to have a tie. I wore it for Margaret Thatcher's funeral. But it had gone missing, so I bought another and then – this is true – I had to go on YouTube to remind myself how it should be done up.

That's another thing I don't get. Who woke up one morning and thought: 'This ruff is annoying me, so instead I shall wrap a bit of silk round my neck'? I'd like to meet him so that I can kill him.

Anyway, my tie was eventually sort of tied and I had found a jacket that was nearly the same colour as my trousers and off I went.

The cards were dealt and our teacher explained that I must let my partner know where my strengths lay. 'Right,' I said enthusiastically. 'I've got a shitload of clubs.'

Apparently this was wrong. You aren't allowed to say what you've got. You must hint at it by saying you'd like the trumps to be clubs and that you've got enough to win one trick. Well, I had the ace, king, queen, jack and 10 so obviously I was going to win way more than one trick. I therefore opened with 'five clubs'.

Apparently this was also wrong. But it did stop anyone else bidding and that meant the game could get under way. My partner began by excusing herself from the game entirely, which was weird. She simply put her cards on the table, face up, and said: 'Good luck.'

'Whatever,' I replied.

Yup. That was wrong too. I was supposed to have said: 'Thank you, partner.' Which was weird, because why should I thank her for simply giving up?

No matter. I had all the heavy-hitting trumps and I needed to win only five tricks. Nope. Wrong again. Bidding five meant that for some reason I had to win 11 tricks. I have no idea why, but I failed completely. And lost.

Or did I? Because at the end of each hand you add up the number of light fittings in the room, subtract the number of teeth in your head, put that number above the line and the number of children you have below the line and then after five rounds there's a rubber and the winner is the player nearest the mantelpiece.

Who the bloody hell thought that made sense? It's as stupid as cricket. You get one run if you do one run, four if you send the ball all the way over there, six if it gets there without bouncing . . . and if it rains it's a draw.

Mind you, it could be worse. The Germans have developed a version of bridge called skat. In that, you have to work out which one of the other two players will be your partner. Imagine that. Playing a team game when you don't know who your team will be.

Perhaps that's what's gone wrong with their national football squad. But, whatever, it won't catch on here, as no one is going to say yes if you invite them round for an evening of skat.

There's another problem with bridge, which became clear as my inaugural evening wore on. Because we were in a beautiful club in St James's where all the other customers were dead, the waiters had nothing to do but constantly fill up my wine glass with a beautiful red.

And since bridge requires you to not participate if your partner made the opening bid of the successful suit and is wearing white underwear, there's very little to do half the time but drink it.

Soon I was a bit sozzled and I was arguing with the teacher, who kept saying that to win I needed to lose. In the same way as John Prescott used to say that the slower you drive, the faster you get there. He didn't make any sense. It didn't make any sense. And what were trumps again?

You can't do this if you want to win. You must concentrate as though you are flying an airliner and all four engines have stalled. If you daydream for even a moment, you've had it.

Which is why I wouldn't use MPs and civil servants to negotiate our tricky exit from the EU. I'd use our national bridge team instead.

21 October 2018

Meghan the scarpering duchess could learn a trick about crowds from me and the Queen

Last week the Duchess of Sussex – that's the American one, if you get them all muddled up – was invited by the United Nations to promote markets by spending 20 minutes touring a market in Fiji. Sadly, after just six minutes she whispered urgently into an aide's ear, and then moments after that she was politely bundled into a black van and whisked away.

No one knows for sure what caused the sudden departure, but some have speculated that the crowd was a bit boisterous and she became nervous.

Yes, well, I don't really buy that.

In the olden days, when I was the first-most-searched-for Jeremy on the internet rather than the sixth, I experienced some fairly heavy-duty fan action while staying in hotels around the world. A few years ago, when news of my visit to Kiev leaked onto the tentacles of social media, many protesters stopped throwing things at policemen, put down their placards and came to lay siege to my hotel. I needed 28 security people to get me out, and it was all jolly scary.

One man was so overcome with emotion, he decided he'd like to take my head home as a souvenir, and, let me tell you, it's tricky signing a million autographs while someone is yanking your ears, especially if the man whose pen you're using really, really wants it back. What's more, everyone wanted a selfie. And everyone was damn well going to get one. Pretty soon my feet weren't on the ground, either literally or metaphorically.

A few weeks later I was in Turin, and as I opened the curtains, I noticed a gigantic crowd surrounding the hotel. It was even bigger than the throng in Kiev, so once again I called my people, who called some other people, who were massive and arrived in black suits, wearing earpieces.

I was told to wait behind a pillar in reception until the meat machines had formed a human gorge through which I could make my escape. And I had to pretend that this was all a terrible nuisance, but the fact is I was loving it. My own security detail to keep the thousands of adoring Italian fans at bay. I mean, come on. That's quite a thing, especially as many were extremely pretty girls.

I knew something was wrong the moment I emerged at speed from the revolving doors. 'Go, go, go,' shouted the muscle mountain to my right, and I did as I was told while wondering why I could hear him so clearly. Where were the Beatle screams? Where were the cries of, 'Selfie, *per favore*'? In seconds I was in the back of the black Range Rover, and as the door slammed, I had my first real chance to examine the crowd close up. And it looked – what's the right word? – perplexed.

I found out later that this might have had something to do with the fact I'd been staying in the same hotel as One Direction. And that the crowd that had been waiting for them were a bit confused when a fat middle-aged man came out, behaving as though he was the president of America.

My point is that I know what it's like to be surrounded

by a seething mass of people who want a slice of your action. I've been there. And I'm sorry but the crowds Meghan had to face in Fiji were more Gerry Rafferty than Led Zep.

She should have been able to cope. All she had to do was get her security team to keep the selfie-hunters and the pervs at bay while she spent a paltry 20 minutes saying, 'And what sort of vegetable is this?' Then she could have returned to her hotel for a bubble bath.

But no. She ran. And that means everyone is grumpy, especially the United Nations, I imagine, because it's lost this once-in-a-lifetime opportunity to hammer home its vital message about the importance of markets.

The thing is, though, I don't think it was the crowd that caused Meghan to flee. Because, as you may have heard, she is currently with child, and that, I'm told, can cause issues 'down there'.

Which brings us on to the most important lesson that the duchess has to learn if she's going to be a prominent and valued member of the British royal family. It's this. The job comes first. Even if you have a gaping head wound, you simply carry on. Always.

God knows how many times Mrs Queen must have felt under the weather when she's been standing around pretending to be interested in the new civic centre's disabled ramps. But she just gets on with it.

Meghan has to learn how to do this, and I have a couple of helpful hints. First of all, you're a very pretty girl and you like wearing snazzy clothes. Well, stop it. Take a leaf out of my book and make sure that you constantly look terrible. Always look ill and worn out, and then no one will know when you actually are.

Then you have to come up with a strategy for coping with boredom. Yes, a Fijian market is not interesting. Nor are the UN's plans for creating more. You'd rather be in Harvey Nichols shopping for baby clothes. I get that. The trick is to know true boredom. I do this by talking to James May. Afterwards I feel able to deal with anything up to and including 40 years of solitary confinement.

So start every day by asking Harry to explain why a D-model Apache helicopter is different from the F model. Then you'll be able to deal with any number of tribal dance routines.

Of course, if you don't fancy looking terrible and being bored for a living, and you're starting to see that the American dream of being a princess isn't all feasting on peaches and peacock, there is an alternative.

Anonymity. Take it now and we won't hold a grudge. Don't, and I'm sorry but you'll never be allowed to scuttle from another engagement, ever.

28 October 2018

The past is another country, and if I ever think of visiting again, I hope they deny me a visa

Is there any more dangerous place to explore than the past? Obviously outer space is fairly tricky, and if you go under the sea there's a chance you'll be eaten or stabbed. But the past is nothing but layer upon layer of guilt, shame and regret. I know this because last week I had to go to Doncaster, which is where I grew up. I had no intention of visiting any of my old haunts, because I'm never particularly interested in yesterday. It's done and gone.

But the actual location we were using for filming was my old prep school. And it isn't a school any more. I'm not sure what it is. It has the feel of a halfway house where prisoners adapt to life on the outside before going home. This made me sad.

And then I don't know what came over me. I decided to visit the house my grandfather built. I'd spent many happy afternoons there, but that was 50 years ago and a lot's happened in 50 years. Mostly to my grandfather's house. I wish I hadn't seen it.

I also wish I hadn't got back into the car and driven past the pub my other grandparents ran – it was selling wine, for God's sake – and then into the village where I grew up. Straight away, I noted the wall I'd been forced to build for some teenage misdemeanour was still upright, but our tennis court and vegetable garden had a house on them.

I peeked through the windows of the converted barn

where my mum had started her business making Paddington Bears and it was being used as a storeroom for junk. There was a Paddington in the window but it wasn't one of my mum's. It was a cheap American copy. And then I went to my old house.

That was the same. Exactly the same. It had the same garage door, the same tiles, the same lamppost in the garden and even the same cotoneaster outside the dining room window. Plainly this was the only property in Britain that had been entirely impervious to Carol Smillie and 'Handy' Andy, and to the Ground Force movement.

But it had shrunk. When I was growing up, it was a very large house. There'd be huge parties on New Year's Eve, and at weekends I'd turn up with 10 or 15 friends, who would all sit round the dining room table for Sunday lunch.

I don't know how this was possible, as the dining room is now box-room tiny. And how did my dad ever cook in the kitchen, which is barely big enough for a cooker? And why were we so excited by the new remote-controlled television when nothing in the drawing room was more than four inches from where someone was sitting?

Even the view is changed. From my bedroom window I used to be able to see five power stations and two coalmines. Today there are only a couple of forlorn cooling towers, but there are hundreds of windmills, sitting out there in the flatlands giving people tinnitus and mincing birds. Ed Miliband is the MP these days. That says a lot.

Having burrowed through the strata of disappointment, I decided I might as well visit my dad's grave. Which was so covered in moss and gunk, I couldn't even read the inscription.

I drove away from Doncaster wishing I'd left the stone unturned. I should have finished my filming and gone. Because the past isn't how I left it. It's been ruined by change and progress and distorted memories.

But then, on the way back to London, I decided to stop off at a hotel called the George of Stamford. It's where we used to stay in the days when you had to open a gate to get onto the A1 and it took two days to get from Yorkshire to anywhere.

Stamford is a pretty Lincolnshire town a mile or so from the A1. It's so unchanged that people from the time of Ethelred the Unready would find it all comfortingly familiar. And so it goes with the George. However, I'd been told when I made the reservation I'd have to wear a jacket and that jeans were not allowed. This is something that makes my teeth itch with rage. It's the problem with the provinces, where eating out is seen as a treat, an event, a shiny bauble to end an anniversary or a birthday. It's not seen, as it should be, as a thing you do because you can't be bothered to do the washing-up that night.

That's why posh provincial restaurants still do that ta-dah thing with the cloche and why they're always silent. The food is king. You're there to genuflect to the chef's magnificence. Even the lighting is designed to highlight the handmade butterscotch in his chive and mushroom froth.

As I tiptoed through the George's oak-panelled dining room, I figured it would be the perfectly miserable end to my tear-stained trip down memory lane.

But no. It was the best supper I've had. The bits and bobs that came free were tremendous, and the beef was carved from a massive slab at the table, and there was a ton of horseradish, and the roast potatoes were perfect, and the wine list had a nice rosé I hadn't tried before and there wasn't a single bit of provincial pretentiousness in anything.

Even the waiter was brilliant. Instead of standing there like a cross between Uriah Heep and that stuck-up shop assistant in *Pretty Woman*, he joined in our chat about the TV show *Ozark*. He acted like a normal person in a normal restaurant.

I ate out a lot with AA Gill, so I know what he liked in a restaurant. And he would have loved the George. Which, of course, made me sad all over again.

This is why I've decided to be more resolute in keeping my head turned towards the future. Because, compared with the past, it's a joyous place full of nothing but Brexit, Jeremy Corbyn, dementia and death.

4 November 2018

I welcome trouble at till for M&S and I pray it finally gives small shops a spark of hope

I have never bought anything from Marks & Spencer. I've used its shops, once or twice, to shelter from the rain, but I've never seen a single thing in any of the aisles that I've wanted to buy. It's all stuff that I need. And that's boring. It's why I've never bought a washing-up bowl.

I am of course aware that Marks & Spencer is where you buy a skirt when you've grown out of Sir Philip Green. It's where you buy trousers when you've grown out of jeans. And it's where you buy your underwear when you are no longer doing sex. It is middle England with cash tills. It's where magistrates shop, safe in the knowledge they won't bump into any of the riffraff they've sent down. And it's in trouble. M&S has entered a world of S&M.

Owing to competition from online giants and budget supermarkets, and the fact that people are wearing jeans and doing sex for a lot longer these days, the ailing giant's half-year profits have risen by 2 per cent, but like-for-like sales of food, clothing and homewares have fallen again. And by quite a lot. As a result the share price dropped last week from a high of nearly 600p in 2015 to just 300p or thereabouts.

I don't understand what these numbers mean, but the management does and it's come up with a plan to turn things round: cheaper prawn sandwiches.

Hmmm. The nicest thing I've ever put in my mouth was a small piece of bruschetta that I bought at a cafe in Bologna. The tomatoes were about the same size as sultanas but each packed the punch of a hydrogen bomb. It was a kaleidoscope of taste sensations, all so vivid that my eyes became crossed and I lost the ability to make noise.

Knowing that nobody would believe a tomato could taste that good, I found out where they came from and bought some. Which caused my eyes to cross all over again, because they cost a little bit more than the car I was driving. I didn't mind, though, because – and this is the thing – they were worth every penny.

Yes, in America you can buy a tomato the size of your head for about one cent and that sounds tremendous. The problem is that this tomato, while huge, tastes of absolutely nothing at all. It's just water with seeds. You'd get more nutritional value from licking some Lego. So which tomato represents the better value? The one-cent watermelon or the five-grand, five-carat seeded red diamond?

This is what M&S must surely understand. If it decides to lower the cost of its food to attract more customers, the people who supply that food are going to have to make it for less. And that is bound to have an effect on quality. Then, pretty soon, the town's magistrates are going to think: 'This prawn sandwich doesn't taste of anything.' And that will be that for one of Britain's best known and most respected businesses.

I can't wait for this to happen. I can't wait for all the supermarkets and chain stores to be wiped out by online competition, because then the little shops will come back selling expensive things in small brown paper bags. And this will be great news for Yorkshire people like me who think value is more important than cost.

At the moment a small shop selling good-quality products cannot survive. Due to idiotic parking restrictions and an unintelligent army of traffic wardens who don't understand what's meant by 'I'll only be a minute', no one can stop off at the butcher and then the greengrocer on the way home. Because that would mean two parking tickets.

So they go instead to the supermarket, where there's a car park, and while they're there they buy some batteries and some lightbulbs. Which means that the small independent electrician's shop is history too. And the next thing you know, the town centre is full of nothing but charity shops, pizzerias and sick.

If, however, we can get rid of these supermarkets by buying stuff we need online, then the small shops will come back to the town centres to sell us stuff we want. Such as tomatoey tomatoes.

You may think I'm talking rubbish and that you want cheap food. But do you, really?

Because think about this in terms of drink. I understand that if you are 18 you will travel halfway across town to find a pub that sells cheap beer. My son is always in a part of London I've never heard of because he's found the elusive £4 pint. But what about water? You could drink that from a tap for nothing, but you don't, do you? And then there's wine. Sure, you can buy extremely cheap plonk that will get you drunk just as quickly as a 1945 Pétrus. But you don't, because you know cheap wine is only for homeless people.

When you are in a restaurant, looking at the wine list, you never buy the cheapest. You buy, if you've any sense, the third cheapest, because you reckon that seems about right. Well, it's like that with food. It's like that with everything.

America has done its best to teach us that the lowest cost is always the best. But unless you're on the dole, it isn't. The cheapest of anything is always the worst. There is, as I've always said, no such thing as cheap and cheerful. It's cheap and nasty or expensive and cheerful.

Retailers just don't seem to have got this message. They're still looking at ways to turn everything into a battery farm. To reduce the price, whatever the cost may be.

It'll be the death of them. And then we can get back to the European system of shopping for what you need from whomever does it best.

Mind you, in Europe the traffic wardens are either more understanding or not there at all. Which helps.

11 November 2018

I don't care if these blasted abbreviations are MIA, AWOL, KIA or DOA. I just want them gone

I received an email last week that said the sender was OOO. And by the time I'd worked out what on earth that meant, he'd got back to his office and sent me another missive, to which I replied: 'So we are all BYY then?' BYY has no meaning. I'd made it up. And I sincerely hope that the millennial on the other end of the exchange had to spend the rest of the day trawling the internet for clues about what BYY might mean. And then the whole evening worried sick that a fat old dinosaur might know more about modern parlance than he did. I'm going to use this trick a lot in future.

I was sent a flow chart the other day, which asked the simple question: 'Is it acceptable to use the phrase "reach out"?' This led to the second question, which was: 'Are you in the Four Tops?'

I liked that, because I hate the expression 'reach out'. If someone uses it to me in an email, I don't reply. It's the same with 'circle back' and 'move the needle', anything that's 'frictionless', 'skin in the game' and 'deep dive'. This means I haven't replied to anyone in corporate America for about two years. From now on, though, I'm going to turn 'there we are then' into an acronym and leave them wondering.

What I want to know about these abbreviations is: what exactly are you trying to achieve by using them? Yes, it's quicker to type OOO than 'out of the office', but since this is an automated message that you need set up only once, the amount of time you save in a lifetime is about half a second.

Whereas the people who receive this message every time your computer sends it will waste hours walking around their office and sucking a pencil as they desperately try to figure out what it means. It's possible, probable even, that someone could have developed a cure for cancer by now had they not been stuck in one of your ridiculous crossword clues.

Some well-known acronyms simply don't work at all. Pin number, for example. Because what you're actually saying is 'personal information number number'. It's the same with those who refer to the HIV virus. Or an ATM machine. Or an LCD display. Or an ISDN network.

Then you have abbreviations that are longer to use than the actual words. Worldwide web, for instance, is three syllables, whereas WWW is nine. And why say: 'Have you RSVPed?' when you mean 'Have you replied?'?

I can see why initials might make sense if you are in the army and people are shooting at you. Better to say there's the threat of an ABC attack and you need AA, because by the time you'd said you needed anti-aircraft support for an atomic, biological or chemical attack, everyone would be KIA.

Or, as Robin Williams put it in *Good Morning, Vietnam*, 'Seeing as how the VP is such a VIP, shouldn't we keep the GC on the QT? 'Cos if it leaks to the VC, he could end up MIA and then we'd all be put on KP.'

Business, though, is not Homs or Raqqa, so using abbreviations is stupid. Elon Musk recognizes this and has views on the matter, saying to staff at his company SpaceX that unless the practice was stopped, there'd be codes for everything and new recruits would have to waste time learning them. He cited the VTS-3, which was an in-house short-form of 'vertical test stand with three legs'. As he pointed out, 'tripod' was easier to say and understand.

And yet he misses the point, because no one is dreaming up abbreviations to save time. They are showing off. By saying VTS-3 to a peer or a junior, what you are actually saying is: 'I know more things than you do. I am cleverer than you. I am better than you.'

So, when you get an email that says the sender is OOO, what it actually says is: 'I have saved half a second of my life and I don't care that you will need a minute or two to figure out what I mean, because my time is more valuable than yours because I'm a more important person.'

It's the same as being late. That's rude because what you are saying is: 'Your life is less worthwhile than mine.' It's almost certain that people who use a lot of acronyms in business emails are incapable of punctuality. And I'm willing to bet they are also the sort of people who use the word 'paradigm' or who adopt a ridiculous French accent when saying 'bouillabaisse'. They are show-offs.

And that's just the start of it. They can't contribute good ideas and they can't win you over with charm or wit, so they use a type of communication designed specifically to exclude others. That's why millennials talk about memes and meh and Milfs. They are speaking in a language, like polari and rhyming slang, that was invented to be impenetrable to you and me. This means they are, in fact, bullies. And bullies, as we know, are the new racists. You should bear that in mind next time you say lol. Because you're being Harvey Weinstein.

Famously, David Cameron said he thought lol meant 'lots of love', and everyone howled with derisive laughter because of course we all knew it actually means 'laugh out loud'. Or is it the other way round? I don't know. And I don't care. Because if someone sends me an amusing picture on WhatsApp, I have the good manners to say: 'I found that funny.'

You try, when you are in a restaurant in Paris, to say 'merci' and 'au revoir', because it's polite. Well, think about that next time you are sending an email that's NSFW. Because the person you sent it to might open it in front of his boss, thinking you had some kind of beef with New South Effing Wales.

18 November 2018

Enterprise, stand by to beam aboard Picard and his Oxfordshire nimbies

As we know, there is a genuine and serious problem for young people living in rural areas. Because after you've stolen a quad bike and then spent the afternoon lolling around in a bus shelter, off your head on spice, there is literally nothing to do. Apart from a bit of light vandalism.

Some say the problem could be solved by more affordable housing, but if a young person gets 40 quid a week for doing some part-time fencing work and spends 30 of that on spice and a tenner on cider, the only price they can realistically afford is nought.

Yes, a £50,000 house is affordable if you are Sir Elton John but if you're on benefits and you look like an extra from *Shaun of the Dead*, it may as well be a billion trillion. And there's no hope if things stay this way because as the bright kids leave for the city, the mouth-breathing agri-yobs that remain will impregnate their gormless girlfriends and there'll be an IQ spiral until it'll be impossible to distinguish between rural people and the potatoes they grow.

Jobs. That's the only solution. Because when someone has a job, they have money. And if you have money, you get to choose how you fill your weekends. And if you have a choice of things to do then the idea of standing around in a municipal shrubbery, drooling, suddenly doesn't seem so appealing.

That's why I was cheered to hear that on a bit of countryside near where I live, an American philanthropist had applied for planning permission to build a car museum. And this wouldn't just be a place where he could take friends on an ego trip to the core of his wealth and brilliance. It would be open to the public and to schools for educational visits.

That would be good for local hotels and restaurants and shops and, best of all, it would create about 100 permanent jobs. And 100 jobs would mean support and income for 100 people who'd stop taking spice and start feeding their children and painting their front doors and not filling their gardens with dead dogs and old washing machines.

No town would say no to the creation of 100 new jobs. It would be madness. But that's exactly what happened with the car museum idea, owing to the intervention of Captain Jean-Luc Picard from the Starship Enterprise. Or to be accurate, the actor who played him, Sir Patrick Stewart.

He and, it's said, 249 other locals banded together and, by using nimby noises and hyperbole, created the image of a super-rich car enthusiast having a 2,000-decibel rev-off with his billionaire mates every Sunday morning.

And as a result the local council seems to have said: 'OK. Sod the jobs and the money and the pretty environmental schemes that our American friend has promised. We would much prefer local people to be fighting in the streets over the one job on offer from whatever charity shop has opened in the town this week.' And so that was the end of that.

Now I know Sir Stewart a little bit and he's a nice chap, a lovable old leftie thesp with a beautiful speaking voice. I also sympathize with him. Because people who live in the countryside out of choice, and not because there's no call for shepherds in Chelsea, are very Prince Charlesish when it comes to change. We don't like it. We have all picked a moment in history where we thought everything was OK – usually around 1867 – and we want everything to stay like that for ever.

But it's got to stop, really. Because when you think about it, people are much better at creating beauty than nature. Yes, I admit, nature, when it girds its loins, can do spectacular. Anyone who's seen Ha Long Bay in Vietnam or the Grand Canyon will testify to that, but by far the prettiest thing in the British Isles is the Humber Bridge. And God had nothing to do with that.

When someone in the 17th century suggested building Goodwood House, I'm sure lots of people lodged all sorts of objections with the local sheriff, saying it would spoil their view and increase traffic – it's certainly done that in recent years – but now people travel from all over the world to West Sussex to see it.

I was in Azerbaijan recently, and in Baku, the capital, there's a gallery and cultural centre that was designed by the late Zaha Hadid. It's not just the best-looking building I've seen. It's the best-looking thing. It's better even than a Riva Aquarama speedboat or the sun rising on a frosty morning or the pinkiness of the snow-capped mountains at dusk in Useless Bay in Chilean Tierra del Fuego.

The view from my cottage in the countryside is very lovely. There are yellowhammers and fields and hills and woods and all of it would be vastly improved by the addition of that cultural centre. In the same way that Bilbao was vastly improved when the Guggenheim arrived.

And Salisbury when someone said: 'Shall we build a cathedral?'

Our American friend with plans for a car museum has now shrunk his ambitions, moved the site and hired Foster + Partners to design the buildings. That's Norman bloody Foster, for God's sake. This is the man whose company brought some zizz to the City of London with the Gherkin and gave Germany a glass dome for its parliament building. And now his practice has been asked to enhance Oxfordshire with a museum. I'd be proud to have such a thing outside my sitting room window. I hope it happens.

Sure, I wouldn't want to be around for the building works and, yes, there will be more cars on the roads. But these will be cars bringing money to the region – and jobs. And these are the twin pillars of rejuvenation. Not cheap houses made from spit and Kleenex. Not charity shops. Not a ban on Londoners owning second homes. Money. And jobs. Lovely.

And even lovelier when they come in a parcel wrapped up by Lord Foster.

25 November 2018

I had my dream house all planned, and then it hit me – there's nowhere to store the Parma ham

The worst thing about Brexit is that when Jeremy Corbyn and his bunch of halfwits come to power, there will be no guiding hand to steady his lunacy. Freed from the European overlord, he'll be free to do as he pleases, filling cattle trains with intellectuals and burning books and insisting the army develops some kind of weird new marching technique.

Unsurprisingly, various regions from across Europe have invited well-off British people to up sticks and start a new life over there. The Portuguese have a 20 per cent income tax rate for Brits who wish to emigrate. The Italians, meanwhile, say if you buy a house in their country there'll be no tax at all – just a flat fee of €100,000 (£90,000) a year. And pretty much no reporting requirements about overseas earnings.

And then you have the Basques, who are offering massive tax rebates to people working in the film and television industry. Well, I do work in film and television, and – I've got to be honest – that sounds extremely appealing. Apart from the dodgy weather, San Sebastian is a tremendous place, and Biarritz, my favourite city, is just around the corner.

It all sounds very tempting – slashing my tax bill and leaving the Brexiteers to wallow around in the communistical misery pit of their own making – but instead of buggering off, I'm literally putting a stake in the ground here by building a house.

I'm told that this is everyone's dream: designing and creating your own living space. We all watch *Grand Designs* with drool puddling on our guts and think: 'God, I'd like to do that.' But so far it's proving to be quite difficult.

I got planning permission ages ago, but then I decided that instead of a slate roof, which the council liked, I'd prefer something made from stone. So I got some new planning permission for that. But last week, in a meeting with the architect and the project manager, I discovered that if I used stone tiles on the roof, it would be nearly the same colour as the house.

This, I figured, would be the same as wearing a jacket that was nearly the same colour as your trousers, so we spent a few hours discussing the possibility of using darker composite tiles instead. And then I decided that, because I'm not John Terry, I didn't want a plastic roof and I'd go back to slate. So now I've got to ask the council for permission to change my mind. Again.

After this lengthy discussion about the colour of the roof, we talked about how much lime would be used in the mortar and the texture of the gravel on the drive, and then it was time to turn our attention to how the lights might be turned on and off.

Now I've said before that no two suitcases are the same. You literally never see anyone in an airport who has one the same as yours. Well, it's worse with companies that make light switches. They do one and then they change the design and do another and so on. This means there are 74 billion options.

There are also some hi-tech alternatives that allow you

to draw the curtains and pilot a drone over Homs. But I have made it very plain to all concerned that, apart from wi-fi, I want no tech in the house at all. Because tech doesn't work. Ever. Not even wi-fi, usually. I've also insisted that the plans are drawn in feet and inches, because I can visualize that. How big is '350 mill'? The length of a pin or two hundred miles? I've no idea.

Eventually, out of boredom, I chose a switch, and then we moved on to flooring. Oak. Yes. Definitely oak. 'Or what about elm?' asked the project manager. 'Or mahogany?' queried the architect. Pretty soon it was dark and still we were sitting there saying tree names to one another.

And then I noticed something. I've been looking at the plans for months. I've worked out where the laundry cupboards will be and even where I can store the vacuum cleaner. Wine fridge? Yup. Ticked. I know where it will be plugged in and what sort of generator will be employed to keep it going should Corbyn's nationalized grid go wrong. I've even angled the house so that on a summer's evening I can sit on the porch with some sipping whisky and watch the sun go down.

But as the team talked about the possibility of planking ebony and holly, and the clock crept past seven, I started to get hungry, so as we discussed the possibility of creating the world's first poisonous floor out of manchineel, I thought about food. And that's when the problem entered my head: there was nowhere for a pantry. I was building a six-bedroom house, but there wasn't even a tiny spot where I could store flour and Oxo cubes.

Plainly this had to be rectified, so we stopped talking about Burmese teak and started discussing what should be sacrificed to make way for the olive oil and the ham. It came down to a choice of three things. Wine fridge. Dishwasher. Or lavatory. The lavatory lost.

Nobody explains any of this to you when you say you're going to build a house. Nobody says that you can't get a costing for the job unless every detail of the job has been talked through in advance. You literally can't start until, in your head, it's absolutely finished. I began in earnest on my house in September, and the schedule says that, even if everything goes smoothly, we will not break ground until September next year. And then it'll take three years to build. And by that time I'll be dead.

And then the house with no downstairs lavatory will end up in the hands of Diane Abbott, who'll fill it with all the people who were too stupid or too poor to bugger off to San Sebastian when they had the chance.

9 December 2018

Houston, I have a problem; it seems any old bearded fool can go into space these days

We've always been told that space flight is difficult and dangerous, and that astronauts need to be comic-book men of steel with supercomputers in their heads and lungs like barrage balloons. If you've seen the film *The Right Stuff*, you'll know what I'm on about. The seven brave fighter pilots chosen for the Mercury space programme had to prove they could keep their bowels under control even when they'd been fed laxatives, and that they could breathe out solidly for half an hour.

They also had to have balls of steel. It's not in the film, but when the seven were invited by NASA to watch a test flight of the Atlas rocket they'd be using, it exploded spectacularly, turning night into day for miles around. As everyone ran around screaming, Alan Shepard turned to his colleagues and said: 'Well, I'm glad they got that out of the way.'

The colleagues, by the way, were John (Glenn), Virgil (Grissom), Scott (Carpenter) and Gordon (Cooper) – ring any bells? Yup, they were the names used years later for the fearless Thunderbird pilots.

And then there was Brains and his mates, the engineers who designed the rocket ships. They were selected to be the best of the best of the best, and each had to know more than all of the world's encyclopedias and be capable of winning any chess game in four seconds.

Obviously, the cost of putting a man into space was so prohibitive that a small country such as Germany could not countenance such a thing. You needed to fit leaf blowers to the letterbox of your space agency and then employ a round-the-clock army to keep them fed with cash. This meant space was a superpower thing.

But then along came *Apollo 13*. I guess you all know the story. Kevin Bacon flicked a switch. There was an explosion. Tom Hanks and Bill Paxton did a lot of acting and we were informed they had only enough power to run a toaster. What's more, they had to use the cover of the flight manual and bits of their spacesuits to make scrubbers to filter their air.

It was like a *Blue Peter* thing: lots of sticky-backed plastic, and I know we were all supposed to be amazed by the ingenuity of both the crew and the boffin boys at Houston. But I wasn't. I just sat there thinking: 'If they can get round the moon and back to a safe landing on Earth, in a can, with less computing power than a modern-day Ford Fiesta, making stuff out of gloves and duct tape, then maybe space flight isn't as difficult as we've been led to believe.'

Of course, Hanks had to do incredible calculations in his head while freezing to death and then had to manually correct the course of his can while travelling at 17,500mph, using nothing but an engine that wasn't designed for the job, so he had plenty of the right stuff, clearly.

But today I follow the International Space Station on Instagram, and the guys and girls who operate it don't look like fighter-pilot superheroes to me. They all look a bit flabby, if I'm honest, with their polo shirts tucked into their chinos. Certainly, I can't see any of them being able to wrestle a Klingon, or rescue Sandra Bullock should debris tear the space station to shreds.

What's more, in 1998, John Glenn, one of the original Mercury astronauts, joined a space shuttle mission. He was 77 years old. And I'm sure this provided great cheer for the world's elderly, but if a 77-year-old can go up there, how hard can it be?

Plainly, the same thing occurred to the marijuana enthusiast and libel expert Elon Musk, because he has embarked on a space programme and seems to be enjoying some success. Then you have Jeff Bezos, who is a wonderful man in every way, with some fabulous shows on his Amazon Prime Video service. He too has a spacecraft and he too is being successful.

These are rich guys. In the world of business, they are superpowers. But they don't have more money than the UK and we couldn't afford a space programme, so how can they? Unless it's not as expensive or as complicated as we've always been told.

Further doubt was cast last week when the record-label boss who discovered Mike Oldfield and his tubular bells put a tourist ship into space. Taking off from the Mojave Desert in California, a twin-fuselage cargo plane flew to 45,000ft before releasing a Virgin Galactic rocket ship from under its belly.

Fuelled by grains of what's basically nylon, this accelerated to more than 2,000mph and a minute later reached peak altitude, before landing safely back on Earth. It's incredible, really, that a man who crashed his boat and his hot-air balloon has made a spaceship that runs on bits of chopped-up anorak. And that it actually works.

Yes, there is some debate about whether SpaceShipTwo reached 'space'. Many say the official start point of the big nothing is the so-called Karman line, which is 62 miles above the Earth. And Sir Richard Branson's bird only got to 51½ miles. But I've watched a video of the flight and the view from the windows at that altitude looks pretty spacey to me. NASA agrees. It awards 'astronaut wings' to anyone who reaches an altitude of 50 miles. Which means it reckons Beardy made it. It has even congratulated him.

So, soon, despite some setbacks and a handful of deaths, he will achieve his dream of taking fee-paying customers up there for a moment of weightlessness. Hanks has already signed up. So has Angelina Jolie – and you could too for $250,000 (£199,000).

As that's about a quarter of what it costs to go from London to Manchester on a Virgin train, it's pretty good value. And it's sad, too, because it confirms what I've suspected since Jim Lovell had his 'problem' on Apollo 13. You can be fat and dim and still go to space. All you really need is the will.

16 December 2018

Lasers, nets, eagles, jammers – it's all pie in the sky. Our only defence against drones is luck

As I write, planes have started to take off from Gatwick and everyone is now wandering about in a state of bewildered impotence, trying to work out who is responsible, how such a thing can be prevented in future and, of course, whether drones should now be banned.

Commentators have pointed out that over a 14-month period one gang alone used drones on 55 occasions to deliver drugs worth more than half a million pounds to Britain's prisons.

Then you have celebrities, who complain that paparazzi are using aerial tech to photograph them mating with other celebrities, and I know of a young lady who found a private place to do some topless sunbathing last summer, only to find that, because of a perv drone, it wasn't private at all.

For sure, they are extremely useful when it's the day before Christmas and you can't think of anything to buy your son. But even here there are issues, because on Boxing Day morning, when you are on the lavatory, his new toy will arrive at the window and transmit live pictures of your No 2s to the internet. And then the next day it will crash into a tree, and that'll be that.

A ban, therefore, makes sense. Except it doesn't, because my film crew uses drones to get aerial shots, and Sir Attenborough does too. Not even the most reclusive monkey or stork is safe now from the prying eyes of the BBC's natural history department. And neither are terrorists. Remember Jihadi John? Well, his last thought was: 'I wonder what that buzzing noise is.'

Then you have rail operators, which use drones to see just how much trackside cabling has been stolen in the night. In China they are fitted with flamethrowers and used to clear debris that's stuck on overhead power lines.

Amazon is working on drones that will deliver stuff to your back garden in less than 30 minutes. And there's talk of the NHS using them in London to move urgently needed medical supplies between the capital's 34 hospitals.

The trouble is that drones are a bit like guns: extremely useful when they're in the right hands but extremely unuseful when they're not. And there's always been a suggestion that some radicalized halfwit will fit a gob of C-4 plastic explosive to a £40 drone and fly it into the left engine of an El Al Boeing that's coming in to land at Heathrow.

To get round this, most drone makers that sell to the public fit their machinery with so-called geofencing, which stops it being flown near a prison or an airport or, I'd hope, a nuclear power station. But to get round that, almost anyone with a laptop and a soldering iron can buy a DIY drone kit that could be piloted right into the conning tower of the nuclear-powered sub HMS Astute.

Or, as we've now seen, into Gatwick. I don't believe the culprit was a terrorist. He could be an eco-freak who thinks Mr Polar Bear is more important than the Christmas plans of more than 100,000 people, but I'm willing to bet £5 that, actually, the man responsible is a fat gamer who lives with his mum and has a hard drive the police would describe as distressing.

I'm not an FBI profiler. I know that. But I also know this guy has a black T-shirt, likes heavy metal and doesn't understand soap. All the police needed to do was find someone in nearby Crawley who'd been downloading a lot of Metallica. Especially if he had a lot of well-thumbed electronics magazines.

Someone like that could easily build a go-anywhere drone that could fly at 5,000ft at 70mph. And not even Lee Harvey Oswald could hit something that small going that fast that far away. It is unshootdownable. Besides, I can't really see the police being allowed to fire their guns at a drone that, when all is said and done, is just being a nuisance. As the BBC put it, 'Marksmen have no control over the bullets.' This obviously is nonsense. But it highlights the problems caused by the very mention of weaponry in the left-wing press.

That's presumably why the Dutch have been training eagles to bring down rogue drones. However, you can be sure that if anyone tried such a thing here, the airborne wing of the Labour Party, known as the RSPB, would put an immediate stop to it.

Jamming the signal? Well, I spoke to the guy who flies the drones we use on *The Grand Tour*, and he reckons that this is extremely difficult. He then talked for quite a long time about gigahertz and megahertz, and when I woke up he was making end-of-chat pleasantries. The upshot is, though, that if you jam all the frequencies that might be used, you shut down the area's mobile phone network, paralyse the police and probably crash the planes you're trying to protect.

Lasers? Really? Sussex police, we now know, turned up with nothing but a boot full of silver blankets and a couple of truncheons. Not even James Bond has an anti-drone laser. And the idea of using an airborne net is even more far-fetched. Apparently, we don't even have the tech to find where the signal is coming from.

In the absence of realistic anti-drone measures, it makes sense to treat them like guns and allow only people with licences to own and operate them. Except, of course, this wouldn't work, because anyone with mischief on their mind could simply build one anyway.

I'm afraid, then, that they've been invented and, like nukes, now can't be uninvented. Which means the only real solution is to thank God we weren't at Gatwick last Thursday. And go through life with our fingers crossed.

I hope you all have a very happy Christmas, and let's hope someone doesn't fly a drone into Santa's sleigh.

23 December 2018

I'm no irrational lover of dumb creatures but we must save Japanese whalers from themselves

The Japanese have had a good old chin-scratch and decided it's probably for the best if the whales that live off their coast are herded into a convenient bay and then stabbed so that they drown in about a million gallons of one another's blood.

You'd imagine that this news would have caused Jeremy Corbyn and his merry band of communists to rush into the street with petrol bombs and some hi-vis jackets. But unfortunately they were too busy telling everyone that when they come to power they will make sure the police are prevented from investigating burglaries and murders and told to crack down properly on foxhunting.

I'm not kidding. On the very day the Japanese made their announcement, the Labour Party's environmental spokesmanwoman was banging on about how rich people who ride horses on Boxing Day should be given some serious jail time.

For once the Conservative Party was a bit more on the money. Michael Gove was so cross with Japan he took immediately to Twitter to say so. And he wasn't alone. An Australian woman went on Sky News to do a bit of weeping, and then there was Boris Johnson – who probably fancies the Australian woman – and a Norwegian called Erik Solheim, whose role in global politics is unclear. But their message to the Japanese was clear. Stop this nonsense or else.

The Japanese, I'm sure, will have looked all these people up on the internet and decided that if Russia can invade Crimea without even getting a small fine, they're not going to wake up and find themselves facing crippling trade sanctions, no matter how many whales they stab.

It actually makes me cross that the world is so pathetic at the moment. Everyone on the entire planet, apart from 16 Icelanders and a handful of Norwegians, knows that it is wrong to kill whales, and yet here's Japan, standing there with its hands on its hips saying: 'Yeah. And what are you going to do about it, pal?'

Weirdly, I don't buy into the usual whale-hugging guff. We are told they are extremely intelligent, but this obviously isn't so or they'd have invented the fax machine. 'Aha,' say some marine biologists, from inside a cloud of Bajan weed. 'They haven't invented the fax machine because they can already send Instagram pictures to one another.' This may well be true. It's been suggested one whale can see something and transmit an actual image of it to another whale.

But that's not intelligence. That's just something they can do. It's like claiming a pigeon is intelligent because when you take it to the south of France it will fly straight back to the crummy shack where it lives in Barnsley. Or that humans are intelligent because we can operate hammers.

Someone once told me salmon are bright because they can navigate thousands of miles back to the very spot where they were born. But I find myself scratching my head at that one because when my children were born, I didn't put their mother in a car and drive her to Doncaster. That would have been idiotic, so we just went to the nearest hospital instead.

There's also a lot of talk about how whales use sonar to detect food. Great. I use the internet and a mobile telephone, and that's much better.

But just because something is daft, that doesn't mean we have the right to kill it. Yes, there was a time when whale oil brought light to the night, but since Azerbaijan worked out how to get crude oil from under its deserts, there's been a better alternative.

And don't give me the food argument either. I've eaten whale – not a whole one – and, while it was very nice, especially when the waiter grated some guillemot on it, it did taste very like steak. And if you want a steak, why not get it from a cow – an animal that's bred and farmed for the purpose? Besides, in Japan whale accounts for only 0.1 per cent of all the meat that's consumed. So it's not really big business.

Then you have those who say whales must be killed for scientific reasons. Well, I've done some checking and it seems all you can learn from a whale you've killed is how old it was and what it'd been eating. And I'm not sure either nugget quenches a human's thirst for knowledge. It certainly wouldn't wash if you used it as an argument for killing your next-door neighbour. 'I knew she was fibbing when she said she was 42.'

The fact remains, though, that if there were no whales in the world, it wouldn't really matter. It'd be the same as having no brontosauruses, and we seem to be able to cope with that.

Maybe they have some eco-purpose and we need them to stop a proliferation of plankton giving the sea the consistency of gravy. Or maybe, if they were all gone, it would lower sea levels enough to give the Maldives a bit of breathing space.

Or maybe the Japanese decision is irrelevant because many whales survive on a diet of fish, and the way those aquatic Spanish vacuum cleaners are hoovering global stocks to almost nothing, Mr Whale will die of starvation soon anyway.

It's all a big potpourri of ignorance, garnished with a lot of what-ifs. But none of that matters. What does matter is that when I see some halfwit from Texas leering at the camera with one foot on the lion he's just shot, I'm consumed by an urgent need to peel him. I feel the same about the nouveau riche of Vietnam who believe that if they snort powdered rhino horn they will have 9ft erections.

But I reserve a special level of hatred for people who sail off into the big blue to spend a week or two killing whales. For absolutely no reason at all.

And on that note, may I wish everyone a happy new year – except them.

30 December 2018

Hey, Tories, you can't bleed all the rich like Corbyn would, so try a vulgarity tax

Look, there's no point beating about the bush, so I'll get straight to the point. Theresa May is hopeless. She talks like a robot when she has a script and like a nervous three-year-old when she hasn't. She laughs like a penguin. She enjoys rambling. She admits the naughtiest thing she did was run through a field of wheat. She talks French like she's joking. And when someone suggested she should dance onto the party conference stage to the accompaniment of Abba, she said: 'What a good idea.' Which it wasn't.

Small wonder she's failed so spectacularly to secure any kind of Brexit deal. Because how can you negotiate with a room full of antagonists when all you can say is 'Strong and stable', and you've arrived at the table like a sort of wooden John Travolta.

The worst thing about her, though, is that she plainly has no vision of what she'd like Britain to be like. Margaret Thatcher had a vision. Tony Blair had a vision. Jeremy Corbyn has a vision. But Mrs May? She knows she can't have what she wants, which is Enid Blyton and red telephone boxes, and Bernard Cribbins running the railway station, but she has no clue what would work instead.

Furthermore, I see no one in the Tory party who's any better. There's Boris Johnson, of course, but he has only two things on his mind: Boris Johnson and the rather attractive filly who works in the Commons bar. And the rest? It's like looking into a tin of minestrone soup.

I was speaking about this with some Conservative friends of mine recently and everyone agreed that the party needs a goal to aim at. Corbyn has 'For the many, not the few', and that works very well. It resonates with voters. And it informs his decision makers on the direction they need to be travelling.

But the Tories? I know they're all transfixed by Brexit, but when that's over, they need something more than 'Well, we're better than Corbyn.' I agree with that. I'd rather put my dog into No 10 than him. But not everyone thinks the same way.

The problem is big. The Conservatives have always championed aspiration. It's seen as a good thing, to strive for a bit of G Plan furniture, a better Ford Mondeo and your council house. But that was in a time when wealth was a very different animal from what it's become today.

When I was growing up I knew about Howard Hughes but he didn't seem real. He was just a madman who lived in the dark and only drank milk. I also knew there were some titled people who lived in extremely large stately homes. But they didn't look very rich to me. Most had 200-year-old jackets and jumpers with holes in them.

I knew only two rich people. Both were local farmers. One had a trout lake in his garden and one had his own swimming pool. And while these things were fantastically luxurious they didn't seem to be impossible goals. Whereas today we regularly read about and see people whose wealth is so huge it seems to be unachievable.

Off every beach at every holiday destination you see boats with helicopters at the front and pools full of Victoria's Secret models at the back. At every airport there's a zone for private jets that are bigger than the plane you and a hundred others arrived in. And in every newspaper there's another young woman with £25,000 breasts, snuggled into the arms of a man whose watch is bigger than your washing machine.

I'm currently hosting *Who Wants To Be a Millionaire?* on ITV. And not that long ago a million would buy you something with pillars and a flower room. Now, though, it's barely enough to get you a one-bedroom flat in Fulham.

If you google Rich Kids of Instagram you'll find a site where youngsters are encouraged to post pictures of themselves literally bathing in actual cash. And when you see that sort of thing, you become very inclined to vote for Corbyn and his much-talked-about wealth tax.

Wealth taxes don't work. History has taught us that. But I can see how they might have some appeal when you're living in a high-rise with five grown-up kids who can't afford to move away, and you're reading about people whose newly built Caribbean holiday house is so vast it affected the world price of teak.

Even I saw red the other day when I met someone who'd just sold his business for £20 million. He was down in the dumps because 'in this day and age, anything less than 200 mil is seen as a failure. Jeff Bezos makes that in a day.'

Comfortable is no longer seen as a goal worth striving for. You don't want a chain of dry cleaners across the northwest. Because on the monetary scale of evolution that makes you a worm. So you may as well vote for Corbyn because he will use rich people's money to pay you to do nothing.

The trouble is he can't target only the non-doms and

billionaires because they'll just live in one of their other houses somewhere else. So he has to go after the ordinary rich, which in his weird head is anyone with a house. Certainly anyone with a bit of money left at the end of the month will have it taken away by his Stasi.

I therefore have an idea that I offer to the Conservatives: a vulgarity tax.

It's very simple. If you live like that woman who runs Bet365 – quietly, diligently and with a philanthropic heart – you will be fine. If, however, you choose to live like Paul Pogba, turning up at nightclubs in a diamond-encrusted Rolls-Royce, then Tommy Taxman is going to come round with a crowbar.

I realize this is bad news for Rolex, Chanel and the people of Cheshire. But it's good news for the soul of the nation. It will also completely undermine Corbyn. And that's more important.

6 January 2019

This trendy new weight-loss tipple is not making me thinner. And it doesn't even get me drunk

Last week thousands of geeky people in terrible jumpers travelled to a massive electronics fair in Las Vegas to get all hot in their underpants over the latest breakthroughs in consumer technology. None of which is useful. And none of which will work.

One exhibitor was displaying a dishwasher that you could use in a car, and I'm sure that was very difficult to achieve. Think of the plumbing and where the water might come from.

But you do have to wonder who on earth has thought: 'Damn. If only there were some way of washing this cup and saucer before I get home.'

Then there was a vending machine that can bake bread. Great. But the whole point of a vending machine is that it delivers food and beverages immediately. Not in an hour and a half.

But the invention that really caught my eye was a belt that warns the wearer when they've eaten too much. This seems unnecessary. I'm wearing a belt now, and although it's very old-fashioned and low-tech, it's perfectly capable of letting me know when it's time to put down the knife and fork.

And it's been doing quite a lot of that ever since I gave up smoking. Yes, this bold move means I get to spend longer on earth as a grey-faced cripple with tubes up my nose, but the downside is: I have become very fat.

The problem is that when you smoke you are an exciting person with exciting friends, so your heart beats more quickly. When you give up, your life has no meaning or purpose, so it slows down.

And this means your metabolism becomes lethargic, which means you become heavier and heavier until your skin can take no more and you burst.

I know that you are all heartily fed up with diet stories and fitness regimes that plague us at this time of year, but since I quit the fags, my waistline has expanded to the point where my belt is sitting there saying: 'Oh, for crying out loud.'

In numbers? OK. I'm now two stone heavier than I was 18 months ago. And at that rate of climb I'll weigh 34 stone by the time I'm 70.

So my decision to act is not some frivolous new-year gimmick. Nor was it brought about by a need to be 'beach ready' or any of that nonsense. No. I've decided to do something because my knees and ankles hurt and I've forgotten what my penis looks like.

Exercise. That's the key, says everyone in the world. But I tried walking home the other day, and after just a few feet the muscles in my back spasmed and I had to get in a taxi. Plus the only people who go to gyms are body-obsessed morons who just want to have sex with the other body-obsessed morons they meet there. Frankly, they'd all be better off in libraries, doing something about their IQ.

Whatever, I can't do exercise until I've lost at least some of the weight, which is why supper last night was some raw fish and lunch today was a banana. Tonight I shall have a bowl of thin broth at six-ish and then test my resolve by not eating even a small piece of the Cadbury Fruit & Nut bar that's in my fridge, a hangover from the fat old days.

There are those who say I should have a diet plan. And you can't go anywhere these days without Michael Mosley sticking his nose into proceedings, saying that he is definitely a doctor and that if you eat nothing for four days and only zinc-based products for the next six he will become extremely rich. I don't buy any of this. Just eat less. That usually does the trick.

The big issue, of course, is drink. I'm not an alcoholic, in the same way as you aren't an alcoholic either. We burst through the door at night and hurtle to the fridge for a gallon of something crisp and invigorating because we've had a busy day and now we want to get pissed.

It's hard to change that, but it's important. I mostly drink rosé, and research has shown that drinking one small glass of this delicious pink nectar has the same effect as eating one of those fatbergs they occasionally find in the sewers and washing it down with some melted lard.

It's therefore been replaced in my daily life by something called water. Used usually for cleaning cars or as a medium on which boats can operate, it contains magnesium, which is used to make the gearbox casing on a Ford Fiesta; silica, which can give you a lung disease; and potassium, which is good for fertilizing soil but can cause nausea, vomiting and an irregular heartbeat.

Despite all this, water is now very popular, especially in America, where you are asked if you'd like some every time you enter a room.

I can report, however, that it tastes of nothing at all. It's like liquid lettuce. And I've noticed that even if I drink it in large quantities, I don't become argumentative or woolly-headed. The other day I had literally four pints of the stuff and still managed to drive a car without crashing into a single lamppost.

It therefore seems to serve no purpose whatsoever, but this morning I climbed onto the scales and the news was odd. Even though I have drunk not a sip of alcohol for the past 10 days and eaten nothing but small quantities of fresh, slimming food, I am now 2lb heavier than I was on New Year's Eve. And the only conclusion that can be drawn from that is: water is fattening.

I am therefore going to cut it out immediately, and I suggest you do the same. Use hi-tech Diet Coke to keep you hydrated, as that contains no sugar, fat or salt. And if you want to lose weight, take up smoking.

13 January 2019

How does my garden grow? With sickly twigs and a threadbare hedge . . . and no bees at all

We like to think that 'researchers' are people in white coats, with pipettes and microscopes. Or that they are to be found in the street, with clipboards and a winning smile, asking passers-by about dog food or aircraft noise. But I'm not so sure.

If, for instance, the National Cheese Council were to announce one day that cheese makes your penis bigger, we'd dismiss the report as nonsense. But if the National Cheese Council were to say a team of 'researchers' had found it to be so, then we'd nod sagely and immediately buy a hunk of red Leicester.

However, I'm fairly sure 'researchers' just sit in a room all day, waiting to be told what to say by their paymasters. They exist solely as a label to make untruths look real. They don't garner opinion or fact. They invent it. They're PR men in lab coats.

Last week they came up with a belter, telling everyone that bees are being saved by the middle classes, whose suburban gardens are full of juicy and nourishing flowers. The presumption here is that upper-class gardens are full of coach parks and gift shops. And that working-glass gardens are full of used needles, broken dishwashers and a rusty Peugeot on bricks.

This, however, is simply not true. A great many working-class people are enthusiastic horticulturalists.

Their gardens blaze all summer long with a smorgasbord of, er . . . and there you go. I'm middle class and I can't think of one single bee-friendly flower. Lupin? Is that one? All I know about flowers is that I like hyacinths, but they only grow indoors, I think, so the bees can't get at them.

My garden in Oxfordshire has no flowers in it at all. There are some bushes down one side, and on the other a hedge the neighbouring farmer likes to ruin once a year. Underneath there's a cesspit that leaks. I don't know if bees can smell, but if they can, they'd almost certainly give the whole zone a wide berth and head off instead to Gary and Sharon's sweet-pea-scented allotment.

However, because the 'researchers' talked about how the 'middle classes' help bees, I'm sitting here on a guilt trip because I don't. And I should.

Gardening, I'm afraid, is not an option, because I don't understand it. I go sometimes to my local garden centre, and all you can buy is a plastic pot full of mud with a dead twig sticking out of it. And when you look at the label, it is always in Latin.

I have occasionally bought one of these twigs and taken it home, and a year later, when it's still a twig, I've put it in the bin. Occasionally a working-class person will come round and explain that it needed more sunshine or less, or that I've given it too much water, or not enough, but the end result is always the same. It stays dead.

Once, I tried to create an actual flowerbed. This meant I had to do manual labour and, immediately, my back hurt. But I persevered and filled the mud I'd hoed with some *Impatiens bequaertii*, and six months later I had a bed full of thistles.

In London I have a balcony with flowers on it, and in summer bees do come and cause my guests to run round in a panic, spilling their drinks and screaming. It's weird. A dog can bite you and give you rabies. But you don't climb on a chair and hyperventilate when you see one. So why do people do that when they see a bee?

We are told that the world cannot function without them and that if they become extinct – which is a possibility if we carry on panicking and making merry with the fly spray – it will be impossible to grow food and we will all die. That theory was almost certainly dreamt up over tea and biscuits in a honey manufacturer's research department, but I don't care. I like bees. They amuse me with their aerodynamic hopelessness. And I want more of them in my life.

It is thought there are about 44,000 people keeping bees in the UK. This means beekeeping is now more popular than being in the Green Party. And it's not just Britain. Beekeeping used to be nothing but an excuse for uptight ladies of literature to wear man-repellent clothing – much like the Green Party in fact – but now Peter Fonda is an enthusiast. So's Morgan Freeman. And Scarlett Johansson was given a hive as a wedding present by Samuel L Jackson.

Bees are the most fuel-efficient creatures on earth. Give one an ounce of honey and it'll have enough energy to fly round the world. Bees also recognize our faces. And they are all different. There are optimistic bees and sad bees. So really, they are like dogs. Except they can manage if you go on holiday.

Unlike dogs, however, which produce only faeces, bees make honey. And how that honey tastes depends on what sorts of flower they visit. I once had some that had notes of peppermint with an overtone of hot handbags.

Apiarism, then, is a hobby that allows you to be even more pretentious than wine enthusiasts. But unlike wine, which tastes only of wine, honey really doesn't just taste of honey.

And then there's beeswax, which you also don't get from dogs. If you use this to polish your wooden floors, your house will smell even more wonderful than a bakery.

So bees are interesting low-maintenance pets that keep on giving. And, in addition, beekeeping seems to me to be a relaxing and gentle way of filling your spare time. And researchers say that is good for you. Along with not relaxing in your spare time. Along with eating tomatoes. And not eating tomatoes. And using bath salts. And not using bath salts. And wanting to be in the EU and not wanting to be in the EU.

20 January 2019

Anointed with Piz Buin and ordained by magical thinking. God save our royal family!

If we'd never had any sort of government and suddenly decided we needed one, it's highly unlikely we'd come up with a system where the position of head of state was hereditary. Imagine trying to sell the notion on *Question Time*. Not even the brilliant and eloquent Diane Abbott could hope to make it fly.

It's nuts that Prince Charles is going to be our next leader simply because his mum was. Lots of people think that way. And I agree that, logically speaking, they have a point. But what if we decided to get rid of the royal family and have a president instead? I think we'd almost certainly end up with a palace full of Ant & Dec. Or, if it had to be a woman – and in the current climate it would – we'd have President Rachel of Countdown.

So while I know that the hereditary system is silly and that we could one day end up being led by someone who talks to his lunch, I still prefer it to the alternative in which you end up with Donald Trump or Vladimir Putin or that bottom feeder in Venezuela.

Did you see what Mrs Queen had to say last week on the divisions caused by Brexit? 'I for one prefer the tried and tested recipes, like speaking well of each other and respecting different points of view . . . and never losing sight of the bigger picture. To me these approaches are timeless, and I commend them to everyone.'

Obviously that is neither possible nor desirable at a football match, but in the country as a whole she's dead right. And I'm glad we have her and her wisdom and not President Dec with his 'Let them eat grubs.'

The problem, however, is that in a hereditary system some poor sod gets the gig simply because he came out of the wrong womb at the wrong time. Imagine having to sit down with your child when they are eight or nine and explain that they will have to spend their entire adult life being polite and wearing a seatbelt and going to Middlesbrough on a Wednesday afternoon to open the civic centre's new disabled lavatory.

Yes, they get a lot of houses and a man to warm the lavatory seat before they use it, but I'd rather live in a tent and do my business in the woods than have some chinless adviser called Nigel telling me that I must marry a clotheshorse and never once go home with a traffic cone on my head. It's not a life. It's a life sentence.

And there's more. To make the whole system work, the royal family have to convince proles such as you and me that there's some mystical reason they are in charge and not, say, Huw Edwards from the 10 o'clock news.

During the actual moment of a coronation, the Archbishop of Canterbury spoons special oil from an eagle-shaped bottle onto the monarch, and to make sure you and I don't see this, it all happens underneath an embroidered tent that's carried to the spot by a gaggle of cross-dressers who were definitely bullied at school.

The reason this part of the ceremony is hidden from the public's gaze is simple. If we actually saw it happening, we'd know the oil was basically Piz Buin factor 10.

And then the whole divine-right, appointed-by-God-Himself thing would be ruined.

It's already ruined, if I'm honest. Most of us don't believe in God, and we certainly don't believe that more than a thousand years ago he found a man called Theo in Germany and said: 'Your sperm, my son, is holy, and it will be used many years from now to provide a system of government in Great Britain.'

We know it's all just a magic trick, and, as with a magic trick, we don't really want to know how it's done. So if they want to claim that someone goes into the embroidered tent as a man and comes out on the other side as a king, fine. As I say, it's better than having Ant & Dec or Donald.

The problem is that when the ordinary person comes out as a king, he's got to keep the whole charade going. He's got to be aloof and covered in medals he didn't win and good at waving, and all his opinions have to be nice and calm and sensible. Everything that happens in his head has to stay there. That's just about doable, but not when you have the tabloids running around saying that the royal family must be aloof and good at waving and so on but that in addition they must be like us.

So now we have poor old William, who's stuck. On the one hand he's got the Nigels telling him that he must behave like a king and be carried around in a velvet-lined sedan chair by six oiled eunuchs, and on the other he's got the *Daily Mail* saying that he must go down to the Dog and Duck on karaoke night and get pissed.

Only last week he spoke in Davos to a roomful of people who are nowhere near as influential as they like to think, saying that the British habit of stiffening the upper lip and keeping calm and carrying on meant it was difficult to deal with the horrors he experienced as an ambulance driver.

Doubtless this is true, and doubtless it was an important message for the nation's mental-health charities. But, while opening up and weeping and talking about stuff is fine for normal people – and especially Americans – it undermines the fabric of royalty.

Happily, there's no serious movement in the UK right now to get rid of the Windsors, but unless they sit down soon and work out how to keep the magic going in a cynical world where there are no witches or unicorns, such a thing might get traction.

It would only take something small like a road traffic accident to get the discussion going, so let's keep our fingers crossed that such a thing never happens.

27 January 2019

Cheat, love, bray – let me put my ass on the line and tell you that the donkey sex scene was real

There's no easy way of saying this, so I'll just jump straight in. While driving through Colombia last year, I encountered a man who was making love to a donkey. Further investigations revealed that he was not an escaped lunatic and that a lot of the men in his village do the same thing when they're bored or lonely.

Now I know the programme that I make for Amazon is supposed to be a car show, but I thought the donkey story was interesting. So we broke out the cameras and filmed one of the men making the two-backed beast with Eeyore. And then we spoke to his mates, who were at pains to point out that they only had sex with the female donkeys, because doing it with a boy donkey would be weird, obviously.

The scene was part of a show that was released recently and almost immediately the *Pop Idol* winner Will Young responded by saying something about how the car I'd been using was gay. Or not gay. Or that it was gay but we shouldn't have said so. I can't quite remember. Everyone else, on the other hand, wanted to know why on earth we'd faked the donkey scene.

Yup. Everyone had looked and listened and then decided that because they had never seen a man having sex with a donkey on their way to work at a warehouse in

Huddersfield, I couldn't have seen it either. So it must have been fake.

This accusation of televisual jiggery-pokery baffled me, because let's just say we'd wanted to film a story that was not true. Why, in the name of all that's holy, do you think we'd come up with the idea that a man would have sex with an animal? And even if we did, then what? Do we just go up to someone and say, 'Hey, mate. I'll give you a tenner if you'll do a bit of roadside bestiality'?

And what do you think the Colombian government would have to say about it? I once put a lavatory in my car in Mumbai, saying that it'd be useful if I got Delhi belly, and now I'm banned from India. Then I said that eastern Turkey felt less safe than Iraq, and now Johnny Turk won't let me visit any more.

So do you really think I'd want to tell a blatant lie about Colombia? Because those guys probably wouldn't send me a polite letter asking me never to come again. They'd send a man to cut off my arms with a chainsaw.

I'm afraid, then, the scene wasn't faked. It was real. The interviews afterwards were real. It was all on television with subtitles. And no one believed it.

I think the problem started with poor old Bear Grylls. Until then everything on the television was true and real because the person doing the talking was Sir Robin Day or John Noakes. A sensible man with sensible clothes and sensible hair. But we learnt that the bear that attacked Bear in one of his camping programmes was actually a member of the production team in a bear suit, and this opened the floodgates.

The BBC was forced to admit that a scene in its epic *Human Planet* series showing a tribal family in Papua New

Guinea living in a tree house had been a setup, and it previously had to concede that footage of a tarantula in a Venezuelan jungle had actually been shot in a studio.

Oh, and then there was 'Wolfgate', when the Beeb said the wild wolf it had just shown was actually a partly domesticated one. Everyone was very angry, and I can't see why.

It costs a fortune to send a film crew to a remote location and an even bigger one to house it and feed it while it trudges about looking for its quarry. You want to pay for that? Or would you rather the producers set something up in advance so that they weren't wasting your licence fee on a scene you aren't going to believe anyway?

It's now reached the point where people don't even bother telling the truth. You had Boris Johnson and his merry bunch of cohorts running round in the run-up to the referendum saying that if we left the EU we'd be able to give the NHS an extra £350 million a week. That was a complete fabrication.

Then you had Donald Trump, who'd seen photographs of the crowd that turned out to watch Barack Obama's inauguration in 2009 and photographs of the measly crowd that turned out to watch his. He knew we'd seen them too, but even so he apparently asked the government photographer to edit the photos to make his crowd seem larger. He's the most powerful man in the world, and he's forever lying.

I look now on the internet at all the stuff that's been written about me in recent times. And a huge amount of it is wrong. So we must assume that a huge amount of the stuff about everyone else on the internet is wrong too. It's scary.

Later this year we will show you a *Grand Tour* programme we made in Mongolia. We will explain that we are in the most sparsely populated country on Earth and that there is not a single shred of evidence in any direction for hundreds of miles that man has existed.

We will drive across this wilderness in a car we have built ourselves, and we will be seen living like animals, for days, in the frozen expanse of nothingness. It is all true and it is all real. And at the end I guarantee someone will write to say that it was faked and that we stayed in hotels.

It's a shame, really, because when we don't trust anything we see or hear, we lose our ability to be amazed. You can't stand back in childlike wonderment at something if you automatically think it's computer-generated imagery. And how can you form an opinion when you don't believe anything anyone says or anything you read?

Sometimes it's healthy to believe that man walked on the moon, that Facebook has some good points and that in Colombia there is a small group of men who shag donkeys.

3 February 2019

Credit card, toothbrush – I'm off on my mini gap year. And on that bombshell . . . goodbye!

When Richard Hammond has a crash and needs to spend a month in hospital being put back together again, it plays havoc with the filming schedule, but we usually cope. However, on the day he returned to work after his most recent accident, I was struck down with pneumonia. And was told to live on a yacht in the Mediterranean for a month.

This threw a whole toolbox into the works, and I knew that no matter how hard we scrabbled to catch up, there would come a time when filming would have to stop so that some actual forward planning could happen. This would mean that for about three months I'd be at a loose end. And I wondered what I would do to fill the time.

I quite liked the idea of eating crisps and watching *Cash in the Attic* reruns until I became one of those comically fat people who appear in the tabloids, being winched into an ambulance. But then I met some friends who'd decided to take their young kids out of school and bugger off to surf in Sri Lanka for a while. And it got me thinking. Maybe I could do something similar.

'So you're going to spend the time learning how to surf?' said another friend. No. I'm too old for that. And I don't like weed. But I did fancy the idea of going somewhere and achieving something.

Helping to build a school in Africa, perhaps, or clearing

some landmines from Cambodia. This appealed, so for a while I looked into the possibility of giving my time to a charity. However, charities tend to view men of my age who suddenly decide to go to southeast Asia with a fair bit of suspicion, and also I'm not very practical. I think if I built a school, it would fall over, so I figured they'd be better off with my money than my time.

The idea of taking a mini gap year still appealed, though. Only a week after I was booted out of school I was working on a local newspaper, so I never got to do what's now considered a rite of passage for every middle-class child in the country.

And I didn't want to wait until I retired, because travelling when you have wonky knees and poor bladder control probably wouldn't be much fun.

What to do, though? I don't want to learn to fly, because that's just maths and weather and a stupid phonetic alphabet. Cooking? Nope. That's just peeling vegetables. Tennis? Not unless I had a boy to pick up the balls. And travelling the world with a small boy is not a good look.

Someone tried to convince me I could learn to paint. But I know how to paint. You dip your brush in some oils and smear it about on the canvas. Anyone can do that. It's just that everything I do ends up looking like a dog.

As I dithered and procrastinated, it was becoming clear that my temporary redundancy would begin in a month and I hadn't even worked out where to go. 'India,' said everyone. But I can't do that because I'm banned. Also, India is nowhere near as amazing as they'd have you believe.

Australia? Been there. America? Yup, all 50 states. South America is ticked off, as is Africa, apart from the

Democratic Republic of Congo, which I don't fancy, mainly because it doesn't sound very democratic to me. For a while I toyed with the idea of taking a gap year at home, but then I read that there will soon be martial law, so that was a no-no as well. Europe was a worry too, in case I wasn't allowed back.

Eventually I decided I would write a book. So I started to think about characters and motivation and plot, and then there were only two weeks to go and I knew what was coming. I wouldn't go anywhere. I'd squander this gift of free time, and I wouldn't write a book either because I'd be too busy watching *Cash in the Attic*.

But then, one day, I awoke knowing that I'd go to Singapore and catch the Eastern & Oriental Express to Bangkok. Full of vim and vigour, I cranked up the internet and discovered that the train is fully booked from now until the end of time. And that it takes only three days, which isn't long enough to write a book. Plus I hate trains.

And then someone pointed out that I'd spent most of my working life travelling and that it would be silly to spend my time off doing even more of it. This was all becoming annoying. I think most of us would love to take a sabbatical, but as it's going to be a once-in-a-lifetime thing, you don't want to get it wrong. Which means you become too afraid to do anything at all.

Then there's the Presbyterian work ethic. When you've had your nose to the grindstone for 30 years, you become enslaved to the concept. In the same way that long-term prisoners struggle with freedom when they finally get out of jail, I was struggling with the very idea of going away. It would feel alien. Weird. So I was making up all sorts of reasons why it couldn't happen.

Then, last Friday, I recorded the last bit of voiceover for the current series of *The Grand Tour* and, with the production team starting preparations for the next one, I went home, turned on *Cash in the Attic* and opened a packet of cheese and onion crisps.

And that night I came up with a plan. So tomorrow I am going to Heathrow with a credit card and a toothbrush, which will probably be confiscated, and I shall look up at the departure boards and simply go to whichever destination I like the look of.

It means I won't be writing this column for a little while. But I'll see you on the flip side to let you know why I haven't finished my book yet. Or started it.

10 February 2019

What I did on my gap year

I am back. My gap year is over. And I achieved nothing. The plan was to spend a couple of months in Indochina, writing a book. But it turns out that writing a book is much, much harder than reading one, so I did that instead. And then, in the heavy, hot, windless evenings, I'd slip into a linen suit and pop into town to sneer at the Chinese tourists.

On one excursion in Laos I lost my mind and decided to visit a temple. This is never sensible, because no temple is interesting and none was built in a spot that's convenient. They're always in a cave or on a mountain. And I never get that. How long would a supermarket last if it were on top of Ben Nevis? Anyway, this one was on top of a hill, which meant climbing 600 steep, narrow steps. And about halfway up I met a million-strong party of Chinese holidaymakers coming the other way.

I squeezed into an alcove to let them pass, and not one smiled or even attempted to say thank you. They just marched past in their stupid pop socks and face masks — an unsmiling, ungrateful and neverending column of worker bees on day release.

Later I found another enormous group of them sitting on a low wall, their minibuses blocking the town as they ate a picnic lunch. And when a klaxon announced that it was time to go, every single one of them simply threw their plastic containers and water bottles over the wall and mooched off.

Elsewhere they scream into their phones, play computer games with the sound turned up and allow their children to do exactly as they please in restaurants. And have you seen Chinese tourists in a queue? No, of course you haven't. No one has.

I'm not alone in thinking this. On my travels I met many guides and waiters and shopkeepers, and none had a single good word to say about their Chinese visitors. They come. They stay in Chinese-run and Chinese-owned hotels. They make a mess. And a noise. And when they go there are always replacements. It's a conveyor belt of awfulness that's ruining the world.

There are many theories on why the Chinese are so badly behaved when abroad. Some say it's because China is corrupt, which fosters a dog-eat-dog, survival-of-the-fittest mentality. Others say that in China's super-cities it's important to be overbearing and shouty or you will be trodden on.

But I believe there's a simpler reason. The Chinese are unused to foreign travel and, as a result, they simply don't know what's acceptable and what's not. And we can't scoff, really, because back in the mid-1960s, when package holidays to the Costa del Sol were invented and we were new to foreign travel, we were just as bad. We spoilt coastlines and filled fishing villages with chip shops and wobbled about in a beery haze, with our red-and-white stripy arms and our propensity for vomiting and fighting.

The Germans were also terrible when they first decided that holidaying abroad was a good idea. They put on uniforms and marched into Amsterdam and Paris, and the world was ruined for years.

Then you had the Russians. Remember when they were

unleashed, strutting about in their tiny swimming trunks, spraying champagne over one another and pulling Putin faces if you appeared to disapprove?

Today, of course, the Germans and the British and many Russians are pretty good tourists. We look at frescos and try the local cheeses and attempt to say things in the local language. But our children are not. This is because they're new to travel as well. All their lives they've been told to sit up straight and put their iPhones away at mealtimes, so when they are suddenly allowed to go to Magaluf and do what they want, they end up in a hospital with an itchy crotch and a tube up what's left of their nose after it came into contact with a bartender's right fist.

For a solution to all this, we should take a leaf from the book of Sri Lanka. I'm told – but the high commission won't pick up the phone or answer emails, so I can't verify it – that Sri Lankan nationals wishing to travel are forced first to attend lessons on how to behave when abroad.

I find this hilarious because of all the places I've visited, Sri Lanka is the most polite and charming. Why would you teach someone with impeccable manners how to queue and look interested when visiting a temple? It'd be like giving Mrs Queen lessons in how to hold a knife and fork.

But imagine if Qatar sat its citizens down and said: 'Look, chaps. When you take your Lamborghini to London this summer, don't rev its engine at four in the morning in Knightsbridge, because in England this is deemed unacceptable.'

Or if the American government took Wilbur and Myrtle into a room at the airport and said: 'By all means chat to other Americans you encounter while travelling, but not across a swimming pool.'

I know the Chinese government is trying to tackle the problem of bad behaviour from its tourists by confiscating the passports of repeat offenders, and I know too that in the fullness of time, experience will teach them the importance of saying 'please' and 'excuse me'.

I hope that happens soon, because then we can go back to thinking of China as a country that hacked its way into the 21st century, grabbed the South China Sea, ripped off the designs it could copy and stole those it couldn't, bullied its way into Indochina and Africa, littered coastline after coastline with terrible three-star casinos and condos that have made property prices skyrocket and almost single-handedly kept the ivory trade going.

14 April 2019

Forget Chris Packham's coup – we farmers speak the only language pigeons understand

Fishing. It's not one of my specialist subjects. I do not want to stand up to my gentleman's area in an icy Scottish river and I'd rather spend my spare time in the pub, with friends, than sitting, by myself, on a damp canal bank with a bag full of maggots. Fishing, really, is for people who hate their children.

But, this morning, I feel duty-bound to come to the defence of the nation's anglists, who are being blamed for an alarming drop in salmon numbers in Scottish rivers. There used to be a time when 25 per cent of all the fish that left their birthplace came back. Today, it's just 5 per cent.

Those who enjoy animal rights say fishermen and fishermen women are to blame, along with farmers and bankers and possibly Mrs Thatcher, and conveniently fail to mention a couple of important points. Almost all the salmon caught by anglers are allowed to resume their journey after they've been landed. And, more importantly, the mouth of every Scottish salmon river is patrolled these days by an armada of hungry seals.

You want to get the salmon numbers up, you must do something about the number of seals. But what? Seals have big doe eyes and puppy-dog faces, and no one wants to see them being beaten to death with bats.

This, then, is the problem with conservation. Protect

one species – and seals are very protected – and it's going to have an impact on another. It's all a question of balance and being sensible. Which, I'm afraid, is hard when our government is being advised by a Swedish teenager and Chris Packham.

Packham is a wildlife presenter on the BBC, and I like him. He's a good communicator, fun to be with, hugely knowledgeable about punk rock and able to tell a corn bunting from a reed bunting at 400 paces. He's also a fine lobbyist. So fine, in fact, that, having teamed up with a former conservation director of the airborne wing of the Labour Party, the RSPB, he was able to convince the government's conservation watchdog, Natural England, to announce that it is now illegal to shoot pigeons.

Now I'm not going to be silly about this. Last weekend, as the sun blazed down, I very much enjoyed sitting in the garden listening to the wood pigeons cooing away. It's a sound that makes me feel warm and fuzzy. And I don't hold with the argument that town pigeons should be hounded to extinction because they crap on your car. They do, but it's not a big issue to get a hosepipe and wash it off.

However, I'm a farmer these days, and one of the things I grow is oilseed rape. I grew enough last year to make 100,000 bottles of vegetable oil.

This year, though, things are tricky, because a weed called black grass, which is immune to herbicides, is ravaging the crop.

And what's left is being half-inched by pigeons. I'm told that I can try scaring them away with loud bangs and kites and statues of Jon Pertwee, but I'm also told by the Viyella army of local countrymen that none of these things actually works. You have to shoot them. And now we can't.

Score one for Packham and Corbyn's RAF. But hang on, because if there's less oilseed rape, that means there's less vegetable oil, which will drive demand for alternatives such as palm oil. And palm oil production is what's destroying the jungles of Indonesia, and with them the orang-utan.

So what the do-gooders have done by helping the pigeon, which is as prolific as nitrogen, is kill more of Borneo's endangered orange monkeys. And that's obviously idiotic. Happily, there seems to be a solution.

For nearly 40 years farmers have been using a so-called general licence to shoot pigeons, because they're protected under wild bird legislation, drawn up to save important stuff like the osprey and the golden eagle and so on.

In short, you could get permission to shoot certain kinds of common and unimportant wild birds, such as pigeons and crows and magpies, if it was bleeding obvious they were stealing eggs, pecking out the eyes of lambs or devastating crops. Well, thanks to Chris Packham's lot, that permission has now gone.

There is one idea for keeping the pigeon under control. Simply remove it, along with the crow and the magpie, from the legislation covering wild birds. Then no special permission to kill it is necessary. It's not as if this minor shift in the law would cause millions to take to the countryside each weekend in weirdo NRA combat strides, because to shoot a pigeon you need a gun, and you still need a licence for that.

But will the government allow a pigeon free-for-all? It

should. It makes sense. We live in weird times, though, when governments in general and ours in particular are entirely detached from the real world. They seem to live in a universe full of unicorns and magic fairy dust. So there's no way Michael Gove, who's running the countryside this week, is going to say, 'Lock and load, Farmer Giles. Let's waste the motherf******!'

So what about this for a plan? We pat Chris Packham on the back and say, with a magnanimous smile, that he has won. A bit like remainers are being urged to do by Brexiteers. But then we carry on as before. A bit like Brexiteers are being urged to do by remainers.

Seriously, can you see the police being that bothered? Really? About the death of a pigeon? And how would they ever know? A shotgun is noisy, but it's not so noisy that it can be heard in the nearest police station, which these days is usually 20 miles away. And only open from nine to five. On a Tuesday.

Plod isn't interested when I have a gate or a quad bike nicked, so I can hardly see a SWAT team coming through the door with an enforcer ram because they suspect the pie I'm taking out of the Aga has four and twenty pigeons in it.

28 April 2019

The Chinese take a wrecking ball to red tape. If only they'd apply it to our crumbling bridges

Barnes is a part of London that fell asleep in 1953 and still hasn't woken up. But hidden behind some period net curtains on the main drag is a brilliant little restaurant called Riva. I tried to go there for dinner last night but, annoyingly, Hammersmith Bridge, which connects me to it, was shut.

I assumed, of course, that it had been closed by the safety and health army so that workmen could safely retrieve a cyclist's dislodged saddle bag. Or because a Swedish teenager was staging some kind of environmental protest.

But no. It had been shut because engineers reckon it's on the verge of collapse. No surprises there. It was built 132 years ago to carry tiny little thin people on penny farthings over the Thames, and now it's being pummelled and shaken to within an inch of its life by the hundred buses that use it every hour.

Still, no bother. This is Britain. Ground zero for engineering. So, Hammersmith and Fulham council, which owns the bridge, only need find someone with overly tight trousers and a pair of heavy shoes and the whole thing would be fixed in a jiffy or, better still, replaced with something strong and wonderful. Maybe we could get Norman Foster to add the finishing touches.

Apparently not. The bridge has been closed 'indefinitely',

which means absolutely nothing is being done to mend it. They've identified the problem and decided to do nothing about it. It's a good job they're not vets: 'We could mend your dog. But we won't.'

The Labour-run council says it can't afford to fix the bridge because of, yawn, government cuts. And Transport for London can't help out because it's spending all the money it will ever have and a trillion more on Crossrail. And it is also being blamed for having steadfastly refused to ensure only one bus ever crossed the bridge at any one time.

So that's that. Thanks to petty party-political pointscoring and a blinkered devotion to Dickensian trains, Edwardian bicycles and postwar omnibuses, one of London's 33 bridges across the Thames is now out of action.

They have a similar problem in America, where a survey last year found that 56,000 bridges are now so worn out they are in danger of falling down.

In China things are different. The Chinese recently had a Hammersmith-style problem with one of their bridges. And do you know how long it took to sort out the financing and get a replacement up and running? A year? A month? Nope – 43 hours. That is not a misprint. Less than two days to knock down a bridge. And build a new one.

Mind you, they do get some practice, because since 2010 they have built just shy of 200,000 road bridges. This means that for the past nine years they've been opening 60 new ones . . . every day.

And it's not as if they're made from box girders and old railway sleepers. Almost all of them are bold and elegant and delicate and mesmerizingly beautiful. And they are

machinegunning this science and this art into the land-
scape once every 24 minutes.

Mind you, the Chinese are not hamstrung by the red-
telephone-box mentality that plagues Britain. When
British Telecom suggested replacing its famous old boxes
with something that smelt less of urine, everyone said it
was the end of days.

Much the same thing would happen if anyone suggested simply pulling down Hammersmith Bridge and
replacing it with something less wobbly. 'Noooo,' they'd
wail. 'You can't demolish Hammersmith Bridge. It's
grade II* listed and beautiful.'

Well, it shouldn't be, because it isn't. The towers are too
low, the pillars are too squat and it's painted the exact
same colour as a Second World War German soldier's
underpants.

Tear it down, I say. Or blow it up. I don't care. Or leave
it for pedestrians and build a new one over the top of it,
sweeping from the A4's elevated section in a graceful arc
all the way to a soft touchdown on Barnes Common. In
China they could have that sort of thing up and running
by Wednesday.

Sadly, though, we can't, because the powers-that-be
would rather sit around in their meetings, calling one
another comrade and blaming Thatcher and Osborne
and the effing Tories. And everyone in power is now
entirely convinced by the Swedish teenager's delusional
notion that we can function as a society while producing
no carbon dioxide at all. Meanwhile, you and I are in a
traffic jam and Barnes is even more cut off than usual.

There is only one solution: we need to get rid of democracy. It doesn't work. America was given the choice of a

woman with a rictus grin or a man with a bath mat on his head. And now a load of its bridges are about to fall down.

Here, it's likely we shall end up with a choice between Pol Pot and Boris Johnson, and to get across London we shall have to go through Bristol.

Back in the Sixties things were much better. You had Tony Benn running amok, and it was all very ugly for anyone with more than £2.50 to their name, but we did get Concorde. He pushed that through. Can you see Theresa May doing that today? Spending billions on a new type of plane?

Benn was also responsible for the Post Office Tower. Sure, it didn't have any stairs, and anyone going to the top floor in the lift would have to spend most of the morning going back down again, but it remains one of our most iconic landmarks.

If we had a benevolent dictator – and I'm thinking really of me – a new Hammersmith Bridge would be nearly finished by now, the leaders of the local council would be in prison for moaning, Barnes would have decimal currency, Donald Tusk would have a thick ear and we'd be out of Europe without a backstop, or with one, or whatever it is that people want.

5 May 2019

We love reaching the places other car shows can't. But thanks to Isis, we're stuck with Slough

There seems to be a general consensus that Isis has been pretty much wiped out in Syria and Iraq, and that in former strongholds such as Raqqa and Mosul, people are now hanging up curtains and tending to the geraniums in their window boxes.

Certainly we are seeing fewer online videos these days of people having their heads cut off, or captured airmen being burnt alive. Which means we've all gone back to worrying about the important things in life, such as clean air in the community, and badgers.

However, the Grand Tour television production team had a meeting last week to decide where we'd go to make our next special. The idea of these shows is simple: we drive unsuitable cars through extraordinary and difficult terrain in remote and largely unvisited parts of the world. It's like Attenborough, only with more falling over and fewer facts.

In the past 18 years, we've been to many fascinating and beautiful places. And Argentina. We've done Botswana and Namibia and Mozambique and Vietnam and Burma and Thailand and the southern states of America. We've been to the North Pole and Mongolia and Chile, twice. In fact, we've done nearly all of South America and, after a gruelling journey from the Iran–Iraq border to Bethlehem, we've pretty much covered the Middle East as well.

The world is a big place, though, so you'd imagine there is still plenty of ground left to cover. And so did everyone in the room as the meeting began. But as it finished two days later, we were forced to conclude that while Isis may have been kicked out of Raqqa (been there already) and Mosul (done that too), it is still making huge chunks of the world unvisitable.

We began by thinking about the Sahara. We'd buy some crappy old hatchbacks and drive them somehow to Timbuktu. Except we wouldn't, because where would we start? Libya? Algeria? Northern Nigeria? None of those places is a haven of peace and tranquillity. And even Timbuktu plays host these days to sporadic and vicious terrorist attacks.

So we looked further east and things were no better. Sudan is a no-no and so is its southern neighbour, the imaginatively named South Sudan. Somalia is even worse, and while Eritrea is fairly stable, the Foreign Office advises visitors not to go within 15 miles of its borders. Which sounds fine, except Eritrea is only about 40 miles across, which means we'd have to go to the dead centre of the country and spend a week not moving a muscle.

At this point James May began what turned out to be a very long story about Lawrence of Arabia. We had some lunch as he talked about various battles and the sort of motorcycles Lawrence liked, and we enjoyed some coffee and biscuits as he spoke of various Arabs with whom Lawrence had fought. And then, over a brandy, he said we should attempt to follow in Lawrence's footsteps from Saudi Arabia to Cairo. This would be an epic journey, except it would mean crossing the Sinai Peninsula and, thanks to Isis, the chances of us all arriving on the other side with heads were slim.

To try to get away from the terrorists' wretched clutches, we turned our attention to those islands that blur into one another between Asia and Australia. But time and again, Google searches revealed nearly all of them have an Isis presence. There was even a bomb in Bali recently. And not a Jägerbomb.

A few years ago there were reports of Isis saying that its goal was to create a hardline Sunni state that stretched from west Africa to the far end of Indonesia. It would be a bigger empire than ours, or even the monster created by Genghis Khan, which stretched from the Danube to the Yellow Sea. And, as it seemed a ridiculous notion, I dismissed it as nonsense. But it's not nonsense.

The group may only have a couple of hundred tooled-up lunatics in Egypt or Timor, but that's all it takes to create a no-go area for Johnny Westerner. And that, I guess, is the very definition of terrorism. The trick, then, would be to find a part of the world where there are no tooled-up lunatics, which is why we started to look at the glorious-sounding Andaman Islands, off the coast of (mostly) peaceful Thailand. But there's a tribe on one of these islands that will kill anyone who lands. They even shoot arrows at helicopters that arrive to collect the bodies.

It's the same in the Democratic Republic of Congo: they don't kill you because they hate Christianity or democracy or women in miniskirts, they just kill you. Borneo? Well, once you've seen all the fallen-down trees and homeless monkeys mooching about, what's left to talk about?

It's all so depressing that after a while the meeting room sank into a pit of thoughtful silence as we wrestled with guilt over the mess our generation has made of everything, and the inevitable consequence. No one dared voice it, although we all knew it had to be said . . .

'Australia,' I muttered.

But of course we couldn't go to Australia, because you set off from one side and absolutely nothing happens until you get to the other. It'd be the most boring show in history. And thanks to the relentless paparazzi, everything we said and did would be reported long before the programme was shown. If Australia's paps had anything to do with it, we'd already know what happens at the end of *Game of Thrones*.

This left us with Europe, which, apart from a small bit at the top of Scandinavia is hardly unvisited and surprising. Driving through Germany in a small Peugeot is not the bedrock of great primetime TV. Plus, by the time we start filming, we'll be out of the EU, which would mean a three-day wait on the M20 for customs to check the carnets.

I guess, then, that next time out it'll be a Grand Tour special in which we travel the entire way across Berkshire. Pity.

12 May 2019

Hook up the lie detector, then tell me the Jeremy Kyle affair isn't about punishing poor Brexiteers

If you host a weekly radio show for 10 years, you will have broadcast millions of words into the homes of listeners. All of them can have been well chosen, thought-provoking and beautifully pronounced, but if the next four you select are, 'He f***** your granddaughter,' you're in trouble.

Inside a courtroom, previous good behaviour is taken into account. But on the outside it's a different story.

Danny Baker entertained millions for many years, but then one day, and for reasons that are unfathomable, he decided to post a picture on social media of some posh people posing with a well-dressed ape. He argued that this was not in any way racially motivated, and I'd like to believe him, but it was no good. No second chances. He was out.

You sometimes get the impression that if a modern-day television or radio executive found that the handle of a drawer in his kitchen had come loose, he'd knock his whole house down.

In recent times we've waved goodbye to Jonathan Ross, *Bargain Hunt*'s Tim Wonnacott, Mark Lawson ... I'm sure there are more but none springs to mind at the moment. And all undoubtedly feel like the hero of that old joke. 'I built a bridge with my own bare hands, but do they call me John the Bridge Builder? No. I make love to one goat ...'

Everyone you know in film, television, politics and business is only one flippant remark or one cross word away from being John the Goat Shagger.

Last week it was the turn of Jeremy Kyle, whose confrontational morning show on ITV was axed following the death of a guest.

As I write, the hyenas and vultures are picking over its carcass, saying that such lowbrow nonsense should never have been broadcast. And that its like should never be seen again.

I see. So what sort of show should be beamed into the plasma-filled homes of the fat and the unintelligent? Repeats of the Richard Dimbleby lectures?

I have not seen the *Jeremy Kyle Show*, but I have been in the Salford studios when it was being recorded, so I've seen the audience, none of whom has read *Architectural Digest*. It's obvious from their leggings that what they want from a TV show is two overweight people slagging each other off until one is escorted from the studio by a security man the size of a Buick. This causes them to moo and low like farmyard animals, both in the studio and in council houses all the way from Wolverhampton to Carlisle. It's modern-day Saturday afternoon wrestling.

And you'd imagine that the soft-left intelligentsia on Twitter would be happy to let the farmyard animals in the north of England have this kind of thing to distract them from mending the latch on their outside lavatory doors or warming up after a chilly dip in the tin bath.

I mean, these good northern people are proper, honest socialists. Except that, now, they're not. They're Brexiteers. Which means they must have their playthings taken away.

Look at the state of the country's pubs. They're closing at the rate of 18 a week. Bitter sales, meanwhile, remain moribund while craft beers gain in popularity. No 6 cigarettes have been replaced with the vape. And this is all fine if you have a disposable income, but what if you don't? What if you are more worried about finding some money for the kiddies' tea than you are about global warming? Let's not forget: to be green, you first of all have to be in the black.

The bright and the sassy may moan about the dumbing-down of television, but they can go out for craft beer and a crafty vape at a whole-food restaurant tonight. Plus, they have all sorts of things on BBC4 to stimulate their neurological route map. And access to Netflix and Amazon and BT Sport and Sky.

It's the same on the radio. The BBC runs two full-time stations for a tiny number of remainers, and absolutely none at all for people who voted Brexit.

Last week a crowd of people in Pontefract cheered and shouted support for Nigel Farage and Ann Widdecombe, who'd dropped in to say a few words. And they were treated by commentators as if they might have some kind of warty plague. I'm surprised there haven't been calls to take their liquorice cakes away from them.

I voted remain. And I still lie in bed at night hoping that some way can be found to turn back time. But I don't hate Brexiteers. I don't want to punish them. Yes, many wanted out because they want less immigration, but that doesn't make them Hitler. And, yes, some are far to the right of the political centre line. But few, I suspect, are as far to the right as Corbyn is to the left.

All of which brings me back to the *Jeremy Kyle Show*

and the ridiculously gleeful reaction to its demise. Sure, a guest went home having failed a lie detector test and, it seems, took his own life. That is extremely sad and it's probably right the show is canned. But it should be replaced with something similar. Something with its eyebrows in its hairline.

Think back. When Michael Lush plummeted to his death while rehearsing a stunt for the *Late, Late Breakfast Show* in the 1980s, someone realized that Noel Edmonds, the presenter, couldn't very well announce Lush's demise and follow that with a cheery: 'But coming up later, a skateboarding duck, and we pour goo all over Olivia Newton- John.' So they axed the show immediately. But they didn't give up on light entertainment, or Edmonds for that matter.

Let me finish with a question. If Cliff Richard had decided to kill himself after footage of the police raid on his home was broadcast, would the BBC have decided to cancel the news? No, I don't think so either.

19 May 2019

Tie the model-railway vandals to the tracks and we'll get this country back on the rails

It is impossible to name the saddest photograph ever taken. There's one in my hall of a gathering of women in Chad. I find it heartbreaking because all the men who should have been in the frame were dead. And doubly heartbreaking because the person who told me that fact was Adrian Gill, who'd been there when the picture was taken.

On a less personal note, we have the picture, taken on that terrible day in 2001, of the upside-down man who'd leapt from the twin towers. And that monk who set himself alight on the streets of Saigon. How desperate do you have to be before you think, 'Right. I can only sort this out by setting myself on fire'?

More recently we had the awful shot of that dead three-year-old Syrian refugee on the beach. That was hard to stomach. And years before that, the little African kid, his belly distended by hunger, crouching over in the parched earth, while in the background a vulture waits, drumming its claws, for the inevitable moment it can start dinner.

Strangely, I'm never moved by grief caused by a natural event. Show me a fat man from the Southern states, wailing at the spot where his trailer used to stand before the good Lord took it away, and I'll turn the page. Tsunamis, earthquakes, tornados and hurricanes – these things come, they cause sadness and they go.

Whereas sadness caused by man-on-man cruelty – somehow that's a whole different story. Show me a photograph of an old boy fighting back the tears on Remembrance Sunday; or Phan Thi Kim Phuc running naked from the effects of a napalm strike; or a bunch of flowers left on the railings outside an off-licence to mourn the victim of a stabbing. That's what'll do it for me. And that's why, last week, I was moved to unmanliness by those photographs of a ruined model railway engine.

It's easy to poke fun at people who have train sets. They're obviously introverts who would rather spend their evenings painting little plastic milkmen and cobbler's shops than talking to their wives. They're friendless and lonely and tragic. But they are part of the patchwork quilt that makes Britain British.

They are a keystone species, like starfish in a Pacific rock pool or wildebeest on the Serengeti. Without model railway enthusiasts, in their comfortable jumpers and their sensible shoes, Britain would be no different from Libya.

On a Monday evening, members of the Market Deeping Model Railway Club meet to chat about how Vauxhall's mustard-yellow paint can be used to create British Rail warning signs and listen to interesting talks on the importance of using a fine saw to separate parts from the sprues. I guess it would be like spending a night in James May's head. And that's fine. These elderly souls, in the autumn of their lives, are happy in their harmless world of fine paintbrushes and tweezers and turning bits of fluff into realistic farmyard animals.

Occasionally they put an exhibition together and take it to venues in the Peterborough area, so children can see there's a world beyond their games consoles and their social media. And that if they don't work hard in school, it's where they will end up.

Last weekend they were staging just such an exhibition in the pretty Lincolnshire town of Stamford, when some kids broke in the night before and smashed the whole thing to smithereens. The little railway buildings, the signals, the points, everything. Engines were hurled to the ground and stamped on. Thousands and thousands of hours of work was ruined in a few minutes of wanton cruelty.

I know the work was pointless. I know that it furthers humankind not one jot and that it's this love of steam trains and Enid Blyton and running through wheatfields that caused Brexit. But it made those old men very happy. And now that happiness has been taken away by some yobs. And I hope that when they are convicted, the judge sentences them to death.

I have a friend who did not go out and did not drink for three years. Every penny he earned, he put into a pot, until he had enough to buy an Aston Martin. Eventually he had enough for a five-year-old example and was beyond happy when it arrived. He immediately went for a little drive and then afterwards wrapped it in a blanket and locked it in a barn.

And the next morning he found that someone had broken in and keyed the bonnet. This is a man who's served in Iraq. He's been under fire and he's fired back. And yet he was distraught. So I hope that when those responsible are found, they get the firing squad as well.

Oh, and while I'm at it. I now have CCTV at my cottage, and when I'm next there I'm going to review the tapes so I can see who broke into my vegetable patch last week and stole my marrow. And be warned: when I've done that, I will find you and I will kill you.

There's a lot of talk at the moment about what constitutes a hate crime. Well, I'm upset by the people who smashed up that train set and by the kids who vandalized my mate's car and by the rambler who stole my marrow.

Britain is about to enter a new period in its history. No one knows how we will get there, but when we do, it would be a good idea to remind people that if they vandalize a train set or a car or a marrow, they are demonstrating their envy of the owner. And that envy is the root cause of all hatred.

Look at all the pictures that have made you sad. Deep down, just about all of them were caused by envy. Acting on it is the worst crime, and anyone who does so must face the consequences – which at the very least will be having whatever you broke shoved up your backside.

26 May 2019

We turn up our noses at invasive species, but at least skunks are spicing up the sticks

Alarming news from north Nottinghamshire. It seems a brace of wild raccoon dogs have escaped and are running about making blood-curdling screams and attacking farmyard animals. Many fear it's only a matter of time before they eat a child.

According to *The Times*, one resident said she had heard a 'terrifying noise like I have never heard before' and that her husband went out with a dog. She didn't elaborate on what sort of a dog he was going out with, or what this had to do with the story, but did add that in a two-hour assault the raccoon dog attacked anything that came near and that a goat emerged from the melee with a sore shoulder.

Hurriedly taken photographs show that the creature looks like the result of some terrible early days teleporter accident. If you've seen *The Thing*, you'll know what I'm on about. It's a hideous-looking teeth-transportation device with the meanness of a hyena and the savagery of a wolf, to which it is related.

Despite this, however, police are simply urging locals to stay indoors and whimper until the situation has normalized. No actual action is being taken at all. This may have something to do with the fact that the raccoon dog lives on small insects, crops and, on anniversaries and special occasions, mice. The only real issue, as far as humans are concerned, is that they are a bit smelly.

So, in fact, they are pretty harmless and I wish them well, in the same way that I wish the small flock of parakeets that flutters in a blizzard of colour around my London flat well. Like the raccoon dogs, they are not native to Britain, but I welcome them as I welcome the Vietnamese people who arrived recently and opened a restaurant in my neighbourhood.

The fact is that Britain has by far and away the most boring collection of indigenous wildlife to be found anywhere on earth. We have no wolves or bison. Our birds are mostly brown and only one of our snakes is even a tiny bit venomous. Australia has kangaroos, Canada has mooses, there are jaguars in America, polar bears in Svalbard, and even somewhere like Italy, which you'd expect to be pretty barren, there are great white sharks off the coast. Whereas in Britain we are so desperate for variety, we make up stories about monsters in lakes and big cats on Exmoor. And we treat the badger as if it's a Bengal tiger.

However, owing to lots of overambitious customers who buy peculiar pets and allow them to escape, Britain is filling up fast with weird and interesting animals.

It's reckoned there are more than 1,500 wild boars running free in the Forest of Dean. They are magnificent – like huge hairy hovercrafts. On an island in Loch Lomond there are wild wallabies and in the Lake District there are coatis strutting about with their priapic tails and their cute foxy faces.

Oh, and then there's the striped skunk. Perhaps the most striking feature of this little fella is the sac of mucus on either side of its anus. If threatened, it will turn and squirt the contents of these sacs into the face of the aggressor. Apparently, the smell is a sick-inducing mixture of garlic, sulphur and sewer gas, and it's so strong there is no creature on God's earth that'll hang around to get another dose. It is the ultimate weapon. The daisy cutter of the animal kingdom.

In the olden days, people would keep skunks as pets, but in 2007, when the government should have been concentrating on sub-prime mortgages, it decided that its time would be better spent introducing a law banning people from removing a skunk's anus sacs. And when this practice became illegal, baby skunks were simply released into the wild, where they live now. Perhaps this is why ramblers always wear cagoules, because they know there's a chance they may get squirted in the face with a gallon of anal skunk ejaculate. Hope so.

Interestingly, the government is not that bothered about skunks running wild in Britain. And it is actively encouraging the reintroduction of beavers. That's probably because these species, like the wallabies and coatis, are seen as either harmless or beneficial, like French chefs and German engineers. However, when it comes to other species, it reacts as though half of Somalia has landed on the beach.

Take the coypu, which is like a big rat. They were first brought from South America to Europe by French fur farmers in the 1880s, but this didn't work as the locals kept eating them. Later, they were brought, once again for their fur, to East Anglia. But when the market for wearing rat skin dried up – can't imagine why – they were released.

And immediately, everyone was encouraged to go outside and kill one as soon as possible. In 1961, 97,000 were slaughtered. The following year 40,000 went to meet their maker. This is because the coypu can destroy marshland. Left to their own devices, they would wipe East Anglia from the map and Norwich football club would be playing matches on Dogger Bank.

It's the same story with the Siberian chipmunk. This is prettier than Brigitte Bardot's nose, and as it sits there, nibbling away at a hazelnut, you can't see a problem. But if you see one, you are urged to contact Defra, the environment ministry, which will be round with a marksman far more quickly than if you rang to say your Syrian neighbours were stockpiling ammonia.

Actually, if you rang to say your Syrian neighbours were stockpiling ammonia, they'd arrest you for being racist. This is what the people of north Nottinghamshire should remember. It's what we should all remember. Racism is still a thing in the animal kingdom, so if you want the police to come quickly, and preferably in a gunship, don't describe the crime that's been committed: simply say there's a Siberian chipmunk on your bird table.

2 June 2019

Higher truths are out there, and you don't need crampons or a death wish to reach them

Last weekend, 94 emergency people with lights on their heads spent many hours trying to rescue an elderly man who had burrowed like a rabbit under the Yorkshire Dales and then broken his leg. And while they were at it, another call came in to say that a rabbit lady in another hole, in Cumbria, had also fallen and badly injured her leg.

Sadly, because of the difficulties in getting him back to the surface, the rabbit man did not survive. But I'm delighted to say the rabbit lady did.

I do not wish to take up caving. The idea of wiggling through a narrow hole that could collapse at any time, hundreds of feet below the surface, fills me with utter dread. But I do see the appeal for those who are not scared of being buried before they're dead. Because that hole where the rabbit man died is unmapped, so who knows? There could be a huge cavern down there, full of luminescent pink fairy dust and diamonds.

This means that caving is actually exploration. And the people who do it are the Abel Tasmans and the Roald Amundsens and the Neil Armstrongs of the modern age. They really are going where no man has gone before. That's why I'm saddened by the death of the old boy last weekend. He was a brave soul and should be remembered as such.

Back in Victorian times, the world was awash with

possibilities for those who didn't want to sit through another piano recital in the village hall. They could go and find the source of the Nile or the middle of Australia. But everywhere has a flag on it now. Which is why, last month, a man with some fizz in his veins drove his submarine nearly seven miles below the surface of the Pacific to the bottom of the Mariana Trench. Some people are wired that way, in the same way as some people are wired to watch *Love Island.*

I also understand the appeal of other extreme sports, such as cycling on one wheel into the path of oncoming lorries. This is a thing in London these days. Hundreds and sometimes thousands of kids take to the capital's streets to wheelie down the wrong side of the road, dodging traffic and doing tricks. 'Knives down, bikes up' is their motto, and I wish them all well.

I don't like skiing. It's very tiring and the prices are as stupid as the boots. But as a man who likes to drive quickly, I can see why someone would want to hurtle down a mountain on the very edge of control. It's a rush.

What I don't understand, however, is mountaineering. I was once interviewing a Frenchman called Alain Robert beneath the arch at La Défense in Paris, when, without as much as a by-your-leave, he started to climb up it. Now I don't know if you've ever examined this colossus, but it's completely smooth. It'd be like climbing up a massive plate-glass window.

Since then, Monsieur Robert has climbed all sorts of tall buildings all over the world, and all he ever gets after reaching the top is arrested. So it all seems rather pointless.

I watched a documentary last week about a wiry

American fella who decided one day that he'd like to climb the 3,000ft Dawn Wall in Yosemite National Park. It had never been done before, so in some ways you could argue that he was pushing the limits of what's possible. But the record for eating baked beans with a cocktail stick currently stands at 275 in five minutes. And, I'm sorry, but if, one day, someone managed to eat more, you could hardly argue that he was the next Sir Ernest Shackleton. And eating baked beans with a cocktail stick is no different from being a fly on a rock face in California.

Less dangerous? Not really. The wiry American fella's climbing partner spent most of the ascent falling off and he didn't die once. All he ended up with at the top were some hurty fingers.

For real danger you need to go up Everest. It has claimed 11 souls this year alone. It's proper mountaineering. You have to clamber over foothills made from the rubbish dropped by those who've done it before, and you have to navigate round all the frozen corpses of those who haven't.

And then you must stand in a half-mile queue of cagoule people, comparing lip balm and debating whether Viagra really does help with altitude sickness (it doesn't – I've tried), before, eventually, you get to the summit and someone takes a picture of you. Or is it you? In all that clobber and with your face behind an oxygen mask and tinted goggles, who would ever know?

I agree that mountaineering is difficult. If I ask one leg to support my weight, it always goes wobbly, and, to make matters worse, my gut means the rest of me is always about 2ft from the rock face. I wouldn't do it. But some people like to set themselves challenges. They don't care that a million others have done it before. They just want to prove that they can be one of them too.

However, if you get it wrong, there is expense and helicopters and using a head wand for the rest of your life. And as a result, surely, you'd be better off using your spare time to do something worthwhile.

It's hard to find undiscovered places, but all around us are scientific truths that have not yet been found. Or even thought about. There's a line in the closing monologue of the breathtakingly good *Chernobyl* series on Sky: '[Truth] is always there, whether we see it or not . . . The truth doesn't care about our needs or wants. It doesn't care about our governments, our ideologies, our religions. It *will* lie in wait for all time.'

This is correct. The truth about everything that we don't yet know will lie in wait. Until someone puts down his crampons and his karabiners. And finds it.

9 June 2019

Change sometimes feels like the big bad wolf, but at least it's made tripe and onions extinct

Russian and Japanese scientists have revealed the almost perfectly preserved head of a giant wolf that's been buried in the Siberian permafrost for 40,000 years. And, crikey, it's a frightening-looking thing, almost twice as large as the head you'd find on a modern wolf – we have to deduce that the damn thing must have been the size of a cow. A cow with yellow, uncaring eyes, teeth like a toucan's beak and a brain bigger than a small-block Chevrolet V8.

No one has been able to work out yet how it died, but since no body has been found nearby, we must presume that it was so vicious it ate itself.

Now, scientists are unable to agree on exactly when mankind first developed the ability to think clearly. But 40,000 years ago we were making beads and burying our dead and doing finger-painting in caves. We had also started wearing clothes, which, I feel sure, we would have soiled extensively had we encountered a cow-sized wolf in the forest.

So I wonder what would have happened if we knew this drooling beast was about to become extinct. Would we have been thrilled? Or would the Pleistocene equivalent of Sir Attenborough have climbed onto a rock and urged everyone to extinguish their fires and stop eating meat so that it could survive? I seriously doubt it.

But that's exactly what's happening now. We have

decided that the world today is exactly how it's supposed to be. All those funny hoppy birds on islands in the South Pacific. All those fearsome bears in the far north. All the little parasites that burrow into children's eyes in Africa. This is the correct balance, we reckon.

Really? So how come it wasn't correct when the dinosaurs were kicking about? Or the woolly mammoths? We get all hung up about the tiger being in danger of extinction, but I bet you any money that olden-day sailors were not that bothered when the helicoprion went west. Because that shark-like beast had a fully operational buzzsaw in its mouth.

It's the same story with our climate. All those halfwits who are planning on bringing Heathrow to its knees this week have decided that the temperatures we have now are what God intended. Right. I see. So what did climate-change enthusiasts think in the last ice age? That Norway was supposed to be buried under a mile-thick sheet of ice?

And what about when the world was formed? Back then there was almost no oxygen in the atmosphere. It was made up mostly of carbon dioxide and nitrogen. So what would have happened if, instead of an amoeba, Prince Charles had crawled from the antediluvian slime? What would he have said: 'To keep things as they are, let's stamp on all these oxygen-generating plant thingies'?

And then there's the countryside. We have it in our heads that fields should be clearly marked out by dry-stone walls, that hedges should be as neatly trimmed and that there should be a lone oak standing majestically in the bottom paddock.

Well, actually, back in the early days, much of Europe

was a forest and the rest was a tangle of impenetrable brambles. Everything you see now is modern and manmade.

I could go on, and so I shall. I have a friend who engaged the services of a much-respected American architect to design an extremely modern house that would be built on a hillside in Oxfordshire. And, immediately, people in the area began to run around as though she were planning on building an exact working model of Chernobyl.

This is because the Georgians told us what a house should look like, and since then we've been wearing blinkers. I am currently designing a gaff in which I'll live when I'm a drooling incontinent, and at first I wanted it to look like Zaha Hadid's cultural centre in Baku, Azerbaijan. Then I decided I wanted a plantation-style job, like Forrest Gump's mother's. And then I bottled out and am now going for something house-shaped.

All of which brings me on to the mess we are in with our politics. We've lived with a two-party system for all my lifetime, so in my head a two-party system is obviously better than the alternatives you have in ridiculous countries where it takes five years to form a government after every election.

I therefore want our system to continue, in the same way that Attenborough wants the Indian elephant to avoid extinction and Charles wants his garden to look exactly like it did in 1870.

But we don't have two main parties any more. Not really. The Conservatives like to think they have unity, but they don't. And Labour is split in half as well. Both are going to have to face up to the fact that soon they must make like a vase that's fallen on the floor. And our voting cards will be longer than a roll of Andrex. Is that a bad thing? I think most of us would say yes, even though it probably isn't.

It's strange. We accept that fashions change. We would not wear the shoes we were wearing last year. My children don't even want to wear the shoes they were wearing this morning. We accept changes in what we eat too. I was brought up on a diet of tripe and onions, and I loved it. But now I like a pho or some bruschetta. Eating tripe is like eating a tyre.

I'll finish with the thorny question of music. Yes, we all rejoiced when the Animals and the Rolling Stones meant we no longer had to listen to the consonant-free nonsense from Bach and Mozart and bloody Bizet. And we rejoiced some more when Genesis and Supertramp came along.

But going beyond that, into a world of drill and hard trance and garage? No. I'm with Charles and Sir Attenborough on that. Sometimes you must draw the line. Sometimes you have to say, 'Enough's enough,' and protect the wolf, no matter how awful it might be.

16 June 2019

A splash of Pekingese, a dash of basset and, voilà, I've crafted a Crufts-conquering Frankenpooch

Figures out recently show that only 98 Old English sheepdogs were registered with the Kennel Club in the first three months of the year. And now everyone is sobbing and mewling and saying that soon the Dulux dog will become extinct.

Now, when a rare bat is in danger of dying out, all housebuilding is put on hold and councils are ordered to devote 90 per cent of their resources to making sure it's saved. Heavily armed patrols are used to preserve the last white rhinos. And because of the polar bears, we all must put our patio heaters in the bin and walk to work in shoes made from potato peelings.

But the Dulux dog is a pet. So the only way it can be saved is by forcing people to buy one, and I'm not sure that's possible. Most people would prefer a Labrador, because, unlike an Old English sheepdog, it can see where it's going. Also, while a Lab is endlessly greedy and will continue to eat until it bursts, it doesn't defecate twice a day into its own hair.

Maybe when Jeremy Corbyn is in power, dogs will be allocated by a government department and you'll have no choice over what breed you get. But he isn't, so you do. And only a tiny number of people are choosing Old English sheepdogs. Maybe if Kim Kardashian or Nicholas

Witchell were to buy one, the decline would be arrested, but that hasn't happened yet.

In the past, many famous people, including the Vanderbilts and the Guggenheims and Franklin D Roosevelt had Old English sheepdogs, but the last famous person to have one was Sir Paul McCartney. And he ate it.*

There's a vault buried deep inside a mountain in Svalbard, Norway, where examples of all the world's seeds are kept, but there is no such thing for dogs. So when the dog-loving public falls out of love with a breed and no celebrity is on hand to make it popular again, it will die out. This has happened many times in the past.

I assumed when I first saw a stuffed example of the now-extinct kuri dog that the taxidermist hadn't been very good at his job. But further research has revealed that it really did have ridiculously short legs. It was also stubborn and had a useless sense of smell. Small wonder it never caught on.

Then there was the Cordoba fighting dog from Argentina, bred, as its name suggests, for fighting. Unfortunately, the breeders were so successful that whenever two dogs were brought together for mating purposes, they tore each to pieces before any impregnation took place. As a result, pit bulls are now used instead.

The Hawaiian poi went west because one day it was forced to become the world's first vegetarian dog. Which meant that, like human vegetarians, it soon became listless and wan, and then its breath smelt so bad that even other dogs wouldn't mate with it.

All these dogs are now gone, but here's the thing. When

---

* He didn't really.

one breed dies out, it's possible to simply create another. That's not easy with monkeys or whales, but, that said, a grizzly bear will occasionally do sex with a polar bear. I'm not sure what this proves. That bears aren't racist? That's about it, though.

With dogs, things are different. In the UK, there are 221 officially recognized breeds. And all of them are man-made Frankenstein dogs that were created by lunatics.

To make a new breed that will be recognized by mad-haired Crufty people, you need to start with two pedigree dogs whose bloodlines can be traced back to William the Conqueror. And what you end up with after an evening of heavy dog love between the Duke of Spaniel and Con-tessa de Alsatian is . . . a litter of mongrels.

Over the following decades, though, the duke and con-tessa will create more of these mongrels, and eventually, when you are very old, you will start getting those to mate with one another. Yes, this means daughters have to get with their dads, and brothers and sisters have to make the two-headed beast while you watch. It's a bit like life in Louisiana.

After a very long time, however, you're still nowhere near getting official recognition for your new breed.

Take the current trend for crossing Labradors and poodles. This was a bad idea because both breeds are prone to wonky hips and any cross is going to end up yachting its way through later life. But it was a brilliant piece of marketing, because who doesn't want a dog called a labradoodle?

Everyone did. And today you can buy third- or fourth-generation 'doodles, but don't think for a minute that it's an officially recognized breed. Because it isn't. In the dog world, it's a parvenu, an upstart – that fat woman who befriended Rose in the film *Titanic*: fun, but not the right sort.

Creating a new breed is like haute cuisine. You start with good, pure ingredients, add a splash of Pekingese if you want extra snappiness, or a hint of basset if you want something that trips over its own ears, and then you use patience and diligence and lots of castration on the dogs you don't want, and eventually you can win Crufts with your 2-inch-tall Siberian tiger dog. Because no one else has made one.

It's easier, probably, to create a new cat breed, because their equivalent of the Kennel Club, which is called – and I'm not making this up – the Governing Council of the Cat Fancy, is run by people who love cats. Which means they'll be lonely and will want to talk to you on the phone.

Dog people are usually too busy to do that because they've got to take Rover for a walk, or feed him, or, if he's an Old English sheepdog, use a comb to try to get some of the dingleberries out of the hair round his bottom.

23 June 2019

Putin might not save Richard Hammond from a smash, but he'd get us all picking up our litter

For the first time in 20 years we weren't able to finish one of our televisual adventures. The ending was to be spectacular and controversial, and it would have wound up the Chinese something rotten, but two hours after we set off, the man in charge of safety and health pushed the abort button.

Months of planning. Many hundreds of thousands of pounds. A great story. All dashed on the jagged rocks of risk assessment and bits of small print in the insurance arrangements.

With hindsight, I admit it was the right call. We had bitten off more than we could chew, the weather was dreadful and there was a very real possibility that, if we'd stiffened our upper lips and soldiered on, someone would have died. And when I say 'someone', obviously what I mean is 'Richard Hammond'.

Which causes me to wonder. Would Christopher Columbus have sailed across the Atlantic if he'd had to fill in a risk-assessment form beforehand? Would Neil Armstrong have reached the moon 50 years ago this week if NASA had had to pass everything through a health and safety department? Would anyone have reached the South Pole?

We read last week about a former soldier who has spent the past few years running about in Syria rescuing runaway girls whose life with Isis hadn't turned out to be quite as glamorous as they'd imagined. He pointed out that no government could do this – and no corporation could either – because when a risk assessment is carried out and you say there's a good chance you'll end up being beheaded on the internet, someone's going to say: 'Let's not bother.'

If the Bible began with the words, 'In the beginning God created the heaven and the earth, and then he filled out a risk-assessment form,' there would have been no light and no dividing of the firmament.

All of which brings me on to Vladimir Putin. While I was away making half a television show to keep the insurance company happy, he rocked up at a G20 conference in Japan having said that the democracies of the West were finished, because liberal policies were very obviously not what the vast majority of the electorate wants. He claimed that the public had turned its back on social tolerance, multiculturalism and immigration. And, before having a small pop at transgenderists, he said that the liberalist enthusiasm for human rights meant that refugees were free to rape with impunity.

Naturally, everyone sank to their knees and sobbed uncontrollably, saying that Captain Botox had really lost it this time. But the trouble is that, when you stop and think about it, he does seem to have a point. Vast numbers of people all over Europe really do want an end to immigration. Given half a chance, they'd also vote to bring back hanging. And while there is a great deal of multiculturalism in advertisements and in box-set television shows, there's almost none round the kitchen tables of middle England.

We are told by those with liberal sensibilities that there are words we may not use any more, but in every pub and club people are still using them. We are told there are jokes we may not tell, but they're still being told. The people in the corridors of power are completely dislocated from what's actually going on.

We don't really care about human rights and we aren't interested in risk assessments or transgender lavatories. We watch politicians making liberal noises on TV and all we think is: 'Have the police found the man who stole my bicycle yet?'*

In Russia, things are different. Yes, it's a democracy, so everyone gets a chance once in a while to vote for Mr Putin. This is a man who at some point in his life at the KGB will have definitely pushed another man's eyes into the back of his head using his thumbs. It's hard to negotiate with someone you know has done that, which is why no one does.

Putin wants Crimea. He takes it. And what is the response from the liberal West? 'Please, sir. Don't push my eyes into the back of my head using your thumbs.' He doesn't have to trouble himself with human rights or how he will look on the world stage if he rains fire on towns in Syria. He just does what he thinks is right and proper, and he's still well-liked in Russia.

Maybe that's what we need here. A benevolent dictator. Someone who's unschooled in the nuances of politics and immune to right-on thinking. Someone who looks at those daft contestants on *Love Island* arguing about whether Italy is in the country of Rome or vice versa, or

---

* They haven't. As far as I can tell, they haven't actually solved any crime since Dixon left Dock Green.

where Barcelona is, and thinks: 'Right. That's it. No one's allowed to leave school until they have a basic grasp of what's what.'

I'm talking about a man or woman who isn't steered through life by editorials in the *Guardian* and what's being said on Twitter. Who works for the mainstream and not the fringe. Someone with the strength to push a man's eyes into the back of his head using their thumbs. And the willingness to do just that to anyone who drops litter.

I can see why this would have some appeal among large numbers of people in Britain, but before you all start asking Tyson Fury to take charge, I would just point out that, while Russia does have strong and firm leadership, the price of its cabbages has risen by 17 times the official rate of inflation. Eggs, grain and onions are all skyrocketing too.

Disposable income has shrunk for the fourth year on the trot and now 13 per cent of the population are living below the poverty line. Which means 20 million people are living on less than £140 a month. And when the liberal democracies in Europe start making good on their promises to stop using oil, things are going to get much, much worse.

14 July 2019

Leave the pointless promenading to the French. A walk is not a walk without a pub at the end

Last Sunday a group of chaps and chapettes met in London's elegant Jermyn Street and set off on what they called 'a walk without purpose, a stroll without direction, a civilized amble without destination'. It might, they said, last five minutes or five hours or five days, and it might end up round the corner or in a cafe in Paris.

Now, in Valencia I've seen people do this a lot. There's a huge walkway along the seafront, and every evening people get dressed up and mooch along it, at a snail's pace, seemingly going nowhere. And in Spain that makes sense, because have you seen their television shows?

I'd far rather climb into a bullfighter costume and walk about in the evening sunshine, looking at all the pretty girls in their thong bikinis and all the pretty boys astride their Vespas than sit at home, watching some trout-faced harridan and a shouty lothario encouraging a studio audience of rural morons to clap along to some mangled old Julio Iglesias hit. Watching people in Spain is a thousand times more rewarding than watching television.

It's the same story in Hanoi. Every Sunday the main road to the east of the Hoan Kiem Lake is closed to traffic, so that people can take a stroll and enjoy the peace and quiet.

Again, this is because there is no equivalent of *Breaking Bad* on Vietnamese television, and walking along with your kids who are flying kites or spinning tops is just a lovely thing to do.

It's preening, really. It's chatting people up without Tinder and meeting neighbours without rowing over a hedge. It's a chance to do business and catch up on gossip and see stuff and take in the sights and the sounds.

Naturally, the French have a word for this sort of thing. *Flâneur.* It means 'a man who wanders about observing society'. And we have words for people who do that sort of thing. 'Weirdo' is one. Others include 'sex pest'. Promenading, which means to take a walk, in public, is something I suspect we'd struggle with.

In the olden days, people used to promenade in Britain. The rich even built long galleries in their homes, and festooned the walls with art, so that when the weather was inclement they could take their evening strolls indoors and have something to look at.

But now? No. There's always a box set to finish, or a new film, or emails to send. And that's fine, except for one thing. Not moving is the new smoking. If you wobble though life with your head nestling in the blancmange of six chins, you don't get sympathy; you get scorn. You're deemed to have let yourself go, which is a sign of a weak mind.

I'm nervous, however, of just setting off and seeing what happens next. AA Gill used to do that. And he'd always find a little statue of a little-known poet in an even less well-known mews. Or a cobblestone that was out of place. Or an arch that would fascinate him for hours.

I'm not like that. I couldn't care less about almost everything, and I've always never wanted to spend two hours stroking the brass of a faded plaque in Spitalfields.

I've tried walking with no purpose. I've simply left my London flat and set off without knowing where I was going or when I'd be back, and I always, always, always end up in the Ladbroke Arms. The other day I was in Mayfair and decided to walk back to Holland Park, which was about three miles away, and I ended up in the Ladbroke Arms, again, using rosé wine to nourish and water my remaining chins.

Let's just say I was French and that I liked preening in public. And let's say I stumbled on a charming back-street cafe where I could spend an hour or so contemplating the meaning of the table and whether the ham in my sandwich was happy, before sauntering home again, possibly with Carole Bouquet. That'd be great. But I'm not French, so the only reason I walk anywhere is because the law won't let me drive home afterwards.

Here in Britain we prefer to go for walks in the countryside, where no one can see us. I'm not surprised. In continental Europe, looking good is more important than looking where you're going, but here we don't walk to be seen; we walk to stay fit, and getting fit requires specialized clothing.

So we pull on cagoules and action trousers, and we set off with some of those silly Theresa May walking poles. And then we are happy when we sweat and our faces turn red. It tells us that we're in control of ourselves. And that our minds are strong.

Of course, walking in the countryside is impossible at this time of year, because I suffer from hay fever. The long grass doesn't just make my eyes water and my nose stream; it causes my arms to come up in a rash and my ankles to itch. I think it's God's way of telling me to have a glass of wine instead. It's certainly a very clear indication that I'm not French. I'm not sure there's even a word in French for hay fever.

In the winter it is also impossible to walk here because it is so very cold. And because after half a mile your boots are so caked in mud that each weighs more than 200 tons.

But there is a brief window, on June 6, at about four in the afternoon, when it is possible to go for a walk in the British countryside without being stung, struck down with a medieval disease or made to feel as if you're Rocky in training for his next fight.

I did a walk then and it was lovely. There were many flowers to look at, and as I walked, a squadron of silent butterflies fluttered ahead like a fighter escort. I heard birds singing, and soon I arrived at a pub with moob sweat and a raging thirst for beer.

That's not promenading. Which is not something we can do. And we shouldn't try.

21 July 2019

Have I Got No 10 for You has a new guest presenter, and Boris better keep us laughing

Brexit is undeliverable. I've said it before and I'll say it again now. One day we shall have to admit the whole referendum was a waste of time because separating ourselves from the EU is as impossible as humming while holding your nose. Or solving a crossword while being attacked by a bear. It cannot be done.

And now, steering us through the stormy waters towards the Kobayashi Maru, we have Boris Johnson.

Unlike every other commentator who's written about Boris in the past month, I do not know him. Yes, I've met him a few times, but I did not go on picnics while we were at Oxford together. We do not have each other's phone number or email address. We've never arranged to meet for dinner. So I know him in the same way as you know him. And, like many of you, I like him.

I guess he first came into our consciousness as a guest host on *Have I Got News for You*, and we liked the way he absorbed Ian Hislop's hand grenades and Paul Merton's dolphin-in-a-bath unpredictability. He just made growling noises and, after a brief spell in Latin, slotted back into gear with a self-deprecating smile and the next question.

Then there were his newspaper and magazine columns. We liked those too, because he used hyperbole to get his point across. When it was discovered that under a Tory government people drank more milk and had more disposable income, Boris translated that into English by saying that if you voted Conservative, your wife would have bigger breasts and you would have a greater chance of owning a BMW M3. This was a language we understood.

When we learnt that he might have been mating with various girls around town, or helping to organize a hit on some tabloid journalist, there may have been a few raised eyebrows at the nation's beetle drives, but the rest of us just thought, 'I must get that Ocado order done.' And then he appeared on a zipwire over London, stuck, and with the harness accentuating his man pouch, and we all thought, 'Good old Boris. I bet he spills egg down his tie next. Oh look, he has.'

Boris was a clown. A clever clown, but a clown nevertheless, and that was fine when he had menial jobs such as mayor of London or MP for Henley or even foreign secretary. But now he's the prime minister, and wherever he is this morning, I can guarantee he'll be thinking, 'What shall I do with the clown act?'

Well, here's my advice. Don't just keep it up. Ramp it up. Don't think that just because you're the prime minister you've got to start making monotone, Theresary platitudes. We never want to hear you say 'in real terms', and we know your hair was born to look like seaweed caught in a riptide, so don't try to tame it. And never wear a hi-vis jacket. You're the prime minister now; no one is going to accidentally reverse over you with a forklift truck.

I can't say 'be yourself', because I don't know who you are under your food-spattered suit. But I can say 'be who we think you are'. Don't try to become Jeremy Hunt.

Look at how he responded when Iran seized that tanker, and use it as a lesson in how not to behave on camera. He sounded like his balls were actually dropping while he was talking. It was pathetic.

The fact is, Boris, that you are charged with doing a job that cannot be done. The only bargaining chip you have is the threat of no-deal, and parliament won't allow that, or any of the shenanigans you may have dreamt up to put it back on the table. You're going to Europe to ask for more and they are going to tell you to eff off. And you will have no retort.

Yes, you could come home to say that things have gone well and that 'in real terms' there's been a 12 per cent rise in backstop concessions, but we've had too much of that. It's why America has Trump and Canada has that weirdo. We don't want the Blairs and Majors any more. We want people who've made us laugh on *Have I Got News for You*.

You're the one who called people 'piccaninnies'. You're the one who said women in burqas looked like letterboxes. You're the one who described gay men as 'tank-topped bumboys', so don't suddenly pretend you're Cherie Blair. If the Lithuanian prime minister is causing problems with your negotiations, tell us. And tell us straight. Say, 'He's being a nuisance, probably because his head appears to be on upside down.' Because then we will look him up on the internet and laugh, because it does.

Of course, the day will come when we are supposed to leave the EU and it won't be possible, and that'll be tricky. But if you've kept us amused in the meantime with some choice observations, a bit of Latin when you're stuck and the occasional public tumble, you will be forgiven.

If you try to brave it out like an old-school politician

with neat hair and a tie that doesn't smell of sherry, you've had it. And then we will end up with Corbyn and Watson and that coterie of evil that lives on the dark side.

That's really it, Boris. Don't bother trying to be conventional over the next few months, because even if you were as skilful a politician as Blair or Obama, you would not survive the failure to deliver Brexit. You'll be gone as a result, and Britain will be plunged into what Dante would have called the 37th circle of hell.

Just remember this. You can't do the job you've been asked to do. So you face a choice. Fail to do it with a straight face and we get Corbyn. Or fail to do it while playing everything for laughs and we might not.

28 July 2019

You take the £15 million yacht, Greta Thunberg, and I'll fly. Only one of us is speeding towards a climate change solution

During the dry season, the Tonle Sap lake in Cambodia is about the size of Gloucestershire. But when the rains come – and boy, do they come in that part of the world – it becomes five times bigger. It becomes gigantic.

I was there last month, however, in what should have been the wet season, and it wasn't gigantic at all. The rivers feeding it were full of nothing but happy cows, and forlorn boats, tipped over on their sides. And as I cycled down what should have been the lake's shoreline, past fishermen's houses on optimistic 40ft stilts, I couldn't even see it.

Of course, in my head, I had a reason for all this. The Chinese have built so many dams upstream of Tonle Sap that there simply isn't enough flow to make those stilted houses necessary any more. But in the back of my mind, I knew there was another reason. It wasn't raining. It should have been coming down in lumps but the skies were blue, and the Chinese hadn't caused that. Well, not with their dams, at any rate. I was forced, therefore, to conclude that the climate is changing.

I'm aware that some people have been saying this for quite a while. But they were all socialists and their goals seemed to be so convenient. No foreign holidays. Less consumption. Less travel. More vegetarianism. More cycling. More hemp. They wanted us all to party like it was Bulgaria in 1959.

And, I'm sorry, but I just didn't trust any of their data. Why should I? Only last week a bunch of them arrived in London to picket the offices of a power company called Drax. Some had brought banners saying they wanted 'No borders, no nations', which meant they were at the wrong event, and then they got the wrong address and chained themselves to the doors of a Norwegian renewable energy firm.

Now, forgive me, but if a group of activists can't get the right banners or the right address, why should we trust them when they tell us precisely what the weather will be doing 50 years from today? And why should we care? Temperatures have been going up and down for millions of years, so why should we all get in a tizzy about what's happened in the past century? Because that's what God would call 'a jiffy'.

You see, I'm doing it again. I can't help myself. Whenever I see these frizzy-haired halfwits blocking roads, or I listen to their exciting plans for flying drones over Heathrow, I'm filled with an urgent need to fire up both my Range Rovers and buy another patio heater.

But I can't really get the faces of those poor fishermen round Tonle Sap out of my head. Yes, it's possible the climate is changing all by itself, but what if it isn't? What if Swampy is right and we are responsible? What are we supposed to do about it?

Put away our foolish things and play conkers instead? Make some dens in the woods? Buy a bicycle? Apparently not. Kids are the most green-aware people on the planet, but a report out last week said they'd rather sit inside with the central heating turned up and play *Fortnite*.

Obviously, the same thing has occurred to the young

Swede Greta Thingumajig. She's become the maypole around which all the eco-loonies now dance and, as a result, she's been invited to speak at the United Nations. Because that makes sense, doesn't it? The UN being advised by a 16-year-old schoolgirl.

Anyway, this means that Miss Thingumajig will have to go to New York, and obviously she can't use a plane, because she'll be called a hypocrite. So this, then, is her opportunity to show the world that there are practical, sensible alternatives to a quick seven-hour flight on a Boeing 747. And she's done just that, saying that she will make the trip on a 60ft racing yacht.

Naturally, this has made all her disciples very happy, but hang on a minute. What's the message? That the half a million people who fly every day from Europe to America should use a £15 million yacht instead?

It gets worse, because if you examine the yacht she's using, it's not as green as you might imagine. First of all, it is equipped with a diesel engine. Ha. You didn't know that I knew that, but I do. And second, it's made mostly from carbon fibre, which cannot be recycled effectively and which uses 14 times more energy to produce than steel. Which can be recycled very easily indeed.

What Miss Thingumajig is doing, then, is precisely the opposite of what she is setting out to achieve. She is demonstrating that there is no practical and sensible option even for the enlightened, such as me, who think we might just be screwing up the lives of Cambodia's fishermen.

Luckily, however, I have a solution. As we have seen, science has been unable to provide viable green alternatives for the way we move about and what we do and what we eat. A Big Mac is just a better, more fun thing than a lettuce. And that will not change until we are desperate.

If you are sheltering from a nuclear winter and have a fridge full of food, you will not go outside to search for supplies until it is empty. Likewise, we did not invent an electronic computer until we absolutely definitely had to crack those Nazi codes.

It stands to reason, then, that we will not have solar-powered airliners and kids clamouring for some conkers until the wells and seams in the ground beneath our feet are empty. This means that to spur on the green revolution, we must use the coal and the gas and the oil as quickly as possible.

And that's why, as you read this, I shall be boarding a flight at Heathrow for a summer-long blizzard of conspicuous consumption. I'll therefore be doing my bit for those poor Cambodian fishermen and I hope you will too. See you on the flip side.

4 August 2019

Don't worry, be happy. It works in every other nation that's a thinly disguised walking disaster

Have you wondered recently how the country is still functioning? There's a very real possibility that in the coming months we will end up with a ragtag government led by a raving Marxist. Absolutely no one knows what laws will apply on November 1. Businesses are stuck. No one's buying houses. And every bit of grain harvested in the past couple of weeks must be exported out of the country before Brexit. Which won't be possible if it rains, because then it couldn't be loaded onto the ships.

If you add all of this up, sprinkle in the low pound and add a dash of uncertainty about what sinister forces are running the nation's unregistered schools, you'd run around in small circles and emit a scream that went on for such a long time, you'd need to take a deep breath halfway through.

The thing is, though, that things are worse in other parts of the world. Brazil. Venezuela. India. Even Greece. And yet it's still possible to lead a fairly normal life in any of these places.

Or what about South Africa? The previous government endorsed a policy of taking land from white farmers and giving it . . . to themselves. Everyone knows what happened when Robert Mugabe did the exact same thing in Zimbabwe. The skilled farmers fled and food production plummeted by 60 per cent.

Today in South Africa, though, the land grab is going ahead, there's almost 30 per cent unemployment, you are more likely to be murdered than to die in a car crash and more than 25 per cent of men questioned in a survey said they had committed rape, nearly half of them more than once.

But it's still a jolly place on the surface, full of happy people who'll take you into their home and lob a bit of beef on the barbecue. Despite everything, then, society still seems to work.

Then there's America. Forget about Donald Trump and the wall and the fact that everyone has a machine-gun. The thing that always surprises me when I go to the States is how often you see a fully fledged lunatic wandering about in the traffic, with his trousers round his ankles and a mouth that looks like an archaeological dig. They don't seem to have any mental health programme over there, and yet people still get up and go to work and stop off on the way home for a beer as though nothing's wrong at all.

Things are even more puzzling in France. I've just spent a couple of weeks in the Dordogne, and after a day or two it became apparent that every single business is shut when you need it. And then, when you don't need it, it's still shut.

We found a lovely riverside restaurant and thought it'd be nice to have some cheese and wine as the sun went down. Nope. Even though it was a lovely evening in August, it had shut at 4pm. Petrol? No, sorry. So what about a sports bar where we could watch Chelsea play Leicester? Yes, there was such a thing, but it opened at the precise moment the game ended. Changing money at a bank? You're having a laugh. The bank opening hours are: never.

We went one day to a vineyard, where the owner explained that by law he is not allowed to water or spray his vines. Think about that. He is actually banned, by the state, from doing any work.

There are similar issues with the civil service. Carefully crafted rules mean that if you work for the government, even for a few moments as a teenager, you will be paid an inflation-linked salary for the rest of your life. It was discovered recently that 30 state employees had been receiving full pay even though their jobs had been phased out in 1989.

One had his own restaurant and had been questioned about whether this was compatible with his non-existent government job. But still the salary kept on coming. Then there was the railway employee who was paid £4,500 a month for a year, despite not working a single day. And the 'general director of services' at Sainte-Savine town hall in eastern France who trousered £450,000 over a decade for doing nothing at all.

And, of course, if any steps are taken to do something about this, the autoroutes are suddenly full of burning sheep, Calais is blockaded, there's manure all over the Elysée Palace and the president is delivering a resignation speech covered in egg and effluent.

But as I drifted down the Dordogne in a kayak I'd rented (from a Scouser), past all the shut hotels and locked bars, I didn't see any turds, the bridges appeared to be well maintained and the villages were idiotically pretty.

So even though everyone's being paid to sit at home smoking French Women and playing boules, it still seems to work as a country. And it's still, amazingly, the sixth-biggest economy in the world.

All of which brings me on to the eighth biggest. Italy. A wise man told me the other day that the economic situation facing the British was serious but not disastrous. Whereas the economic situation facing the Italians was disastrous but not serious.

And that seems to sum it all up. The Italians know that everything is corrupt and broken and that their leaders are hopeless and on the take, but they have learnt to just get on with it.

It's what we need to do. Hang on to the general sense of wellbeing that you had last weekend, when the sun was blazing and we'd won a game of cricket and someone was bringing you another glass of chilled rosé.

Were you worried about unlicensed sharia schools then? Or what Boris Johnson was up to in Biarritz? Or interest rates? No, because when you're happy, interest rates are actually not interesting at all.

The alternative to doing this is to strive for a more ordered, cleaner society where everything works and the grass verges are mown and there's no corruption and no tramps and no one is stabbed. But if you do this, you'll end up with Switzerland, and no one wants that.

1 September 2019

If cows protect my fields from ramblers and keep the grants rolling in, I'll be over the moon

After Sir Oliver Letwin gave a debagged Boris Johnson six of the best last week, and Jeremy Corbyn revealed himself to be a deranged and dishonest Marxist coward, it'd be easy to imagine that the machinery of government had, with a groan and a burst of steam, ground to a complete standstill.

Not so. A nice chap from Natural England, which sounds like an organic yoghurt but is, in fact, funded by the Department for Environment, Food and Rural Affairs, arrived on my farm the very next day to explain why I couldn't plough up my 350 acres of grassland and use it to grow food. Which, I figured, the country was going to need sooner rather than later.

He sank to his knees and pointed to what you and I would call a dead weed. 'See that?' he said. 'It's marjoram. And that? That's an orchid.' He then switched to Latin, explaining that another plant, wilting in the late summer sunshine, was sepsis, or psoriasis, or something like that.

And then he paused for a moment before saying: 'How many acres did you say you have like this?' When I told him, he was genuinely staggered. He reeled with the excitement and wonderment of it all. 'This is exceptional,' he explained. 'It's rare to find places like this in southeast England. It's fantastic for beetles. It's fantastic for birds. It's . . . oh my God . . . that's fairy flax.'

Imagine a daisy that's been shrunk by a mad scientist and then somehow grafted onto what looks like the stem of some lily of the valley. It was, after I'd broken out the most powerful magnifying glass in the world, extremely pretty, and further research has revealed it to be a useful laxative. Although, as it's only a millionth of a millimetre across, I suspect you'd have to eat several hundred thousand before you'd be able to bomb Swirl Harbour.

'So I can't plough these fields up, then?' To get an idea of how he reacted to the question, imagine how the curator of the Louvre would look if you asked for permission to draw a moustache on the Mona Lisa. 'No,' he replied sternly. 'You cannot plough them up. And if you do, you could go to prison.'

Interestingly, I also cannot leave the fields to their own devices. If I want to keep on getting grants, I must make sure that the whole area is as well maintained and manicured as Jennifer Aniston's hair. This, according to the government agent, means getting some livestock.

That surprised me. I thought there was a general sense among the gentlemen and gentlemanladies of ecology that farm animals are bad because they consume more energy than they produce when they arrive at the dining table, dripping with gravy.

Yes, but in order to keep the fields rich in the flora and fauna necessary for the bees and the birds, it's critical we use them to feed animals. But not sheep, it seems. Sheep are like woolly lawnmowers. They are horned locusts and will turn even the thickest rainforest into the Sahara in two hours flat.

Cows are much better, it appears. Cows mooch through a field like we mooch through a box of chocolates. They find something that looks good and then they spend a few hours savouring it before going in search of the hazelnut cluster.

However, if the world's most paralysed government has rules and regulations on how a micro-daisy should be treated, can you even begin to imagine how much it would interfere if I wanted to start producing Sunday roasts? Or even milk? It doesn't bear thinking about.

So I've been wondering. What if I promise not to put them into the food chain? Would that be OK? Could I get a flock of cows and keep them as pets? Yes, the badgers would immediately give them tuberculosis, but there is an upside I can think of straight away. If we have cows as pets, we will be less inclined to eat them. And that'd be good news for our bowels, which would be less prone to turning cancerous.

Sure, it is not possible to house-train a cow and they do produce a staggering quantity of turd, so your sitting room will become extremely aromatic. Also, a cow will not bark if it detects a burglar. But then neither will a horse, and people keep those for no good reason I can see.

Like a horse, a cow is an accomplished jumper, so you could theoretically enter it for various Pony Club competitions, but, unlike a horse, it does not need to sleep in a stable and it does not need a set of expensive new shoes every week and you do not need to wash its penis. Also, a cow will lie down to warn you that rain is on its way. No horse can do that. No weatherman can, either.

Consider this, too. When you go on holiday, you must give someone you don't know many pounds to look after your dog or your cat or even your fish, but a cow won't even miss you. It'll just stand in its field, turning what you don't need into fertilizer. And scaring the living daylights out of any right-to-roam ramblers that may heave into view.

Obviously, by now, you are sold on the idea and will be wanting to know about costs. Well, it depends, of course, on what sort of cow you buy, but I reckon you could get one for £1,200. Which is only a tiny bit more than you'd pay for a dog. And a dog will do nothing for your marjoram or your fairy flax or your psoriasis. Apart from roll on it.

I'm tempted, then, to get some cows, but there is a worry. That bearded fool Jeremy Corbyn has already said that, when he achieves power, he will confiscate all farmland and implement his hunger plan.

This means the next time I get a visit from a government agent, he will be wearing a brown shirt and tall boots and he will kill my cows because all animals are . . . equally unimportant when space must be found for Hamas terrorist training camps.

8 September 2019

For God's sake, archbishop, get off your belly. We're not to blame for the massacre of Amritsar

The ruler of Cambodia, Hun Sen, insists that minions address him as 'lord prime minister and supreme military commander'. And his wife as 'most glorious and upright person of genius'. Idi Amin decided that his official title would be: 'His Excellency, president for life, Field Marshal Al Hadji Doctor Idi Amin Dada, VC, DSO, MC, lord of all the beasts of the Earth and fishes of the seas and conqueror of the British Empire in Africa in general and Uganda in particular.'

Obviously, we have no time for such nonsense here in Britain, unless you are talking to the Archbishop of Canterbury. He leads an organization that represents the views of 30 or 40 old people who believe their imaginary friend is better than the imaginary friend of Mr Sadiq down the road. But, despite this, he is known as 'the most reverend primate'. Yup. This guy reckons he can lord it over not just you and me but all of the world's lemurs, apes and monkeys as well.

Last week he was to be found lying prostrate on the ground in India, while begging forgiveness from the locals for a massacre that happened 37 years before he was born.

The atrocity in question took place in a walled garden in the Indian city of Amritsar. British troops blocked the narrow entrance and then opened up on those who were trapped inside. In just a few minutes, 1,650 rounds had been fired and a thousand people, including women and children, were wounded. A soul-destroying 400 or more died.

His Divine Magnificence Justin Welby felt such shame over the incident that he was compelled to sink to his stomach, before saying he was 'personally very sorry' for what happened.

Right. I see. So let me ask your Divine Magnificence a question. How do you feel about the antics of Richard the Lionheart? He spent most of his life attempting to make everyone in the Middle East believe in his imaginary friend, and when they wouldn't, he got very angry. So angry that on one occasion he ordered the slaughter of 2,700 unarmed prisoners. Are you 'personally very sorry' for that as well?

Or how about this one? On March 31, 1904, British soldiers invaded Tibet and were told by their superiors to 'make as big a bag as possible'. Since they had Maxim machineguns and the Tibetans had nothing but pointed sticks, the bag turned out to be vast. As a result, his Most Serene Excellency should get over there as quickly as possible, so he can roll around on the ground, sobbing.

Then, after a quick stop-off at Croke Park and Culloden, he could pop over to Guangzhou in China, where, in 1925, the British, French and Portuguese shot and killed at least 52 people for no especially good reason. Follow that with a quick trip to al-Bassa, where our troops put 20 Palestinians on a bus and made them drive over a landmine. And by the next morning he could be in South Africa, where we invented the concentration camp to keep the pesky Boers in order.

Except, of course, 'we' did not invent the concentration

camp, in the same way that 'we' did not use mustard gas in the First World War or murder any innocent civilians in Kenya. British people who lived back then did these things, but holding us responsible is like sending someone to prison because their grandad was a murderer.

You don't have Mongolians rolling around on the banks of the Danube apologizing for the black death they brought to Europe or the pyramids they made from children's skulls. Because 'they' didn't do it. And when I meet a German, I don't ask him to apologize for bombing the East End, because he wasn't in a Heinkel.

I do not hold people to account for the actions of their forefathers, or else I'd hold Welby to account for the actions of his distant relative, the Protestant-burning King James V of Scotland.

Almost every country has, in its history, some disturbing episodes. In fact, there's only one state I can think of that's never fought off a colonizing power or done any colonizing itself.* I'll tell you at the end, so you can try to work it out. Or prove me wrong.

Yes, the British Empire was responsible for some eye-watering acts of cruelty and barbarism. And by lying on the ground in India, the Effortless Bag of Genius is doing a pretty good job of reminding everyone. But I'm not sure it's helpful. Because what Welby's actually saying is: 'The British are useless today, but it was not always thus. In the past, we were nasty sons of bitches as well.'

I urge him, then, to stop and to come home to his palace so that he can tend to the needs of the 30 or 40 old ladies who are busy embroidering church kneelers and

* Thailand, I reckon. Can't think of any others.

handing out hymn books on a Sunday morning. This is what he should be doing. Smiling and saying nice things to his flock; not lying on the ground in India saying he's personally sorry for something he did not do.

Three years ago, the archbish discovered his real father was not the drunk who'd brought him up but some double-barrelled, Oxford-educated fighter pilot who ended up as Winston Churchill's private secretary. It's possible that in this wildly exciting life, old Fotherington-Sorbet got up to all sorts of mischief and devilment. But Welby's not responsible for any of that either.

Interestingly, however, he was responsible for many of the oilfields in the North Sea and off the coast of west Africa. Because, before he found God, he worked for a French oil company and then for an operation that was employed to exploit the assets of British Gas.

So, Welby, you had nothing to do with the deaths of more than 400 unarmed Indians in 1919, but, if Greta Thunberg is to be believed, you definitely have something to do with the death of the entire planet. Maybe, then, if there's any flat-on-your-face apologizing to be done, it should be to her.

15 September 2019

Give McDonald's a break, good burghers of Rutland. Your fortunes depend on the Big Mac

In the olden days, you always got what looked like a dingleberry in a box of Black Magic chocolates. It was there to make absolutely sure the contents weighed as much as the packaging said they did. You found the same sort of thing on rock albums when eight-tracks were all the rage. There were short songs that had been composed and recorded to make sure one 'side' was the same length as the other. Anyone familiar with the 90-second 'Aisle of Plenty' at the end of Genesis's *Selling England by the Pound* will know what I'm on about.

Making up the numbers happens on a bigger scale too. When Europe had fought its wars and sorted out its borders, there was a small patch left over that no one wanted. So the world got Luxembourg, a pointless little state ruled now by a jumped-up little man who, infused with an industrial bout of small-man syndrome, thinks it's acceptable to be rude to the leaders of bigger, more important countries. He even has a beard.

All of which brings me on to Britain's equivalent of the scrap of chocolate and Luxembourg and the tiny Genesis track. The county of Rutland.

Back in the 1970s, everyone realized this accidental gap between proper counties served no real purpose and tried to turn it into a reservoir, but some of the landmass remained, and today it's home to almost 40,000 souls.

Many of whom, it seems, suffer from 'prime minister of Luxembourg' syndrome.

McDonald's has recently applied for planning permission to build a drive-through restaurant close to the bypass round Rutland's biggest town, Oakham. But instead of the investment and the job opportunities being welcomed, all hell has broken loose. Locals are saying this plan would not be for 'the greater good'. Weapons are being stockpiled. Cloaks are being distributed. All the farmers, and all the farmers' mums, are packing heat.

Residents point out that they do not want the 'obvious eyesore of a high-profile golden arch' – forgetting, perhaps, that the flag of Rutland shows a giant golden horseshoe. They also say that Rutland is the only county in England without a McDonald's, as though this is somehow a good thing. It's like saying: 'We are the only county without wi-fi.'

And now they're desperate to keep it that way. One campaigner claims it will affect house prices. Yes, it will. They'll go up. But she's having none of it, saying things will get worse, with 'youngsters in their cars tearing down our streets at all times of night and day'. Honestly, you read stuff like that and you understand exactly why this country is in such a muddle. Because although she didn't say 'and they'll employ foreigners', you can bet your arse she was thinking it.

My two daughters have never, as far as I know, eaten anything made by McDonald's. This is because they were taught in school, before they could read or write, that Ronald is killing children and trees and baby seals for profit, and that if you have one of his burgers, you will immediately explode and become a fatberg in a sewer.

I, on the other hand, will have a Big Mac fairly often. This is because I have a hangover fairly often and there is simply no better cure. I've seen people juicing nettles to clear their heads and munching their way through handfuls of pills. I once even met someone who'd had an actual blood transfusion in an effort to feel better, but I know this from many years of experience: nothing beats a Maccy D's.

There were all sorts of murmurings in the rectory when news came that both Aldi and Marks & Spencer were planning on opening supermarkets in my local town. I may have been party to some of those murmurings myself. But the fact is that, when I want some fresh noodles, or a packet of tongue, I can now buy them all day long, whereas previously I could not.

I recently applied for planning permission to build a small barn on my farm, from which I could sell stuff that happens to be in season. And I was told by a local lady last weekend that it will 'kill the village'. I couldn't see the logic, really. It wasn't as though I'd applied for permission to do a low-level helicopter gunship strafing run down the high street. It'd just be a barn with some vegetables in it.

The trouble, of course, is Britain's morbid fear of change. That's why the Brexit debate is unsolvable, because you have old shire people who want everything to be the same as it was in about 1789. And you have young metropolitan people who want everything to be the same as it was five years ago. Both sides have a point. And I can't see either giving in.

Except here's the thing. Small communities don't have to be backward-looking and small-minded. Rhode Island drove the bus that created the United States. It was the first to renounce its allegiance to the British crown and the last to ratify the constitution that followed. It was little but it thought big. And now it's Rutland's chance.

So, people of Oakham, go and try a McDonald's. It won't be like anything you've tried before, and it won't do you any good unless you've overdone the sherry, but I think you'll like it. I certainly think you'll like the prices. Then talk to the Lithuanian behind the counter and the Somalian having a fag round the back. They may not be up to speed on hunting etiquette or the dress code for dinner at the nearby George of Stamford hotel, but they'll have some stories to tell – that's for sure.

And then, if you think it actually is for the greater good, put down your capes and your green ink and be the jewel that makes the crown.

My mum spent her last few years in the Rutland area and she hated the idea of fast American food. Right up until the moment she put some of it in her mouth. Up to that point, she'd have been a Little Englander. Afterwards, she wasn't.

22 September 2019

Take those chocks away, Biggles – your noisy little plane's a pain in the alpha, Romeo, sierra, echo

Is there anything quite so selfish as taking up a hobby that ruins life for everyone else? For example, how many babies have been born at the side of the road because the car taking the mother to hospital was stuck behind a teenage girl doing 4mph in a gigantic horsebox?

Then you have that view across the Camel estuary in Cornwall, spoilt completely by the 18 lime-green splodges of artificial awfulness that is St Enodoc golf club.

And then there's motorcycling. Yes, it's very noble to wear an all-in-one leather bag that keeps all your valuable and much-needed internal organs in one place when you fall off. But the noise you make as you hurtle towards the pearly gates is horrendous.

The absolute worst offenders, though, are those who fly around in light aircraft. When I first moved to the countryside 20 years ago, I'd occasionally hear a Piper Cherokee forging a lonely path through the sky above my house. It was a mournful sound, like that of a sad dog, and it was fitting, really, because I just knew the pilot was a friendless and unhappily married lost soul who wanted to spend his free time totally alone.

Today, though, things are very different. I spent a few days trying to film at my house recently and there was not a single moment when we could record anything, because of a constant conveyor belt of airborne miserabilists. The sound recordist would hold up his hand, waiting to give the all-clear, and then as one Piper finally went out of earshot, another would come along. And so it went on until dark.

The figures are alarming. There are now 28,000 people with private pilot licences in the UK, and 21,000 light aircraft, which between them clock up 1.3 million hours of pointless noise pollution every year. And as aircraft get cheaper and less complicated, the growth is likely to accelerate.

I understand the need for helicopters, because they are used to take people from A to B quickly and conveniently. But, as a general rule, light aircraft, and appalling microlights, are flown for what the owners call 'fun'.

Let me explain what this entails. They turn up at the airfield where the plane is kept, imagining that they're Douglas Bader. They wear flying jackets bought as Christmas presents by their wives, who desperately want them out of the house. And they spend most of the morning sitting outside the club house, chatting to other Eeyores about their 'old kites', imagining that at any moment a bell will ring and Trevor Howard will tell them to scramble.

Eventually, after this hasn't happened, they will climb into their stupid plane and do pre-flight checks, which makes them slightly aroused. And then they will key the radio so that they can talk in a weird phonetic code to a man in a jumper, who's located in a nearby hut, imagining he's Kenneth More and he's responsible for keeping the Jerry hordes at bay.

Our hero will then take off, and fly into the wind, which means he has a speed over the ground of about

14mph. He's even being overtaken by horseboxes. For miles in every direction, sound recordists are holding up their hands, millions of pounds are being wasted and peaceful picnics are being ruined, but Biggles isn't bothered about any of that. He's now talking to Kenneth More about vectors and remembering to use acronyms and say 'niner' instead of 'nine', and he's so excited by all of this, he's actually got two joysticks.

Soon he will land at another airfield, where he will have a terrible cheese sandwich and a mug of tea, and he will sit about with the pilots based there, swapping stories about near misses and how you need to vector your VIR round niner niner at Biggin, and then he will have to rush to the lavatory for a bit of me' time before flying home again.

Yup. Tens of thousands of people have had their days ruined by the noise, and the man who isn't Douglas Bader has ended up back where he started, having produced nothing. Apart from a bit of unnecessary carbon dioxide. He hasn't even had any excitement.

No land-based creature can think that this is acceptable, and yet when an airfield near where I live was threatened by plans to build a Norman Foster-designed museum housing a collection of pre-war French cars, a staggering 180 or more local people objected. Are they mad? Because even if all the prewar French cars ventured onto the small track at the same time, they would create less din than a single one of the Biggleses.

Happily, the council agreed that the car museum was a good idea and planning permission was granted. But now the local MP, Robert Courts, has stepped in and referred the matter to the secretary of state.

I went to see him to argue my case, but when I noticed the back of his car was festooned with RAF roundels and the back of his phone case bore the insignia of Brize Norton, I figured I might be in for a spot of heavy disappointment.

It got worse when he told me that the transport secretary, Grant Shapps, is very much in favour of keeping as many airfields as possible out of the hands of developers. This may have something to do with the fact that Shapps is a keen amateur pilot and has a light aircraft of his own.

So now, here I am, wondering what on earth to do. I don't want light aircraft to be banned because banning things is mean-spirited and socialist. I suppose I could ask the local flying clubs to go and do their practice restarts and their droning somewhere else, but that shifts the problem. It doesn't solve it.

So I've decided that in my advancing years, I'm going to take up a new hobby of my own. It's called 'shooting light aircraft down with a surface-to-air missile'.

Of course, after I've got the hang of it, it's possible there won't be any targets left. Which means it's win-win.

29 September 2019

The Beeb's editorial police chief has always been a fair cop. It's a crime to throw him under the bus

Last week the BBC tied itself into a new kind of completely inextricable knot when it announced very firmly what it thought it should be saying, and then, when everybody got cross with it, decided very firmly that it shouldn't be saying what it very firmly believed it should be saying.

Here's the history. A few months ago, Donald Trump told some Democratical ladies of colour that they should stop whining about the awfulness of America and go back to where they came from to sort out the mess there.

This was discussed on a BBC sofa by two of the corporation's news stars: a man whose name has gone from my head and a woman called Naga Munchetty, who said such remarks were 'embedded in racism'.

At a rough guess, I'd say about 95 per cent of the population would agree with her. I certainly do. But someone from a rest home for retired Brexiteers in Eastbourne did not, and complained to the BBC, which, after an investigation, partially upheld the complaint, saying: 'Our editorial guidelines do not allow for journalists to ... give their opinions about the individual making the remark or their motives for doing so. Those judgments are for the audience to make.'

All over Islington, people went crazy. They were frothing at the mouth and twitching so violently it looked as though they'd caught rabies. And at the BBC it was much the same story. People were incredulous. A woman of colour had been reprimanded for questioning the motives behind Trump's remark. 'Of course he is racist, for God's sake,' they cried. 'And racism is worse than paedophilia. It's nearly as bad as being a climate-change denier.'

So in stepped the director-general, who said that the complaint should not, in fact, have been upheld, even a tiny bit. Which is a bit like a defendant listening to what the judge has to say and then leaping onto the bench to announce: 'Actually, I'm not guilty after all, and now I'm going home.'

I get the problem. We all live in a bubble, surrounded by people who think like we do. It's why I was absolutely convinced 'remain' would win the referendum. And it's why no one at the BBC could get it into their heads that people in their own building had sided, albeit partially, with the halfwit in Eastbourne.

What disturbs me most of all about this sorry saga, though, is that the BBC has thrown its chief of editorial policy (ed pol), a man called David Jordan, under the bus.

It's well known that, towards the end of my time at the BBC, I was embroiled in many noisy arguments with various bits of the management machine, but in all my time there, I never had a single cross word with David or the department he ran.

When I left *Top Gear* and signed with Amazon, everyone said: 'It must be great to be out of the BBC, because now you're free to say what you want.' And I always used to reply: 'Have you actually watched *Top Gear*? Right. So how could we have caused such upset every week if we'd been in a PC straitjacket?'

Of course, I couldn't just say or do what I wanted and then hand the DVD to a divorcee in a cardigan, who'd slot it into a big machine and press a button marked 'Transmit'. Everything had to be scrutinized by the ed pol police – but they were never the enforcers of management diktats. They were the guardians of free speech, and now their boss is under a Routemaster simply because he and his team analysed what Munchetty said, calmly removed the hysteria of the subject matter and concentrated only on the issue of impartiality. I watched them do this every week for 10 years.

Once, we asked ed pol if we could team up with a production company that was shooting a cinema remake of *The Sweeney*. We wanted to make a *Top Gear* film about how we filmed the movie's big car chase.

Think about that for a minute – that's us, using licence-fee money to make a car chase to slot into a non-BBC film, which would then go on to make profits for someone else. Where on earth do you place your first foot in that political minefield?

Believing it to be an unsolvable riddle, we went to ed pol, and the arrangement it went on to construct between us and the film company was so huge and complex you could see it from space. But using grey, painstaking diligence, it got the BBC and the film company to a position where each would share equal benefits. Which meant we could go ahead and blow up some caravans.

The ed pol department is like John Gielgud in *Arthur*. It runs everything, but its personal opinion is never known. It may be thinking behind its passive face, as you describe something you want to do, that it's the stupidest nonsense ever to come out of a mouth, but you would never know it, because its job is to stick to the rules. And that's it.

I've worked elsewhere, where a management type will call to say: 'Can you take that comment out? Some people in the office were offended by it.' But at the BBC, ed pol is always on hand to stop all that nonsense. It uses its cold detachment and lack of opinion to make sure the boat stays upright.

People complained after the Munchetty ruling that the ed pol police were not considering what the situation felt like for a woman of colour. The truth is, though, that when they come to do their job, they don't see colour. They just see a BBC news person implying the president of America is racist.

There may be only a few hundred people in the country who think Munchetty is wrong. But it is not the BBC's job to ignore them or their views, abhorrent though they may be. Management often loses sight of that simple fact, but ed pol never does. And proroguing the department on a whim, no matter how popular that whim might be, is foolish.

6 October 2019

He's not around to beat me, so I'll say it: Ginger Baker was only the world's second-best drummer

The drummer Ginger Baker died last week and everyone was very surprised because we all assumed the drug-addled wild man from Cream and Blind Faith had shuffled off this mortal coil years ago. It's customary, of course, when someone dies to gloss over their shortcomings and concentrate instead on their work for charity and their heroics in the war. But this is nigh-on impossible with Baker, who was almost certainly the most unpleasant man ever to grace a stage. He pulled a knife on Cream's bass player, Jack Bruce. He used his fists to settle almost every dispute. He broke the nose of the director who made a documentary about him with his walking stick.

Then, of course, there was the naked 11-year-old girl featured on the cover of Blind Faith's only album. That's such a difficult issue these days, none of the obituaries even mentioned it.

Instead, everyone concentrated on Baker's skills as a musician – but even here people missed the point, because despite what he claimed, he wasn't the best drummer the world has ever seen. Thanks to Mitch Mitchell, who played with Jimi Hendrix, he was the second best. I'm on Twitter if you want to argue.

Baker, however, could keep perfect time, even when he was full of heroin, which is quite an achievement. And he could maintain four different cross rhythms with each of his limbs. This is like rubbing your tummy, patting your head, pumping up a lilo and playing hopscotch all at the same time.

I have a drum kit. It's an enormous Pictures of Lily limited edition replica. And after several years of weekly lessons, I developed a profound admiration for drummers, because they're doing something I can't do.

We can't admire people who can do what we can do. I don't admire anyone who can drive fast while shouting, but when I watch a dry-stone-waller creating a natural barrier using nothing but experience and big, warty hands, I become a statue of wonderment held upright by nothing but the tingling in my hair. That's what happens when I hear a drum solo.

A columnist last week said that words cannot begin to describe the 'unstoppable misery' of the 'nightmarish' drum solo. Plainly, he is the sort of man who thinks drummers are like houseflies. That they come, they make an annoying noise and then they die. And I literally could not agree less.

A drum solo allows the audience to marvel at the technical wizardry of the drummer. It allows us to concentrate on his incredible ability to get a whole arm from one side of the kit to the other faster than it takes a Formula One car to change gear. And to do it in perfect time.

It's been suggested that Ginger Baker invented the drum solo so his bandmates could have a moment to go backstage and top up whatever was missing at that moment from their lives. I doubt this, though. He didn't really like other musicians that much.

It's been reported that he called Mick Jagger a 'musical moron'. But that's not true. What he actually said was that the Stones were like 'a load of little kids trying to play black blues music and playing it very badly'. It was George Harrison he called a musical moron. And he dismissed Paul McCartney too, because, unlike him, McCartney could not sight-read music. Led Zeppelin? If you even mentioned them in his presence, you'd get a thick lip. He only really liked people we've never heard of. Phil Seamen was a hero of his, for example. And Art Blakey.

So no. Baker was on the stage doing his solos simply so we could hear how he'd fused the jazz music of his heroes with an altogether new and busy way of playing. He despised the 4/4 beat of rock and pop music, but it's possible that, because of what he did with Cream, he's partly responsible for it.

His solos were often more than 10 minutes long and were mesmerizing. And soon drummers everywhere were trying to outdo him. Led Zeppelin's John Bonham did a 17-minute epic on the track 'Moby Dick', and then you got – whisper this, because I'm friendly with Nick Mason and Roger Taylor – my favourite drummer, Phil Collins, duetting with Chester Thompson. They started out hitting bar stools and then moved to their kits for a drumming shootout. It's the best thing on YouTube.

And now? Well, there was the movie *Whiplash*, which everyone, apart from me, thought was weird – but on stage? In real life? There's nothing. The drum solo is dead.

I find that odd. There are still bands and some still have drummers, so why don't these people want the audience to see and hear them doing their thing? Isn't that like being a goalkeeper who never wants to make a save?

The only explanation is that they actively hide at the back behind the bass and the guitar and the flashy vocals because they're not that good.

This sort of thing has happened before. Between 1750 and 1820, the world heard from Schubert, Mozart, Beethoven and Haydn, but since then, apart from a couple of little spurts, there's been nothing of any great consequence. And today? There's a woman in Iceland who turns drawings of turnips into classical music and there's Ludovico Einaudi, who provided the soundtrack for many of the *Top Gear* films I made. But that's about it.

Could it be that the same thing has happened with drumming? That we as a species were only ever any good at it between 1958 and 1978, and now we have lost the ability, in the same way that penguins have lost the ability to fly?

Luckily, however, we still have the recordings from the days when drumming wasn't just an electronic *nn tss nn tss nn tss nn tss* and I've been listening to a lot of it all week. That's why I ended up revisiting 'Can't Find My Way Home'. You played on that one, Ginger. And now you have.

13 October 2019

I want an old-fashioned shop with an old-fashioned sign – and a ban on newfangled billionaires

I wonder. Has anything ever been improved by having way too much money thrown at it? HS2, for example. Will it be dramatically better than what we have now? I suspect it probably won't. Then there's football. In the olden days, when Blackburn's Billy Harbuckle pulled on a stout pair of boots, sparked up a Woodbine and ran about in a quagmire, before adjourning to the pub with his fans, the game was played for fun. But along came Captain Cash, and now the only fun to be had is watching teams with too much of it fail.

In Formula One motor racing Mercedes has just won its sixth successive constructor's championship and the reason you don't know that is simple: money has made the sport unwatchable. And horsists can shut up, because what you do on a wet Tuesday at Lingfield isn't any better.

In the world of commerce, though, things are especially bad because, so far as I can see, absolutely everyone who starts a business these days is only thinking of one thing: when can I sell it? No one wants to provide a decent living for themselves and their family. They don't want to make 50 quid. They want to make £50 billion and then move to Monaco with some bikinied-up boat meat.

When my mum started making tea cosies and draught excluders in the spare room, she didn't think: 'Right. I shall sell four and then I shall sell the enterprise to a furniture conglomerate for millions.' She just wanted enough money to buy my sister and me some new shoes.

It was the same story with me. In the mid-1980s, when Margaret Thatcher was extolling us all to go it alone, a friend and I started a business, selling road tests to local newspapers. The idea was that we'd have enough at the end of the week to buy some beer. Not a whole brewery.

Today it works very differently. You have an idea for a vegan drinks additive or an app that provides directions to that day's nearest eco-protest, and you then borrow a huge amount of money from someone whose job is to lend huge amounts of money to people like you.

One in a million of these businesses will succeed, and in order to turn the large fortune that results into an even larger fortune, the man who created it will pay people to lend his money to people who have a new idea for a clockwork dog.

This is what's become of capitalism, and if you do the maths, you will very quickly work out that one day, one man – or one woman – will own every single business in the world. And then it isn't capitalism any more. I don't even know what it is, because not even the Catholic Church managed to pull off such a feat.

Shows such as *The Apprentice* give us a graphic demonstration of all this. Gelled-up wide boys and pouting *Love Island* cast-offs giving 10 per cent more than is mathematically possible so that they, one day, can be like that Thomas Cook boss who trousered a couple of million as the business failed. He's their pin-up and it makes me feel sick.

There's talk that, after Brexit, Britain will become a low-tax haven for commerce – like Singapore – and we all nod as if we know what that means. But I reckon that we should have a reboot and go the other way, back to the days when you started a small business because you wanted enough to live on and fancied being your own boss.

I'm reminded at this point of a conversation AA Gill had with a bouncily keen young Thatcherite MP who was squeaking away about how everyone needed to invest the money they'd made from gas shares into an entrepreneur's wet dream.

Adrian piped up to say that he started a business shortly after leaving school. The MP beamed and bounced some more. 'Good man,' he said. Adrian went on to explain that he worked long hours, late into the night, until eventually the Tory boy asked excitedly: 'And what was it you did?'

'I was a drug dealer,' he replied.

I read today about these so-called county line gangs that deliver spliff and charlie and horse around the shires. These are often run by young kids who, having been excluded from school, face a life on the dole, but instead they've helped create a £500 million-a-year industry supplying drugs to middle-aged people who have no theatres and no cinemas to take their minds off the fact that, once again, there's nothing on television that night apart from a documentary on transgenderism.

I'm not advocating the use of drugs or the use of slavery to sell them. I am merely pointing out that large numbers of people in the provinces like to get high and someone has worked up a business plan to sate that demand.

I'm about to do pretty much the same sort of thing. Not drugs, obviously. Or slavery. Well, not much. I'm going to start a small shop. I do not need to borrow a penny to get it going, but, according to the business plan, it should generate about £20,000 in the first year and maybe treble that in the second. I have no intention of selling it, ever, because I want to pass it on to my children.

That makes me feel all warm and fuzzy, knowing that one day, when I'm JR Hartley, I'll go outside with some Humbrol and paint some words on the sign outside my business premises that you rarely see any more: 'and son'.*

If more of us did this – started a business for the long term – then the spectre of Jeremy Corbyn with his anti-commerce and anti-inheritance policies would be far less scary.

But as things stand, practically the only people who will not be voting for him next time round are the hooded entrepreneurs who turn up on your doorstep with a bag of ecstasy on a Friday night.

20 October 2019

---

* Or 'and daughter'. I'm not bothered either way.

Keep a stiff upper lip when all about you are losing theirs, and you won't be a Yank, my son

When Obama Barrack came to Londonshire in 2016, he put on a serious face and told us that we'd better stay in the EU or else. And I remember being so incensed that my nose swelled up and my teeth moved about. Because how dare he come here and lecture us on what we should and shouldn't do.

Last week, it happened again. Meghan, Prince Harry's wife, went on television to tell us that instead of keeping a stiff upper lip and bottling up our feelings, we should vomit them out in a torrent of snot and tear-stained, shoulder-heaving sobs.

Well now, look, Meghan. That might work for you, because you are an American and programmed to weep and wail at every little thing, but we are programmed to do the exact opposite.

This was evidenced at Wimbledon in 1981, when John McEnroe had his famous 'You cannot be serious' meltdown. American viewers heard nothing of the tantrum because they had five excitable commentators, all shouting over one another as they speculated on what kind of punishment the emerging champion was likely to receive. British viewers, on the other hand, heard everything McEnroe had to say. And only when he told officials they were the 'pits of the world' did our commentators see fit to interject with a quiet harrumph.

Dan Maskell was a master of this. All sorts of mayhem could be happening around him and all we ever got was, 'Oh, I say.' He had the stiff upper lip. His son died in a plane crash. His wife drowned. But he did not bleat about these things. He filed them away in his head and got on with his life, best foot forward. Because he was British and that's what we do.

A year after the McEnroe match, a British Airways jumbo jet on a night flight over the Indian Ocean roared at 500mph into a cloud of volcanic ash that wasn't visible on radar. Moments later, all four engines stopped.

Now we all know, of course, about Captain Sully – Chesley Sullenberger – and his Hudson River landing, and all those Mercury astronauts with the right stuff, so I'm not going to say a US pilot would have run up and down the aisle, screaming: 'We're all going to die.'

But I'm willing to bet he wouldn't have been quite as calm as Eric Moody, the BA chap, who announced to passengers: 'Ladies and gentlemen, this is your captain speaking. We have a small problem. All four engines have stopped. We are doing our damnedest to get it under control. I trust you are not in too much distress.'

Think about that. He's doing maths in his head and working out that a fully laden Boeing 747-200 has a glide ratio of 15 to one, meaning it can cover 15 miles for every mile it drops. So, at 37,000ft, he had 105 miles to work out why the engines had stopped and how best to restart them. But despite all this, he didn't panic and, crucially, he didn't forget his manners. I'm willing to bet, in fact, that if Alan Sugar had been on board, Moody would even have started his announcement by saying: 'My lord, ladies and gentlemen . . .'

A lot of this calmness has to do with the classical edu-
cation boys received in the public-school system. Pupils
were taught that if they took a lead from the Spartans,
who loved a bit of discipline and self-sacrifice, they'd be
able to cope more easily with freezing dormitories, the
unwanted attentions of slobbery mouthed geography
teachers and the regular beatings from sixth-formers.

Then, after chapel, they learnt about the Hellenistic
philosophy of stoicism and how it could be found in
Hamlet, Rudyard Kipling, the teachings of Marcus Aure-
lius and, best of all, in the short poem 'Invictus': 'In the
fell clutch of circumstance / I have not winced nor cried
aloud. / Under the bludgeonings of chance / My head is
bloody, but unbow'd.'

To be honest, we liked the Boy's Own sound of all that.
If your best foot is blown off in a battle, you promote the
other one and hop on. And you most definitely do not
finish a game of bowls early just because the Spanish have
sent an armada. That would be poor form.

Put it like this. If Captain 'Titus' Oates had been an
American rather than an Old Etonian, we can be fairly
certain he would not have left the tent saying he 'may be
some time'. He'd have laid there, screaming and begging
for his mother and some counselling. He'd have told his
tent-mates not to judge him and written in his diary how
he'd bravely sobbed and drooled to the bitter end.

Of course, the British are capable of shedding a tear or
two. We cried at the funeral of Diana, Princess of Wales.
Well, I did. We cried when Winston Churchill died. And
we cried when they buried Lord Nelson. But we don't cry
when our neighbour's dog dies or because of something
on the news. We may be upset, but we then employ a

phrase not used anywhere else in the world. We 'get a grip'. Not being able to get a grip is like being really fat. It's the sign of a weak mind. It's an indicator that you aren't able to control yourself and that you may be French.

I don't mind Meghan having the need to open a window to her soul every five minutes. But she can't tell me to do the same thing, because I'm not made that way. It'd be like going to Germany and ordering them to be funny. Or telling the Japanese that blondes have more fun. Or insisting that bees stop making a buzzing noise when they fly.

Let's not forget what happened when Morgan Piers went to America and lectured them on gun ownership. They put a flea in his ear and sent him packing, and now he has to earn a living from behind a veil of orange make-up on breakfast TV. If Ms Meghan doesn't learn a lesson from that sorry tale, she may well end up in exactly the same boat.

27 October 2019

It gets birdbrains in a flutter that wildlife is booming on my green and pheasant land

I was up early the other day because I was keen to write about the Britannia Hotels group's incredible achievement of being voted the UK's worst chain for the seventh year running. Imagine. You're told you're rubbish once and then you keep on being rubbish for six straight years. I wanted to comment about such an extraordinary level of commitment to slack-jawed slovenliness.

But then I noticed that the survey had been done by Which?, an organization that is really only interested in reaching adenoidal people in action trousers and sandals who contribute to TripAdvisor and run the neighbourhood-watch scheme. As a general rule, I've always reckoned that if something does badly in Which?, it's probably pretty good.

As I sat, deciding which side to take in the great hotel debate, I was distracted by an annoying man on Radio 4's *Farming Today* show. He was from the airborne wing of the Labour Party – also known as the Royal Society for the Prevention of Birds – and he was talking about how he thought shooting game birds might be a bad thing.

The RSPB has always been prevented by its royal charter from campaigning against the shooting industry – Mrs Queen likes to strangle a pheasant or two at Christmas time, as we know – but it has worked out that it can comment if it reckons shooting is done by rich bastards in Range Rovers.

Now, the columnist Charles Moore said recently that the actress Olivia Colman had a 'left-wing face'. I won't comment on that, but I will say that Martin Harper, the man the RSPB sent to Radio 4, had a left-wing voice. Chris Packham has both a left-wing voice and a left-wing face, and he wants us all to stop using fly spray.

Anyway, Martin reckoned that if you release 50 million non-native game birds into the British countryside every year, it's bound to have an effect. When pressed by the interviewer for a specific effect, he said: 'Er, climate change.' That was lucky for the Britannia Hotels chain, because I immediately abandoned my original plan and decided to write about shooting instead.

The first thing I did when I started a small shoot was plant several acres of so-called cover crops. Maize, sunflowers and something called kale, which can be eaten by humans if they are very deranged. These crops provide warmth, food and a place to hide from Johnny Fox, not just for my pheasants but a whole squadron of other birds too.

We keep reading about how endangered the yellowhammer is these days; well, not on my farm it isn't. Since I started my shoot, the skies are black with them. And goldcrests. And wrens. And skylarks. The dawn chorus used to be nothing but the occasional squawk of a murderous crow, whereas now it's positively philharmonic.

Research has shown that if you run through a field of crops planted by a shootist, you are 340 times more likely to encounter a songbird than if you do a Theresa May and run through a field of grass.

So, Martin, if the RSPB does manage to ban shooting, then, yes, you will be championed as a class hero throughout the vegan strongholds of Islington and Shoreditch, but you will also be responsible for the deaths of a million linnets. Which, as far as I know, isn't why the RSPB was founded.

And then there are the woods, where the pheasants are held until they are old enough to forage on their own. Woods are beautiful and still. They're places to shelter from the endless drone of light-aircraft enthusiasts. Mine are full of roe deer and muntjac and squirrels and badgers, and at this time of year there are many mushrooms too. I love to spend an evening down there as the leaves turn golden, giggling. Everyone likes woods, except if you are in a horror film.

But they generate no income. So if shooting were banned, I'd have to get Brazilian on their arses and turn them into farmland. Is that what you want, Martin? Because I fear that would create a damn sight more climate change than my Range Rover.

Of course, I'm well aware that some people might bridle at the sight and sound of eight hedge-fund managers in tweed shorts, braying their way through a pint of sloe gin while brandishing a pair of £20,000 shotguns, but what good comes from making them take up golf instead?

There are many hobbies that inflict far more pain and misery on others: light aircraft – I'm not giving up on that – the violin, motorcycling, strimming, morris dancing and so on, so why pick on one that's good for nature and good for the way the countryside looks?

Pointedly, it's good for birds too. Not just songbirds, but the kind of stuff that makes kids point at the sky and squeak with joy. Birds of prey. Since I started a shoot, I have seen a huge increase in the number of kestrels and buzzards over my farm. I even think I spotted a peregrine falcon the other day, and that made my heart soar.

Was it here because it likes eating my pheasants and partridges? There's some debate about that, but the truth is I don't really care if it does take a few. Because I like having it around.

So stop persecuting me, Martin, and concentrate instead on the people who do real damage to these magnificent creatures. Seriously. If you put down your Jeremy Corbyn picture book for a moment and do some actual work, you'll learn that peregrines like to hang out on top of churches and cathedrals. Because the height gives them the ability to reach the speed they need in an attack dive.

But, because of bell-ringers, it's noisy and scary up there. So if you really want to help these birds, don't target the shooting community, which is doing its bit already. Target the real villains: the nation's campanologists. That's what I want to see – the RSPB and the country's bell-ringers at war.

3 November 2019

Private jet on the runway. Sweaty hand on your back. Say ciao to Andrew's entitled Eurotrashers

Shortly after Prince Andrew claimed he didn't indulge in public displays of affection, we were bombarded with a million photographs of him doing just that. There were so many, it started to look as though he'd had his hand on the arse of everyone in London and had even gone into battle in the Falklands with his tongue in his co-pilot's ear.

The problem is, however, that in the world he inhabits, this is the done thing. When you are introduced to a woman, you don't shake hands. You run your fingers delicately up her exposed back and she responds by resting her head on your shoulder. And then, later, you mate.

The first person I met from this weird world was a translator we once used in Italy. She was idiotically pretty, all freckles and blue eyes – like a Cadbury's Flake girl who'd washed up, under a mane of just-out-of-bed hair, in a Timotei waterfall. And she spoke about 17 languages. 'Where are you from?' I asked squeakily. 'Er . . .' she replied.

That's the thing about these people. They're not ever from anywhere. Her mum was an American diplomat in Buenos Aires, her dad was an Italian architect and she'd been born in France and educated in England, and lived mostly these days in Switzerland.

This is why most of her friends would have a 'de' or a

'von' in the middle of their name. To give them some kind of anchor. It's why Andrew fits, because the man he calls Dad is Greek and his mum is German. But he's the Duke of York. I'd be Jeremy of Doncaster. I actually call these people the 'ofs and froms'. But everyone else has a different name for them: Eurotrash. And you can spot them at parties because they all have wandering Eurohands.

They emerge from their mother's birth canal on water-skis, with a golden suntan. By the age of four, they are fully qualified helicopter pilots, and by six they've won several motor races. They never double-fault on the tennis court, never ski on a piste and, like Andrew, have no discernible source of income. The odd one may have an art gallery in Zurich or a private equity operation in Mayfair, but, by and large, they live an impossible life on invisible means.

It's a carbon-heavy life of parties, mostly. They alight in Rome for Alain de Biarritz's wedding to Alexandra von München and then, after a day of recovery by the pool, they all share a secret signal and whizz off to Moscow for Hugo von Duesenberg's 40th. In many ways, they're like starlings. And, like starlings, they socialize and travel only with their own kind – people who are in the same boat. Or on the same boat, usually.

Sitting at a dining table with these guys involves a lot of shouting, because each has such a long name that the place card is 3ft wide. Which means you are always miles away from the person sitting next to you. Not that they will talk to you, anyway, because of your miserably short name. And because you're an insect in a room full of antelopes.

The men never wear socks. The women never wear much of anything at all. And while they are all able to converse fluently with waiters in any country on Earth, they all communicate with one another in English, but with an accent that sociolinguistic professors would place halfway between Milan and Kentucky. The word they use for 'party', for instance, has a 'd' in it. And when we say 'PJs', we mean pyjamas, but to them PJs are private jets, which is what they all use when the lead starling suddenly decides everyone needs to be in St Moritz. Or Juan-les-Pins. These people, who are only ever photographed with a glass of champagne in one hand and a woman's arse in the other, are all basically beholden to Peter Sarstedt.

You might think they'd never allow a girl from the back streets of Naples to join their gang, but that's not true. Yes, the men must have private means, but they also need boat meat for the summers in St Tropez. And anyone will do, as long as she is visually striking and 7ft tall. Her only job is to appear at the dock in a bikini that's two sizes too small. And to not suffer from heat rash. These are the mystery women who appear in the James Bond casino scenes. And in the background of all those Andrew pictures.

And it all sounds very idyllic for everyone concerned. The women just have to be pretty and they get a racehorse for Christmas, which they keep for a laugh. And the guys never have to mate with anyone who's fat.

No one ever has to buy a washing-up bowl or fill a car with petrol. Which all sounds great, but none of them owns a dog – it'd be too much of a nuisance dealing with it when Air Starling decided to head to pastures new.

They don't have jobs for the same reason. And this means they have no concept of responsibility.

Marriages, in their world, are like houses. You move in and then you move out again. They do the wedding thing because they fancy hosting a party, but at the reception the bride will get a lot of Eurohand action, and the only reason the groom doesn't notice is that he's upstairs, snorting coke off the back of the girl from the back streets of Naples.

They never really had much of a connection with their parents, either, because they were sent off to boarding school four minutes after their umbilical cord was cut. And they only ever met Mum subsequently when they passed in the general aviation terminal in Nice.

All of which means that, while their lives are glamorous and exciting and filled with sunshine and princes, they contribute nothing and achieve even less.

Plus, they never experience the most important thing of all: love. It's why so many of them are such enormous bell-ends.

24 November 2019

Mozzies, heat, upset tummies and all-day drinking – even Jeremy Corbyn's taxes are better than life abroad

After Mr Corbyn wins the coming election – and he will, because all your children are going to vote for that weird Lib Dem hamster woman – a great many rich people will decide to emigrate. If the top 1 per cent of taxpayers do that, then Corbyn will have 30 per cent less income tax revenue to spend. If the top 5 per cent go, then he will lose half of what HMRC gets now. Half. The country will go bankrupt, simple as that.

And this time we can't send Princess Margaret to the White House to borrow some dollars, because she's no longer with us. And because that bit of *The Crown* wasn't true. We can't send Prince Andrew, because the FBI will probably arrest him at the airport. And we can't send Harry, because he will probably have emigrated as well.

I've certainly considered it, and so have many of my friends. But where would we go? Portugal seems to be a popular option because it is offering disaffected Brits extremely good tax arrangements. So is northern Spain. And so is Italy. But the problem with these destinations is: they're hot. And if you have been brought up in the Tupperware box that is Britain, you will not be able to cope.

Think back to your last summer holiday. Think of the faff of getting your children to put on sun cream after breakfast. Think of the heartache it caused you and the pain it caused them when they won the argument. And then imagine doing that every single day, for the rest of your lives.

Then think how much work you'd get done. You'd open the shutters every morning to reveal another endless blue sky, so you'd walk straight past your laptop and go to the beach. This is why the economies of hot countries such as Greece and Spain and Italy are failing: faced with the choice of going to the office or going for a swim, everyone pulls on a swimming costume.

And, of course, shortly after pulling on a swimming costume and sploshing about in the sea, you will want a beer. At first you may impose a midday curfew on that, but within a week you'll relax it to 11, and within a month you'll be pouring vodka on your cornflakes.

Not that you can buy cornflakes when you are abroad. Or HP Sauce. And when you have the craving for a chicken madras with some pilau rice, you will be sorely disappointed by the cherry tomatoes and bread that are produced instead. We all think we want to live on a healthy Italian diet but the truth is: we don't.

Then there are the wasps. You tend to dial them out of your Mediterranean memories in the same way your head uses time to dial out pain, but think how many lunches were ruined because someone in your family has insect panic and rushes about screaming every time a wasp comes within 3ft. Which is constantly.

It's hard to enjoy mealtimes with your children here because of their addiction to social media. So imagine how difficult it would be if they were on Instagram with one hand, and creating a wasp-incinerating flamethrower from your deodorant and a lighter with the other.

I was in Madagascar last month, and it is, without any

doubt, the most beautiful place on earth. I didn't know what the colour green was until I saw its jungles, and I didn't have any concept of what a deserted white beach looked like until I saw its northeastern coastline. The Seychelles are lovely but this was better still.

However, five minutes after our 70-strong crew arrived, all of the under-25s took to their beds with upset tummies. I mocked them, of course, for their millennial frailty, but two days later I too was struck with an urgent need to visit what passed on our campsite for a lavatory. I have a cast-iron constitution. I could lick a Turkish urinal dry and not suffer any ill effects, but there I became a human hosepipe.

And then there were the mosquitoes. All around the world they tend to avoid beautiful people – you never see a supermodel coming out of the sea with red welts on her legs – but everyone in Madagascar is fair game. The Guy Gibson of mozzies got James May on the end of his nose, and then, a day later, one climbed into my shirt and, having broken out its best cutlery, began to eat my back. It's two weeks since I got back but it still looks as though I've been at the wrong end of a firing squad.

And I can't scratch the wounds as much as I'd like because my fingernails are constantly employed dealing with the heat rash on my arms.

So, yes, if you move to a hot country to escape the wrath and idiocy of Corbyn, you will save a great deal of money and that's tremendous. But on the downside you will be eaten by insects, you will do no work, you will become an alcoholic, your children will be in agony, you will have loose stools and when you go out at night everyone will think you are Joseph Merrick because of the constant scratching.

My current thinking is that it's better to stay here. But I do have a plan to make that work. The well-off should form a sort of trade union, and if the tax demands become too bonkers, we will simply go on strike. We will refuse to pay our taxes. We will have picket lines. We will point out that we are paying for half the country's services already. We will light braziers and we shall throw stones at the policemen who are sent to make us repent.

That'd blow a fuse in his head. He can say no to a millionaire in a suit, but if that same man put on a donkey jacket and waved a placard in his face? I bet he'd back down in a heartbeat.

1 December 2019

Giant tortoises are slow of foot but quick of wit, while I struggle to keep up with my sheep

For many years the giant tortoise was seen as an easy-to-catch lunch. After a long voyage to the tropics, sailors would disembark and immediately peel one of these giant beasts, which, they said, were delicious. Plus, the creature's hard-to-digest wrapping paper could then be sold to a Victorian doctor's wife as an exotic centrepiece for the hall table.

Later, after various animal enthusiasts decided the tortoises shouldn't be eaten, no matter how wonderfully buttery their fat might be, Hollywood turned up and gave them another role. We've all seen *Jurassic Park*. Well, the grunting noises made by the velociraptors were actually recordings of giant tortoises doing sex.

Today they are protected and their porn noises may not be used in films. Children cannot ride around on them and they cannot be turned onto their backs for a laugh. We have all fallen in love with their enormousness, and when it was reported in 2012 that the last of one species – a chap called Lonesome George – had died, there was international sadness.

It's always interesting to try to figure out why some animals work their way into our hearts while others do not. I've long suspected that unless it's cute, magnificent or delicious, we don't care two hoots if it becomes extinct. But boffins in Japan may have come up with another reason the giant tortoise is so universally adored. Yes, it's slow-moving and has the metabolic rate of a stone, but they reckon that behind the placid, Volvo-y exterior, it's actually quite clever.

Ten years ago they taught a group of captive tortoises in Vienna zoo that if they bit on the end of a particular coloured stick, they would get no food, and that if they bit on a different coloured stick, they would. When the scientists returned nearly a decade later, three of the creatures were tested again. And they could still remember which stick did what. So now scientists are saying that a giant tortoise is basically Sir Tim Berners-Lee with a shell on his back.

I already knew this, because think about the human being. The Vikings had visited France and north America but reckoned that the slate-grey slab of frozen rock we call Iceland would be a much better place to raise a tribe. Then you had the Romans, who could have lived under a wisteria tree in Tuscany but decided Doncaster would be better. And Genghis Khan? He was raised in the bewitching open spaces of Mongolia but dreamt of the day he could move to Kiev.

We saw none of this idiocy from Johnny Tortoise. God knows where he started out as a species, but today he's found only in the Galapagos Islands and the Seychelles. This means he must have walked, at half a mile an hour, through forests and deserts and moorland. And then swum, with his house on his back, for hundreds of miles, across open ocean, until he found what are probably the two most beautiful places on earth. Coincidence? I doubt it.

I've been to the island in the Seychelles where thousands of giant tortoises womble about, eating leaves and thinking about cold fusion. And it only took me about no minutes to see yet another example of their intelligence.

The island has a grass runway, on which planes carrying noisy and annoying tourists land. Now think about that. You walk halfway round the world in search of paradise, and then, when you're about 150, the serenity is shattered by a steady torrent of honeymoon couples.

To solve the problem, the tortoises have decided to live on the runway. They can't be shooed away because, well, they're tortoises. And they can't be carried because they weigh nearly half a ton. This means they've been more successful at closing an airport than those Extinction Rebellion halfwits at Heathrow.

I don't think tortoises are the only animals that have genuine intelligence either. Look at your dog. He can fetch a ball and answer to his name and he knows not to urinate on the furniture. But what he knows most of all is that if he behaves in this way, like a human simpleton, you will give him biscuits and a bed by the Aga.

Left to his own devices, he becomes Alan Turing. Look at those wild dogs you see in places such as India and Burma and South America. Look at how quickly they walk. It's like they have a purpose, like they know where they are going and why. Their ears are alert. Their tails are up. You rarely see humans in these parts of the world moving with such intent. I reckon that when we are not looking, dogs read books.

And I'm not sure that sheep are far behind. They are widely reckoned to be the stupidest animals on earth, but I've had a flock for a few months and I'm beginning to wonder. They are perfectly happy to pretend that they are hemmed in by the electric fences and walls we build, but when they want to move on, they just do. Our manmade obstacles are nothing to them.

And I think they have a sense of humour. I spent two hours the other morning running around, trying to get them into a new field. And three minutes after I succeeded, they all jumped clean over a Becher's Brook of a wall and back into the field they'd just left. So I spent two hours rounding them up again, and three minutes later they jumped the wall again. After a third time, I knew they were doing it for a laugh. To humiliate the idiotic, out-of-breath biped.

There's more evidence of animal intelligence too. When they need a new leader, monkeys and zebras and lions don't sit around arguing about who'd be the best man for the job. The two candidates put forward their case, and there is always unanimous and immediate agreement afterwards.

Humans, however, listen to the candidates for months, and then half of us decide to vote for the person who'll definitely lead the tribe into a fiery pit of brimstone, bankruptcy and despair.

8 December 2019

I've some divan inspiration for hotels – you don't need to stop mattress thieves, just the mattress

It's hard to know when hotels were invented. According to Guinness World Records, the first was in Japan in AD705, but plainly that's not true, because 705 years earlier than that we know Gullible Joe and his mysteriously pregnant wife, Mary, attempted without success to find room at an inn in Bethlehem.

What's more, we have to assume that hostelries go back even further than that, to the days when people started to move about on horses and needed somewhere to rest them for the night. That's 5,500 years ago. That's when the premier inn was. And what's interesting is that in all this time, no one has managed to get a hotel room right. Until now.

Today there are more than 17 million hotel rooms in the world and all of them are wrong in some way. Some smell so powerfully of extreme cleaning products that your septum starts to bleed. Some are several miles from reception. And many have doors that are opened by electronical key cards that don't work. Ever. So then you have to go back to reception and prove to a sceptic in a stupid waistcoat that you're the same person who was there only two minutes earlier.

However, I was at the Dakota in Manchester last weekend and, unusually, it had rooms that had plainly been designed by someone who'd stayed in a hotel before.

The light switches did what I was expecting when I pushed them. You didn't need a degree in astrophysics to open and close the windows. The temperature was maintained at a level that felt like there was no temperature at all. And the shower controls were located by the door to the cubicle, not on the other side of the icy jet that starts the moment you turn the tap.

As it's in Manchester, where even the postmen get dressed up like the Chippendales before they go out, and homeless ladies look like Ivana Trump, I was expecting a lot of unnecessariness and orange diamante. But the decor was halfway between businesslike and what I'd put in my house. I had a look around the room and some of the stuff I would happily have stolen.

I worked with a chap for many years who did this as a matter of course. He argued that he had paid for the room, so everything in it was therefore his. I tried to reason with him but it was no good, and every morning he'd leave with all the towels, dressing gowns, sheets and pillows, as well as any ornaments that took his fancy. Obviously, he couldn't have the drinks from the minibar because management had that covered, but in his mind the fridge itself was definitely fair game.

He was missing a trick, though, because last week hotel chiefs reported that the latest craze is for guests to steal the mattresses from their beds. This sounds nuts, but in posh hotels with good beds and lifts that go directly to an underground car park, it makes perfect sense.

Or does it? Because, think about it. Sure, you could be stealing something that cost upwards of £20,000, but it's been in a hotel room since the day it was sold, and every night it's been slept on by someone you don't know, someone who has a skin disease, perhaps, or some kind of lung disorder.

I went through a period after I stopped smoking when my gums leaked at night and I'd wake up in the morning to find my bedding soaked in blood. Would you like to steal that? And I haven't yet got to the other things that come from ladies and gentlemen when they are in hotel rooms together.

Once, I stayed in a hotel just outside Kampala in Uganda. The sheets didn't look so bad, apart from the fact that they were pink and made from nylon, but I pulled them back to reveal a mattress that remains the single most revolting thing I have ever seen. Many of the stains were green. And God knows what manner of thing had caused that. Maybe a previous guest had spilt some Thai green curry. But I doubt it.

I'm fairly sure that even with light staining, a used mattress would have no second-hand value at all. Which means people are stealing mattresses for themselves. And that's like stealing used underpants to wear.

So how can hotel chiefs solve the problem? It's probably unwise to warn customers that all the mattresses have been drizzled with body waste. That may be off-putting.

Nor can cheap mattresses be used, to minimize the cost of buying replacements, because nobody likes to sleep on horsehair. I did it for five years at boarding school, so I know.

I suppose it might be possible to arrange a lift's algorithms to ensure it always stops on the ground floor and the doors always open. Because knowing he'd have to stand there with a stolen mattress, in full view of reception, might embarrass a would-be thief into thinking twice.

Don't be so sure, though. A few years ago, a gang of four men wearing brown store coats walked calmly into the ballroom at a well-known London hotel and rolled up a gigantic and very valuable Chinese rug. They even asked the guests, who'd assembled for some early-evening function, if they wouldn't mind stepping over the enormous silk sausage they were creating. And then they carried it calmly to a waiting van and drove off.

That's the kind of front the hotel industry is facing. But don't worry, chaps and chapesses, because I have a solution. Fitting a mattress to a bed is a one-time gig, yes? So why not put it there and fix it to the frame with something that cannot be undone with pliers, a linoleum knife, a heavy-calibre gun or even explosives? Such a thing exists. It's called a ratchet strap.

If you think a ratchet strap can be undone or adjusted, then please write to me at 'The *Sunday Times*, London', marking your envelope: 'I'm weird.'

15 December 2019

Northerners are gagging for the Boris bounce, but who do they think will fill all the new jobs?

I was with like-minded friends when the exit poll was announced, and immediately we decided that we should head into the night to taunt a Trot. We needed to find Steve Coogan or someone of his ilk so that we could pretend we were sad for them, while smiling the smile of someone who absolutely wasn't.

In the end we found Lily Allen, and she was crestfallen. As I bit the inside of my cheeks in a desperate bid to stem a fit of giggles, she explained that the Tory victory would mean piles of dead children in the streets and Muslims being openly poked with sticks by shaven-headed gangs of far-right thugs.

She also mused that capitalism needs cheap foreign workers to exploit and that, as a result, immigration will rise, not fall, in the coming months and years. Which is exactly the opposite of what the new Tories on the Northern Wall want. On this point I'm in agreement with her.

On election night I made a coherent argument to all my friends that the 'red wall' would not crumble, because the memory of Grandad dying from a lung disease in his pebble-dashed, National Coal Board house would prevent any northerner from voting Tory, no matter what they'd told the pollsters. 'A northerner could cut off his own head with some garden shears more easily than he could vote Conservative,' I bellowed. And, amazingly, it turned out I was wrong.

In those polling booths they had dead Grandad on one shoulder and the hated spectre of Thatcher on the other. But despite every fibre of their being telling them to vote Labour, they did not. They didn't even go halfway and vote Lib Dem.

When I was growing up in the Don Valley constituency, it was inconceivable that it'd ever go blue. Not unlikely. Impossible. And yet it has. And it's the same story in Rother Valley. If you'd said, in a Maltby pub 25 years ago, that you'd voted Tory, you'd have gone home wearing your bar stool as a hat.

But now – and I still can't quite believe this has happened – many did. And are saying so, out loud and in public. That's how desperately they wanted Brexit.

And don't be fooled by what the *Guardian* says. They didn't want Brexit because of trade deals or fishery protection. Nor do they care a tinker's cuss about the Good Friday agreement or farm subsidies, and if you explain that Britain could become a freeport like Singapore, they will almost certainly throw you into a canal.

Make no mistake. They voted for Brexit, and they voted Tory to make sure Brexit happens, because they want immigration to stop.

That, for Boris, is a serious problem. It's so big, it'll become known as Boris's Big Problem. Because many people who voted for him in those northern towns think that, any minute now, he's going to come along with a magic Boris brush and make the area as racially mixed as it was before the Romans arrived. At the very least, they'll want to see barbed wire and signs saying, 'Achtung – Minen', to make sure 'things don't get any worse'.

But Boris can't do anything like that for three reasons. One, he doesn't want to. Two, it's impossible. And three, as Lily Allen says, we actually need immigration to keep everything running smoothly. I mean, where is Boris going to find all his new nurses? In a secret nurse box in Tunbridge Wells? Or in Africa?

To take everyone's mind off the Big Problem, Boris has promised to invest in the north, and that's a good idea. The gap between the broken engine room of the empire and the south, where there are exquisitely lit art galleries on most street corners, is far too large. And if it gets any larger, someone will drive a revolution through it.

However, investing in the north means attracting more people. And is Nigel Havers going to move to Rotherham? No. But if there are a couple of grants to get a training shoe company off the ground, you can bet your bottom that entrepreneurial types will be off like a shot. Soon they'll need a high-speed rail link from the docks at Hull to South Yorkshire just to keep the factories fed with Latvians.

This will infuriate the people who only want a pie fo' wife and a pint fo' whippet. They will say Boris has let them down. They will say they feel like outcasts in their own land and that they're imprisoned by the weird and woke machinations of the south.

We are no longer allowed to sympathize with this view. It is a racist view. But can you imagine what it might be like if a village in Hampshire or Devon were being overrun by Martians whose cooking smelt different, and who had illegal underground schools for their children, and didn't speak English? Imagine if you walked into the pub and it had become a Martian court.

Outwardly you'd call it multiculturalism and you'd be happy, but inwardly you'd probably scuttle into a polling booth and vote for a man who you thought could turn back time. And if he didn't, or couldn't, or wouldn't, you'd be pretty cross, and you certainly wouldn't trust anyone from his party ever again.

I offer this, then, as a crumb of comfort for Lily Allen. The red wall has not crumbled. It's just melted temporarily. And when immigrants keep on coming, people will drift back to the party where racists feel most at home: Labour. Then, the wall will be back.

Until that happens, though, let's enjoy the calm and pause for a moment to thank our lucky stars. The pound has soared, restaurants are full of people paying £100 a head for lunch, no one's house has been confiscated and even the most ardent remainers have now put down their megaphones. It should be a peaceful Christmas. Let's hope so, and a happy one too.

See you on the flipside.

22 December 2019

It's no wonder we can't find the middle ground. Social media has stolen it

Last week, my oldest daughter announced that she is now bulking up, ready for the all-out war against men. I'm not quite sure why she's gone from being a well-meaning feminist to Defcon 1 in a matter of moments, but this sudden escalation has become the norm in the past 10 years. And as we enter a new decade, it's got to stop.

There was a time when I found socialists quite amusing. I worked with one when I was a trainee reporter on the *Rotherham Advertiser*, and we'd joke over a couple of pints at lunchtime that, come the revolution, we'd meet at a village halfway between our houses and have a shootout. Then we'd have a couple more pints and he'd tell me about the Workers' Revolutionary Party training centre he'd attended in Derbyshire. And I'd laugh at that too. A bunch of lefties with pipe-cleaner arms, using sticks for guns in the woods. Like I said, socialists were funny in those days.

Now, though, I can't stand them. And they have grown to hate the likes of me. On election night, when I was genuinely worried that Jeremy Corbyn might actually win, I turned down one party invitation because I thought he might have supporters there. And I couldn't face the thought of watching them preen and crow.

And it's not just me, and it's not just politics. Young people have decided to hate those who aren't any more. They think old people have messed up their world with our cigarettes and our foreign travel. And we've grown to dislike them for their laziness and the way they leap onto every bandwagon, no matter how stupid it might be.

There was a time when I would have laughed if a 12-year-old had told me you can choose what sex you are, rather than looking in your underpants to find out. But now, when I hear easyJet is banning its pilots from starting messages 'Ladies and gentlemen . . .', in case they upset a transgenderist on board, I radiate rage.

And what good can possibly come of this? I realize kids have always despaired of their parents, but we are on a different level now. It's not just the way dads dance or the Abba songs that Mum likes. Emboldened perhaps by how perma-cross Greta Thunberg glowered at perpetually angry Donald Trump, kids now look at an old lady on the bus with undisguised hatred because she once had a Hillman Avenger. And she glowers back at them because they take a day off when they are ill, rather than soldiering on like she did back in the Fifties.

Brexit was a big one. When David Cameron called the referendum, I wrote a column saying how nicely I thought it was going. I noted that, without party politics in the mix, the debate seemed to be intelligent and free of rancour. But look what happened. After the result was declared, the spittle glands of those who'd voted remain went into overdrive. There was no respect for those who'd voted to leave, no attempt to understand their reasons, just wild-eyed hatred.

And now we get to the point where my daughter, who has campaigned for women's rights for many years, has suddenly decided that instead of using a toffee hammer to break the glass ceiling, she must wheel out the nukes.

In the Seventies, people would say things such as: 'I

really don't like President Nixon.' Whereas now, people
say: 'I absolutely loathe Trump and I hope he dies in
agony in a vat of boiling acid.' My grandfather once threw
his shoe through the screen of his television because 'that
man Wilson was on it'. Were he still with us, he'd throw
his actual TV at Corbyn, I suspect. He'd certainly throw
it at Nicola Sturgeon, and I'm sure half of Scotland would
throw their sets right back at him. Because that's another
debate that now drips in bile.

And I think I know why reasonable argument is no
longer possible. It's social media. When you had to
express your displeasure in the past, you wrote a letter,
and you enclosed your address so that someone could
reply. This meant you had to watch your language and
your manners. Not any more. Now you can hide behind
a blanket of anonymity and say anything you like.

Today, you can see the messages other people have left,
and to stand out, yours has to be more gruesome and
vitriolic. Until eventually, a man in a black Iron Maiden
T-shirt pops up to his mum's loft and fires off a message
saying he hopes you are in the vat of acid with Trump,
and that they put a toaster in it.

I could go on Twitter this afternoon and say I hope
Boris Johnson has a lovely holiday in Mustique, and I
guarantee I will be bombarded with messages from people saying they hope his plane crashes. Social media has
taken away the middle ground. It's a world of nothing, or
everything; a world where there are no catapults or pis-
tols, just intercontinental ballistic missiles.

It's been argued Twitter and others of its ilk democra-
tize communication. They give the little man in his
mum's loft just as much space as they give the president

of America. And this is supposed to be what? A good thing.

Because the little man in his mum's loft has no checks and balances. He's unhinged and stupid and frightened and a bully, and he encourages others to behave as he does until we reach a point where even the president of America joins in and becomes nasty too.

What's to be done? Well before the election, a friend said on Twitter that he could not vote for Corbyn and was swamped with abuse. So, what he did was ask his wife to dress up in a short skirt and stockings and read them all out to him. That, it seems to me, is the only solution. And on that note, have a happy new year.

29 December 2019

The World According to Clarkson

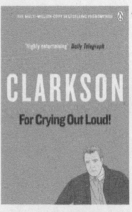

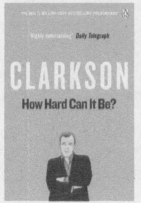

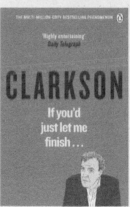

Available Now

He just wanted a decent book to read ...

Not too much to ask, is it? It was in 1935 when Allen Lane, Managing Director of Bodley Head Publishers, stood on a platform at Exeter railway station looking for something good to read on his journey back to London. His choice was limited to popular magazines and poor-quality paperbacks – the same choice faced every day by the vast majority of readers, few of whom could afford hardbacks. Lane's disappointment and subsequent anger at the range of books generally available led him to found a company – and change the world.

'We believed in the existence in this country of a vast reading public for intelligent books at a low price, and staked everything on it'
Sir Allen Lane, 1902–1970, founder of Penguin Books

The quality paperback had arrived – and not just in bookshops. Lane was adamant that his Penguins should appear in chain stores and tobacconists, and should cost no more than a packet of cigarettes.

Reading habits (and cigarette prices) have changed since 1935, but Penguin still believes in publishing the best books for everybody to enjoy. We still believe that good design costs no more than bad design, and we still believe that quality books published passionately and responsibly make the world a better place.

So wherever you see the little bird – whether it's on a piece of prize-winning literary fiction or a celebrity autobiography, political tour de force or historical masterpiece, a serial-killer thriller, reference book, world classic or a piece of pure escapism – you can bet that it represents the very best that the genre has to offer.

Whatever you like to read – trust Penguin.